Targeting Pronunciation

The Intonation, Sounds, and Rhythm of American English

Sue F. Miller

Santa Monica College

Houghton Mifflin Company

Boston New York

Director of ESL Programs: Susan Maguire
Senior Associate Editor: Kathleen Sands Boehmer
Development Editor: Angela Castro
Editorial Associate: Kevin M. Evans
Senior Project Editor: Kathryn Dinovo
Manufacturing Manager: Florence Cadran

Cover design: Harold Burch Designs, NYC
Cover image: Harold Burch

Credits

Chapter 3: Lyrics and music to,"Getting to Know You" by Richard Rodgers & Oscar Hammerstein from *The King and I.* Copyright © 1951 by Richard Rodgers and Oscar Hammerstein II. Copyright renewed. Williamson Music owner of publication and allied rights throughout the world. International copyright secured. Reprinted by permission. All rights reserved.

Chapter 6: "What Did You Say?" by Sue Miller. Reprinted by permission of Sue Miller.

Chapter 7: "Timothy Boon" from *Fairies and Suchlike* by Ivy O. Eastwick. Copyright 1946 by E.P. Dutton & Co., Inc., renewed © 1974 by Ivy Olive Eastwick. Used by permission of Dutton Children's Books, a division of Penguin Putnam, Inc.

Credits continue on page 270.

Printed in the U.S.A.

Library of Congress Catalog Card Number: 98-72063

ISBN: 0-395-90331-9

10 11 12 13 14 15 -PO- 05 04 03 02

As part of Houghton Mifflin's ongoing commitment to the environment, this text has been printed on recycled paper.

Contents

To the Teacher

Targeting Pronunciation is a comprehensive text for introducing pronunciation to intermediate and advanced ESL students. Whether you are experienced or inexperienced at teaching pronunciation, you will be comfortable with the clear explanations and the communicative approach. The text builds pronunciation awareness and provides extensive practice with all aspects of pronunciation—intonation, sounds, rhythm, and stress.

Targeting Pronunciation is organized around ten practical pronunciation goals, or targets, that are easy to teach and learn. Most of these targets are suprasegmentals, such as word stress, sentence focus, and intonation. Segmentals are also well-covered, both in the text and in Appendixes C and D. The targets presented early in the book are recycled throughout the chapters as students increase their ability to monitor their speech and gain more speaking experience and confidence.

Goals

- to promote clear effective communication, with the understanding that native-like speech is neither essential nor realistic for most people learning a new language
- to reach beyond the classroom by addressing what students can do outside of class on their own to make lasting changes in their pronunciation
- to encourage students to take responsibility for their pronunciation changes by discovering their own errors, identifying their most important targets, practicing on their own, and slowly incorporating the newly learned pronunciation into everyday life
- to promote self-confidence and increase the student's comfort when speaking English

Features

- Assessment tools for analyzing pronunciation and prioritizing targets include a goals survey, a pre- and post-listening survey, and student and instructor profiles.
- Songs, poetry, and chants engage students and help them internalize speech rhythm and intonation.

- Tips suggest ways to pronounce English more clearly and practice effectively with the audio tapes.
- Home assignments reinforce the work presented in class and solidify pronunciation changes.
- Communicative activities called Talk Times direct students to use pronunciation targets in real-life situations.
- Appendixes provide practical forms for classroom use as well as additional practice with consonants and vowels that students can use in a language lab or at home.
- A Web page includes an answer key, spelling tips, and additional practice material.*

Chapter Organization

The chapters are broken into small segments under alphabetized headings making it easy for you to proceed through the whole book, or to omit or repeat specific exercises to meet classroom needs. Students can easily isolate sections that need additional practice.

Chapter 1, Improving Your Pronunciation, *has three parts.*

- Part 1, Getting Started, includes a goals survey, a listening-to-English survey, and a list of the ten pronunciation targets.
- Part 2, Checking Your Pronunciation, includes a taping assignment where students record a speech sample, describe a picture, and read a paragraph. You listen to the tape and help set priorities.
- Part 3, Making Your New Pronunciation a Habit, is a self-contained unit that can follow Part Two or can be postponed. It outlines practice tips for the audio tapes and brings pronunciation into everyday life by introducing Talk Times.

Chapters 2–12

These chapters build pronunciation awareness and provide practice. They include:

- teaching and listening sections
- a progression from controlled and guided exercises to more communicative activities such as role plays, information gaps, discussions, and short oral presentation assignments
- many opportunities for students to work in pairs for more speaking practice
- choral practice with poems, chants, and songs
- a Finishing Up section at the end of each chapter comprised of a review segment, a Talk Time activity, practice and recording assignments, and a helpful hint

*The Houghton Mifflin ESL Website address is: http://www.hmco.com/college

Priorities

- Suprasegmentals. These play an important role in speech intelligibility and effective communication.
- Listening. Careful listening precedes other types of practice.
- Multisensory approaches. Students trace stress and rhythm patterns, tap their hands or their feet, or move in a way that helps them to internalize the new speech rhythm. Many pronunciation experts believe that in order to shift from the speech rhythm of their original language to the rhythm of a new language, people need to accompany speech practice with some kind of rhythmic gesture.
- Learner-centered classroom. Students frequently work in pairs to provide more speaking practice. They monitor their own and their partner's speech, and exchange feedback and suggestions.
- Student responsibility. Students learn to discover and correct their own errors. They control their own progress by how much they practice and how many risks they take trying out new pronunciation.
- After-class activities. Students practice with the audio tapes, make recordings of their speech, keep a personal pronunciation glossary, and carry out communicative activities in real-life situations.

Audio Tapes

Practicing with the companion audio tapes for *Targeting Pronunciation* is an integral part of this program's approach to teaching pronunciation. The amount of listening and practicing provided in class is usually not enough to move students beyond the awareness level. Students need access to a tape recorder for both listening to the text tapes and for recording and listening to their own speech. Day-to-day speaking goes by too quickly for most students to successfully monitor their speech. The tapes provide the opportunity to replay and focus on what they could not hear the first time.

Instructor's Manual and Answer Key

The Instructor's Manual for *Targeting Pronunciation* provides practical suggestions and explanations for the exercises as well as teaching and correction strategies. You will find an Answer Key for the exercises both in the manual and on the Targeting Pronunciation Web page.

To the Student

So you want to change your accent. Is this realistic?

You may be surprised to hear that there is nothing wrong with an accent! An accent tells us a little about who you are and where you may be from. People from other countries are not the only ones with accents. Native speakers of English within each country often have accents that give clues about their cultural backgrounds or where they grew up.

Pronunciation training is not meant to hide all signs of your original language and culture, nor is it likely to eliminate all of your accent. The primary goal is clear effective speech. Few adults with noticeable nonnative accents can ever sound exactly like native speakers in any new language. The most important thing is how competently you communicate and how easily people can understand your pronunciation. It is possible to be a confident effective speaker and still have a nonnative accent that does not interfere with communication.

What is an accent?

People vary in the ways they pronounce a language. Around the globe, even where English is not the primary language, there are variations of English and differing English accents. These accents are influenced by regional native languages. In each country there are English accents that native speakers find the easiest to understand. Learning to speak more clearly in English often means learning an accent that is easily understood by a majority of speakers in a particular area.

Why do I have pronunciation problems?

People who learn a new language are often left with pronunciation problems. After working hard to master the vocabulary and grammar of English, many people still have trouble conversing comfortably. They have not received much instruction in the subtle rules of pronunciation that are needed for effective oral communication.

Pronunciation problems can have a variety of causes. For one thing, when English is not your first language, there are particular speech sounds and intonation patterns that are not part of what could be called your *speech memory bank.* Some of the consonants and vowels used commonly in English may not exist in your native language. At an early age you established strong tongue and muscle movements for the rhythm patterns of your original language. If your memory bank does not include the sounds or rhythm patterns of English, it is understandable that you will have difficulty with pronunciation.

Many accent problems come from the difficulties of pronouncing English from looking at the written word. Inconsistent spelling patterns make it difficult to predict pronunciation from spelling, especially for vowel sounds. Although there are only five vowel letters, there are fifteen vowel sounds in English with many possible spellings. The pronunciation of the vowel letters, *a, e, i, o,* and *u* varies in different words. For example, the letter *a* in "at," "ate," "all," "agree," and "any" all sound different. Furthermore, you can't tell from reading which syllables or words to stress, where to change pitch, or how to link words into groups.

How do I make my accent easier to understand?

Learning a new way of speaking is a little bit like learning to play the piano. It requires months of practice and attention. You need to train new muscle patterns as you would in perfecting an athletic skill. There is also an element of taking on a new role, like the role in a play. Learning new pronunciation habits is a gradual process that takes time and patience.

Most people need to start by refining their listening skills. There is a relationship between how clearly you hear a new language and the way you pronounce it. Listening carefully to your own speech, called *self-monitoring,** is an essential part of changing your pronunciation, so you need to become more familiar with your own voice speaking English.

You may not realize that when people can't understand you, it is usually because some aspect of your intonation† is distorted. Individual consonant and vowel sounds can contribute to your accent and the lack of speech intelligibility, but improving your intonation and speech rhythm is more critical.

Help is on the way.

The information you learn in *Targeting Pronunciation* will clear up many misunderstandings about pronunciation and will make you more aware of English intonation and sounds. You will learn why people don't always understand what you say and strategies for helping your listener to understand you better. This training will help you to break down the pronunciation of English into small, manageable units. You will learn what specific aspects of your pronunciation you can target that will make the biggest difference in your speech.

*"self-monitoring" in relation to speech/pronunciation was first used by Joan Morley in *TESOL Quarterly,* Vol. 9, No. 1, March 1975 (pp. 83–86).
†**intonation:** The melody of speech.

The information itself, however, will not change your speech. You will need a plan of action that involves practicing regularly, listening to yourself more carefully, and trying out your new skills in real-life situations. Don't wait until you think your English pronunciation is perfect before you use it. Those who take risks and initiative make the most progress.

Is this a self-help program?

Although you can use *Targeting Pronunciation* and the audio tapes to practice and improve on your own, with professional guidance you should improve more quickly. The instructor will guide you in the use of the tapes, help you to choose appropriate pronunciation targets, and make sure you can say the targets correctly. Your ability, however, to help yourself by practicing regularly and trying out your new pronunciation is the most important part of the program.

How long will it take to modify my accent?

People modify their pronunciation gradually. It takes time to change old habits. The length of time varies with the individual, but here are five factors that affect your progress.

- If your original language is very different from English, your list of pronunciation targets may be longer. The more sounds and intonation patterns you need to work on, the longer it may take.
- People who realize the importance of improving their pronunciation are more motivated to work on it and more likely to take risks and initiative in using new speech patterns. Motivation is one of the most significant factors affecting your progress.
- The more regularly you practice outside of class and the more carefully you listen to your own speech, the more progress you will make.
- The more frequently you converse in English, especially with native speakers, the more quickly you will progress.
- The more natural ability you have, the easier it may be. How good is your ear? How well can you imitate speech sounds? How well can you monitor your own speech?

Here's the good news.

The important thing is that you really *can* change your accent. How many changes and how long they take will vary, but you can learn to express yourself clearly and get your point across in English, whether or not you sound exactly like a native speaker.

Pronunciation training can help you to speak clearly and understand rapid speech more easily It will help you gain confidence and increase your comfort level in new speaking situations. It can further your career opportunities and improve your performance at work if your job requires communication in English. As your pronunciation changes, all speech should be easier to understand, including speech on television and in the movies.

You can enrich your daily life by communicating more comfortably and effectively in the most common language of international communication. Start improving your English communication skills right away. One by one, target the parts of your pronunciation that will make the biggest difference in your speech.

Key to Symbols

The following symbols are used to show you the important parts of English pronunciation as you learn to say them.

STRESS

- **Word stress**

Capital letters represent stressed syllables in words, and stressed words in phrases and sentences.

Examples APple aPARTment underSTAND

I FOUND a NEW aPARTment.

- **Strong stress and light stress**

Occasionally two levels of stress are shown in the same word. In these words, the strongly stressed syllable is indicated by large capital letters and the lightly stressed syllable by small capital letters.

Examples BLACKBOARD apPREciATE

- **Focus**

Bold type indicates the word with the strongest stress in a phrase or sentence.

Examples I'd LIKE the **PUR**ple one.

The DEsert is **BEAU**tiful.

UNSTRESS

- In words of more than one syllable, the unstressed syllables are left unmarked.

  PRACtical imPROVE I'd like some des**SERT**.

- Vowels reduced to schwa are sometimes shown by a slash through the reduced vowel.

Examples adJUSTment appliCAtion (with ə over the reduced vowels)

What do you think? (with ə over "do" and "you")

- X's show silent letters.

Examples picked gates

Don't ask me. He found his wallet.

INTONATION

- Rising and falling lines show the pitch direction of sentences.

Examples That's not my bag.

That's not your bag?

- Lines showing *steps* and *glides* indicate end-of-the-sentence intonation.

Examples *Glides:* I heard it again.

Do you want to leave?

Step: I can see a rainbow.

SOUNDS

- Consonant sounds are shown in small grey boxes. Boxes with a squiggly underline indicate voiced consonants with vibrating vocal cords. Plain grey boxes indicate voiceless consonants.

Examples

Voiced		Voiceless	
z	zoo	s	Sue
b	bill	p	pill
g	goat	k	coat

- Consonant sounds are different from consonant letters. The consonant sound in the grey box may be spelled differently in different words.

Examples	Consonant sounds	Consonant letters
	k	keep candy back bake
	s	sit cent miss face
	f	fat phone staff laugh

- Vowel sounds are shown in small grey boxes. Vowel sounds are different from vowel letters. The vowel sound in the grey box is often spelled differently in different English words.

Examples	Vowel sounds	Vowel letters
	ey	make pay rain vein
	ə	cup some what trouble
	I	him busy gym women

OTHER MARKS

‿ shows linking.

Example My glove‿is gone.

Slashes (/) indicate pauses in longer sentences with more than one focus word.

Example I'd like two fried **EGGS** / and a cup of **COF**fee. /

⟶ means *sounds like.*

Example short or tall ⟶ shorter tall

🎧 indicates a recorded segment.

Acknowledgments

I am indebted to a number of people who have helped to make this book possible. In particular, I am grateful to the wonderful editorial team at Houghton Mifflin Company, especially to Susan Maguire and to Kathy Sands-Boehmer for their ideas, guidance, and support, to Craig Mertens for his efforts with permissions, and to Kevin Evans for his important assistance behind-the-scenes.

Special thanks to Angela Castro for her care and attention to detail during the development of the book, to Herbert Nolan for his dedication and precision in coordinating the production and design, and to Carol Keller, who was responsible for the art.

My appreciation to the following people who have offered valuable suggestions along the way: William Acton, Janie Duncan, Janet Goodwin, Pat Girard, Linda Grant, Anne Isaac, Karl Lisovsky, David Miller, Janet Miller, Kathy Sucher, and Ann Wennerstrom.

I am grateful to the following reviewers for their immeasurable contributions: William Acton (Nagoya University of Commerce), Janet Anderson-Hseih (Iowa State University), Delores Avila (Pasadena City College), Sue Doyle (University of Oregon), Janet Goodwin (University of California, Los Angeles), Gail Kellersberger (University of Houston), Patricia Pashby (University of San Francisco), Patricia Rice (Long Island University), Scott Stevens (University of Delaware), Mary Nance-Tager (LaGuardia Community College), Ann Wennerstrom (University of Washington).

Special thanks to Donna Brinton who started me on the trail to publication and to Barbara Bilson for her generous help. Thanks to my students who taught me how they learn and what is important. My ongoing admiration to those whose leadership in teaching pronunciation has paved the way for us all, especially to Judy Gilbert and Joan Morley.

Finally, my deepest appreciation to my husband, Lee, with his life commitment to the creative process.

1

Improving Your Pronunciation

Part 1. Getting Started

Targeting Pronunciation and the speech models on the tape introduce you to the basic principles of North American English pronunciation. Adapt this book to your personal needs. Take notes in it. The vocabulary is useful for anyone who wishes to speak English more clearly, whether in the United States, Canada, or around the globe. Although variations of English are spoken in different places, they are more alike than different compared to variations of other languages. The underlying principles of English pronunciation can be applied to all of them. You will be learning a form of spoken English that a large number of native and nonnative speakers can easily understand.

Improving your pronunciation can be fun if you are not in a hurry and realize that it can and will happen. Start by reading To the Student, page x. Then answer the following questions.

1. What is one of the reasons you may have pronunciation problems?
2. What is "self-monitoring"? Find the answer in the section called *How do I make my accent easier to understand?*.
3. There are five factors listed that contribute to how long it may take you to modify your accent. Which factor seems most important to you?
4. There are various benefits to pronunciation training described in the section called *Here's the good news.* Which of these is most important to you?

Goals Survey

What do you hope to accomplish regarding your pronunciation?

General Goals

- Read this list of possible goals. Find the three that are the most important to you. Put a "1" next to the goal you think is the most important. Put a "2" next to the second most important goal, and "3" next to the third most important.

  a. ____ to eliminate my accent completely and sound like a native speaker

  b. ____ to communicate in English clearly, effectively, and naturally

  c. ____ to speak so that others can understand me much more easily than they do now

  d. ____ to learn what I can do to clear up misunderstandings in the middle of a conversation

  e. ____ to gain confidence in new speaking situations

  f. ____ to understand rapid speech more easily

  g. ____ to improve my career opportunities

- Some of these goals may not be important or realistic. Put an "X" next to any that you think are neither important nor realistic.
- Discuss these goals with the class and the instructor.

Specific Goals

- Think about times when you would like to speak more clearly and comfortably. List three situations that are the most difficult for you. Here are some examples: giving a talk, making conversation at a party, ordering in a restaurant, business and social phone calls, job inquiries and interviews, meetings at work, other?

  ____

  ____

  ____

- Compare your goals with those of your partner or the other students in your group. Are they similar or different?

Name ________________________ **Date** ______________ **Listening Score:** ________%

Listening to English

This survey will tell you how clearly you hear some of the important parts of English speech. Count the number correct and multiply times 2 to get your listening score.

1. Syllables. Write the number of syllables you hear next to the word or phrase. [6 points]

Example forget it. _3_

1. ____ illustrate
2. ____ crashed
3. ____ returned it
4. ____ academic
5. ____ idea
6. ____ magnification

2. Important endings. For each question, you will hear either sentence (a) or (b). Check (✓) the sentence you hear. [6 points]

Example a. _✓_ **I'll look at the letter.**

b. ____ I've looked at the letter.

1. a. ____ I'll call him every day.
   b. ____ I've called him every day.
2. a. ____ They look over all the documents.
   b. ____ They looked over all the documents.
3. a. ____ He'll decide about it after the meeting.
   b. ____ He decided about it after the meeting.
4. a. ____ It makes me laugh.
   b. ____ It made me laugh.
5. a. ____ They said they'd call before it started.
   b. ____ They said they called before it started.
6. a. ____ They pack up the suitcases for you.
   b. ____ They packed up the suitcases for you.

Name ______________________________ Date ______________

3. Word stress. Listen to the following words. Circle the stressed syllable in the word. [6 points]

Example pencil. allowance. First you will hear the key word, then the sentence.

1. forgot (I forgot her name.)
2. visitors (Do they allow visitors?)
3. application (I filled out the application.)
4. important (It's an important decision.)
5. appreciate (I appreciate your kindness.)
6. understand (He doesn't understand me.)

4. Missing Sounds. Listen to the sentence. Decide if the speaker says the underlined word or if the speaker says a similar word that does not make sense in that sentence. Check (✓) the word you hear the speaker say. [4 points]

Example	My bike is broken.	____ bike	✓ buy
1.	The phone is ringing next door.	____ phone	____ foe
2.	Last week he made a lot of money.	____ made	____ may
3.	Please move your car out of the way.	____ move	____ moo
4.	My insurance rates went up this year.	____ rates	____ ray

5. Reduced Speech. Write the sentence you hear. You will hear each sentence twice. [5 points]

1. ______________________________
2. ______________________________
3. ______________________________
4. ______________________________
5. ______________________________

6. Focus Words. Listen to the dialogue two times. Underline the one word in each sentence that gets the most emphasis. [8 points]

Example A: What are you doing? B: What do you think I'm doing?

A: What shall we do this weekend?

B: I'd like to go to a movie. What do you want to do?

A: I'd like to go to a movie. But only a funny movie.

B: We did that last weekend. I'd rather see an exciting action film. How does that sound?

Name ________________________________ Date ________________

7. Focus Words. You will hear a sentence. Listen for the word that gets the most emphasis. This word affects the meaning and the response. Check (✓) the appropriate response. [3 points]

Example Jane's birthday is September 28th. ____ I thought it was September 29th.

__✓__ I thought Marie's birthday was the 28th.

1. I'd like to rent a car. ____ What about renting a jeep?

   ____ How about buying one instead?

2. Jim is getting married next month. ____ Not this month?

   ____ That's nice.

3. I looked under the chair. ____ Try looking on the chair.

   ____ Try looking under the table.

8. Phrases. Read silently the following sentences and responses. Then you will hear either sentence (a) or sentence (b) in each pair. Check (✓) the appropriate response. [4 points]

Example **There's a hot dog.** **__✓__ Give him a drink.**

There's a hot dog. ____ I want one for lunch.

1. a. What's he doing in the darkroom? ____ He's developing pictures.

   b. What's he doing in the dark room? ____ He's sleeping.

2. a. Who lives in the White House? ____ The President does.

   b. Who lives in the white house? ____ I do.

3. a. Use "drop out" in a sentence. ____ Don't drop out of college.

   b. Use "dropout" in a sentence. ____ He's a college dropout.

4. a. Use "print out" in a sentence. ____ Please print out four copies.

   b. Use "printout" in a sentence. ____ Give me the printout of the application.

Name ______________________ Date ____________

9. Thought Groups. Read silently the following sentences and responses. Then you will hear either sentence (a) or sentence (b) in each pair. Check (✓) the appropriate answer. [3 points]

Example "Tracy," said the teacher, "was late." __✓__ **Tracy was late.**

Tracy said, "The teacher was late." ____ The teacher was late.

1. a. Tom bought a new car, phone, and radio. ____ Tom bought a new car.
   b. Tom bought a new carphone and radio. ____ Tom did <u>not</u> buy a new car.

2. a. The twenty $9 books are left. ____ The books cost $9 each.
   b. The $29 books are left. ____ The books cost $29 each.

3. a. Nancy said, "My brother is a doctor." ____ Nancy's brother is a doctor.
   b. "Nancy," said my brother, "is a doctor." ____ Nancy is a doctor.

10. Intonation. Questions and statements. Check (✓) the one you hear. [2 points]

Example ____ Jim's leaving. __✓__ **Jim's leaving?**

1. a. ____ She's happy about it?
   b. ____ She's happy about it.

2. a. ____ That's not your book?
   b. ____ That's not your book.

11. Intonation. In one sentence, the speaker is finished talking. In the other sentence, the speaker is not finished and has more to say. Check (✓) the sentence you hear. [3 points]

Example I bought some milk. __✓__ **finished**

I bought some milk . . . ____ not finished

1. a. I found an old letter. ____ finished
   b. I found an old letter . . . ____ not finished

2. a. I'd like to attend the conference. ____ finished.
   b. I'd like to attend the conference . . . ____ not finished

3. a. The package contains a note and some candy. ____ finished
   b. The package contains a note and some candy . . . ____ not finished.

Small Talk

Small talk is brief, impersonal conversation that can take place anywhere. You can make small talk with someone you don't know at all or with a casual acquaintance. It is a way of greeting people and communicating with them in an informal, safe way. Americans are often uncomfortable with silence, but, surprisingly, speaking to someone you don't know or just met about impersonal topics is considered friendly and appropriate.

Listen to a Teacher Talking

Listening plays a big part in learning to pronounce English more clearly. Start by listening to a teacher's taped lecture about a way to improve your pronunciation. Careful listening for specific things about pronunciation is called *monitoring*. Careful listening to your own pronunciation is called *self-monitoring*.

1. Listen for content. As you listen to each part of the teacher's lecture, think about the answers to these questions.

Part 1

- What is small talk?
- What is one of the specific small talk suggestions that the teacher makes?

Part 2

- What does the teacher describe as "tempting"?
- What are two safe topics for making small talk?
- Who should take charge of your pronunciation training?

2. Monitor for the important words. Some of the teacher's words are easier to hear than others. They are called *focus words* because they point your attention to what is important. The stressed syllables of the focus words are in bold type. The speaker pauses or slows down where you see the slashes (/).

Example You've all been **TELL**ing me / how **EA**ger you are / to improve your pronunci**A**tion. /

- Listen to your instructor say these sentences from the taped lecture and emphasize the focus words. Repeat what you hear.

    1. That's a cool **BACK**PACK / you're **CAR**rying./
    2. There sure are a lot of **PEO**ple / who want to see this **MO**vie. /

3. I wonder when the **BUS** is coming./
4. Do you **KNOW** / where I can find the **TU**na FISH? /
5. There's always such a long **LINE** here. /
6. What a beautiful **DOG**./
7. What do you **THINK** / of all this **RAIN?**/

- Replay the tape and listen to the lecture again. Pay attention to the focus words. Then proceed to number three to follow.

3. Monitor for word stress. In addition to emphasizing the focus words in each sentence, English speakers stress one syllable in each word.

- Listen to your instructor say the following words from the teacher's talk. Count the syllables and write the number of syllables next to the word. Draw a big dot over the stressed syllable in each word. Notice the stress in these words the next time you listen to the lecture.

Example peॱople _2_

movies ____	around ____	weather ____	places ____
conversation ____	improve ____	complain ____	beautiful ____

There are words in the teacher's taped lecture that are made up of two smaller words. They are called *compound nouns.* Even when they are spelled separately, compound nouns are pronounced as if they are one word. The following compound nouns made up of two separate words are written inside brackets. Listen and draw a dot over the word that gets the strongest stress. Is it the first word or the last word?

supermarket [bus stop] [tuna fish]

- Replay the tape of the lecture. Pay attention to compound nouns and stressed syllables. Write other compound nouns that you hear in the lecture or ones that you think of on your own.

____

____

Partner Work: Small talk plan

1. Talk to a partner about places where you might make small talk in English. List some of the places and some sentences you might say to start the conversation. Have you tried any of these already?

Places	What to Say to Start a Small Safe Conversation
____________________	______________________________
____________________	______________________________
____________________	______________________________
____________________	______________________________
____________________	______________________________

2. Compare making small talk in your native country and in English-speaking countries.

- Check any of the following topics that would be appropriate for small talk in your native country with someone you recently met.

____ weather
____ your religion
____ health
____ current news event
____ movies/TV/books
____ pets
____ your politics
____ family/children
____ your salary
____ food/meal that you are eating together
____ personal appearance (face, eyes, body)
____ sports
____ how much something costs
____ work/occupation
____ compliment (clothing, home, a known accomplishment)
____ critical comments about appearance, speech, or behavior

- Discuss which of these topics might be appropriate for small talk in English. How is this different from small talk in your native country?

---

pronunciation tip **People who speak English frequently make more progress with their pronunciation than people who speak their own language most of the time. Look for opportunities to converse in English, if possible with native speakers.**

Name ______________________ Date ______________

Talking about English

This questionnaire asks about some of your experiences and attitudes about English. Fill it out at home to discuss in class. All answers are correct.

1. What is your earliest memory of hearing English? How did it sound to you?

____

____

____

____

2. How does it sound to you now?

____

____

3. Why did you decide to learn to speak English?

____

____

4. Different cultures in the world have had a variety of experiences, both good and bad, with English speakers or English-speaking countries. Which of your culture's experiences do you think of first? How might these affect your attitude toward English?

____

____

____

5. Do you think English pronunciation will be easy or hard? Why?

____

____

Background Information

- What language do you speak at home? __________ At work? __________
- How long have you been speaking English? __________
- In what country did you first study English ? __________ What was your teacher's native language? __________
- Identify your communication needs. How important is it to you to improve your pronunciation in the following situations? Write a 1, 2, or 3 next to each situation.

  1 = the most important 2 = important 3 = not that important

  ____ home ____ social ____ work/business ____ international travel

  ____ general community (shopping, using government offices, banking, asking for information, etc.) ____ other (explain)

Pronunciation Targets

Look over the following list of ten key pronunciation goals that you will learn about in this book. Think of these goals as targets—as something to aim for. As you aim for these targets you will be mastering the sounds, intonation, and rhythm patterns that can make your English speech more effective.

At first you may need help selecting the specific targets that will make the biggest difference in *your* speech. When you are more familiar with the pronunciation of English and your own speech patterns, you will be able to hear and identify these targets on your own.

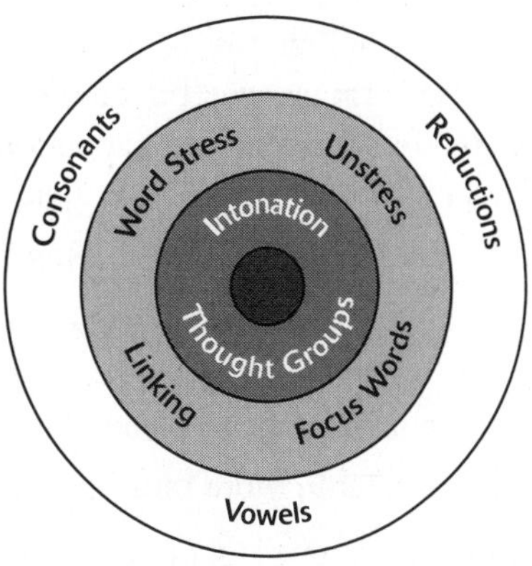

Key Targets

Target 1 Word Stress. Say all the syllables in a word. Signal the stressed syllable by making it longer, louder, and higher in pitch. The unstressed and lightly stressed syllables in a word are shorter and lower in pitch than the stressed syllable.

See Chapter 2, Stressing Syllables and Speaking Clearly.

Target 2 Linking Words and Finishing Syllables. Link the words in a phrase into one connected chunk of speech. Say all the consonant sounds at the ends of syllables and words, especially important endings such as final "s" and "ed."

See Chapter 3, Pronunciation Basics, Chapter 6, The Speech Pathway, and Chapter 10, Important Endings.

Target 3 Thought Groups. Divide longer sentences into phrases, or *thought groups,* to make your speech easier to understand. Each thought group has its own focus word and melody, and is followed by a slight pause. Signal the end of the sentence with the biggest pause and change in pitch.

See Chapter 2, Stressing Syllables and Speaking Clearly, Chapter 3, Pronunciation Basics, and Chapter 12, More Thoughts About Thought Groups.

Target 4 Focus Words. Emphasize one word in each thought group to focus attention on what is most important and to highlight new information. Focus words are easier to hear than other words because the stressed syllables sound longer, slower, and louder.

See Chapter 3, Pronunciation Basics, and Chapter 4, Speech Rhythm: Stress and Unstress.

Target 5 Sentence Stress and Unstress. Stress the content words. They provide most of the meaning. Unstress the structure words, but don't leave them out. They are important to grammar and speech rhythm.

See Chapter 4, Speech Rhythm: Stress and Unstress.

Target 6 Reductions. Shorten the unstressed words used in everyday speech. Native speakers often say a schwa * vowel in these shortened, or reduced, words. Sometimes sounds are omitted.

See Chapter 5, Vowels and Speech Rhythm, and Chapter 11, Putting Words Together.

Target 7 Speech Melody. Use intonation to organize your speech and to express meaning beyond the words themselves, for example, to sound friendly, or confident, or surprised. Target specific melody patterns for asking questions and finishing sentences (end-of-the-sentence intonation).

See Chapter 2, Stressing Syllables and Speaking Clearly, Chapter 3, Pronunciation Basics, and Chapter 8, Sing Along, The Melody of Speech.

Target 8 Specific Intonation Patterns. To make your speech easier to understand and more native-like, pronounce the correct intonation and stress in compound nouns, descriptive phrases, names, and phrasal verbs.

See Chapter 9, More Intonation Patterns.

Target 9 Clear Vowel Sounds. Although there are approximately fifteen different vowel sounds in English, the most important thing about pronouncing vowels is to emphasize the stressed vowels. You may also want to target specific vowel sounds that you find difficult.

See Chapter 5, Vowels and Speech Rhythm, Chapter 7, More About Vowels and Consonants, and Appendix D, Vowels.

Target 10 Consonants. Target consonant clusters or pairs of voiced and unvoiced consonant sounds that you find difficult, such as f and v; ch, j and sh; th; r and l; w and v. Distinguish between sounds where the air stops, and sounds where the air continues to flow out.

See Chapter 6, The Speech Pathway, Chapter 10, Important Endings, and Appendix C, Consonants.

On Your Own

1. Replay the tape of the teacher discussing small talk. Listen several times.

- Monitor for focus words, for pauses, and for the word stress in the words on page 8.
- In addition, monitor for speech melody. The melody of speech and the melody of songs are similar. A speaker and a singer both move up and down in pitch with their voices. Does this teacher use a lot of melody in her speech or does she talk on one tone or monotone? Does this teacher sound friendly?

* **schwa**: The short unclear vowel sound heard in unstressed syllables and words.

2. Complete three small-talk conversations this week. Report what happened on a form called "Small-Talk Report" in Appendix B, page 240.

Suggestion: One of these conversations could be a "phone meeting" to talk in English about pronunciation with another student from this class. This is a good way to start getting acquainted.

3. Tape-record yourself answering the first two questions in the questionnaire Talking About English. Speak naturally without reading your answers. Listen to your tape and answer the following questions:

- Write anything about your pronunciation that you heard when you listened. Give an example.

  ____

  ____

- What do you like or dislike about listening to your speech on tape?

  ____

  ____

Part 2. Checking Your Pronunciation

My Speech Tape

Make a tape of your speech in order to help you and your instructor to identify your personal pronunciation targets and to set priorities for working on your pronunciation. Listen to your tape to start monitoring your pronunciation and to become more comfortable with your own voice speaking English.

Before you begin, write your name on the tape and on the plastic container. Use a good quality cassette that is either new or cleanly erased.

1. Speech Sample

Speak informally using natural unrehearsed speech. Do not practice or write out your answers.

1. Background Information. Start out by saying

- your name
- the city and country you are from
- why you decided to take this class
- how often you converse in English and whether or not it is with native speakers

2. Topics. Look over these topics and choose one to talk about. Talk for two or three minutes.

- Talk about moving. For example, describe how often you have moved and what you see as the advantages or disadvantages of moving. Describe one experience in your life when you moved.
- Talk about work. For example, describe your first job, a past job and/or a present job. Tell which job is your favorite and why. Tell what kind of work you hope to do in the future, and why you are interested in this type of work.
- Talk about the community where you grew up and an experience you remember from your childhood.

3. Pictures. Look at the following series of four pictures and think about the story they describe. Tell the story shown in the pictures. Add ideas of your own. Then tell how you think the story ends.

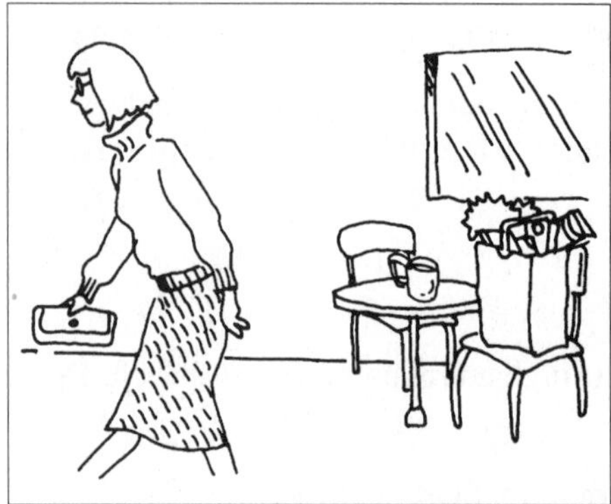

2. Reading

Read silently the following paragraphs. Then record *one* of the paragraphs. Don't try to change your pronunciation in any way. **This is not a test.**

(Photocopy this page and turn it in with your tape.)

Name ______________________________ ______________________ **Date** ______________
Print Your **Last** Name **First** Name

City & Country of Origin ______________________________ ______________________________

My Exercise Program

I used to love to sleep late on weekends until I watched my neighbor getting exercise every day, looking very physically fit. Now I wake up at 5:30 in the morning, put on my exercise clothes and tennis shoes, drink some orange juice, and take off. By 7 o'clock I've walked over sixteen blocks to the gym and worked out for sixty minutes in an aerobics class. After that, I jog at least fifteen minutes on a treadmill and ride my bike to my friend's house. When I finish exercising, I'm unusually hungry, and arrange to stop for an early lunch. Yesterday I ate a cheeseburger, a large green salad, some sliced cucumbers, two bags of potato chips, a milk shake, rice pudding, and five delicious chocolate chip cookies. I decided to keep a record of my workouts and to record my progress in a notebook. I have been doing this for several weeks now. My friend who is a professional trainer doesn't agree with my ABCs for physical training and says I'm probably better off sleeping late and skipping the huge lunch. Maybe I *am* better off sleeping late.

Paying with Plastic

People have always used cash and checks for purchasing things, but in our lifetime things are changing fast. Now, instead of cash, people's wallets are often stuffed with various kinds of plastic credit cards, debit cards, and ATM cards. It is estimated that Americans charge more than $18 billion a year on credit cards and that there are already more than 700 million cards of various kinds in circulation. Sometimes card companies have problems collecting overdue payments. Although most people intend to record ATM transactions and debits as they spend money, it is easy to use the cards without keeping good records. Cardholders who may be tempted to buy things that they can't afford can end up with high monthly payments beyond their budgets. This explosion in the use of credit cards has brought with it huge amounts of personal debt. The card companies are often financially responsible for goods or services illegally charged to businesses. However, it's not the company that pays. It's the consumer who ends up paying for these losses with increased prices or higher interest. The card companies are enthusiastic about the switch to a credit card economy because they earn a small percentage of each transaction. What do *you* think about "paying for it with plastic"?

(Photocopy this page and turn it in with your tape.)

Name ______________________ ______________________ **Date** ______________
Print Your **Last** Name **First** Name

City & Country of Origin ______________________ ______________________

3. Reviewing Your Recording

1. Listen to your tape and write the answers to these questions.

- Which part of your speech sample sounds the best?

  ____

- Write three words that you say on your tape that you think might be hard to understand.

  ______________ ______________ ______________

- Write one phrase that you say on your tape that you think might be hard to understand.

  ____

- How do you think listening to your speech on tape may or may not be helpful?

  ____

  ____

2. Rewind the cassette "My Speech Tape" back to the beginning so that it is ready for your instructor to play.

4. Setting Priorities

Your instructor will help you set priorities for targeting your pronunciation. Discuss how clearly you communicate in English and what you can do to improve. Find out if you and your instructor agree about your speech effectiveness level.

Speech Effectiveness Level

What is clear, effective speech?

In order to be an effective speaker, pronunciation and language skills need to develop together. Good oral communication skills include clear pronunciation as well as accurate grammar and vocabulary. How clearly do you think you communicate in English? Decide which of the following six levels of speech effectiveness best fits your speech:

Level 1 People understand only a few words of my speech.

Level 2 People understand less than half of what I say. I frequently need to repeat things. My vocabulary and grammar are limited. Conversations are slow and difficult.

Level 3 People understand more than half, but not nearly enough, of what I say. I need to repeat and clarify many things. My pronunciation, sentence structure, and vocabulary are all a problem.

Level 4 People understand most of what I say. Conversations proceed with minimal interruptions. However, my pronunciation and occasional errors in grammar or vocabulary are noticeable and sometimes interfere with communication.

Level 5 My speech is fully understandable. My slight accent and any isolated variations in vocabulary or grammar may be noticeable, but they do not interfere with communication.

Level 6 My speech is fully understandable. I use correct grammar and appropriate vocabulary. My communication is clear and effective, and almost native-like.

What is your target level?

Color the graphs with a highlighter pen to indicate where you think your speech is now and what speech level you are aiming for.

Present Level	**Target Level**
6	6
-	-
5	5
-	-
4	4
-	-
3	3
-	-
2	2
-	-
1	1

The speech effectiveness levels were adapted from Joan Morley, "EFL/ESL Intelligibility Index," "How Many Languages Do You Speak?" Nagoya Gakium Daigaku: Gaikokugo Kyoiku Kiyo No. 19, Jan./Feb. 1988, by permission of Joan Morley.

See Appendix B for the Instructor Observations form, page 241, and My Speech Checklist, page 242. These checklists can help you to identify your pronunciation targets and set priorities. They can be copied and used as you make more speech tapes.

Part 3.
Making Your New Pronunciation a Habit

Where do I start?

Learning a new accent requires refining your listening skills and establishing new muscle patterns. This takes time and a plan of action that goes beyond what you do in class. Your instructor will help you develop this plan. Look at this overview about improving your pronunciation that starts in class and ends on your own. It will give you a better idea of how you do it.

In Class

Gain pronunciation awareness.

- Set realistic goals.
- Learn about English pronunciation.
- Learn what will improve your speech.

Shape your new pronunciation.

- Learn how to say the targets.
- Start monitoring your own speech.
- Learn to discover your own errors.

On Your Own

Practice the skills you learn in class.

- Improve your ability to monitor.
- Discover your own errors.
- Correct your own errors.

Make your new pronunciation a habit by using it in your daily life.

- Use what you have learned.
- Listen for what you have learned.

Talk Times: "Use it or lose it"

Make your new pronunciation a habit by using it in your everyday life. These changes happen gradually. You began by making *small talk*, brief impersonal conversation that can happen anywhere. The main purpose is to gain more experience using English in order to build your confidence and increase your comfort level. See page 7 to review *monitoring* and *small talk*.

Now you are going to practice pronunciation during speaking activities called Talk Times that you carry out on the phone or in your community. You will be planning things to say and where you can say them to practice specific pronunciation targets. A target is something to aim for. For a list of pronunciation targets, see page 11.

Preparing for Talk Times

1. Listen to the sample Talk Times conversation. Replay the tape. Pay attention to the stressed syllables in capital letters and the focus words shown in bold type. There are slash marks (/) where the speaker slows down or pauses. After you listen, practice the conversation with a partner. Switch roles.

D = driver looking for the airport A = gas station attendant

Where's the Airport?

D: Ex**CUSE** me. / I'm TRYing to FIND the **AIR**PORT. / Can you **HELP** me? /

A: **YES**,/ take the NUMber 10 **FREE**WAY / going **SOUTH**. / Get off at HARbor **AV**enue. / Turn **LEFT** / and FOLlow the SIGNS to the **AIR**PORT. /

D: Can you **SHOW** me / where that **IS** / on this **MAP**? /

A: (looking at a map and pointing) **WELL**,/ let's **SEE** . . . / The GAS STAtion is right **HERE**. / There's the **FREE**WAY. / This is the diRECtion you're **TRA**veling ,/ and there's the **AIR**PORT. /

D: Thanks a **LOT**. / I apPREciate the **HELP**. /

2. With your partner, make a list of places in your community where you can ask for information. For example, you could telephone or visit a store or business in your neighborhood, or an office here at school. Start with people and places that are the most comfortable, and a target that is easy to monitor. What information do you need?

Places to ask for information	**What to ask**
Example gas station	**Example** Can you give me directions to the airport?
____________________	____________________________________
____________________	____________________________________
____________________	____________________________________

3. Role play a conversation with your partner. Ask for information from one of the places you listed above. What do you want to find out? Target word stress in this conversation. List several words with more than one syllable that you will use in your conversation. Draw a dot over the stressed syllables. Check with your instructor to make sure the word stress is correct.

Example directions

____________________ ____________________ ____________________

Talk Times on Your Own

You will find a Talk Times activity at the end of every chapter. Your instructor will tell you when to begin doing these on your own. Copy the Talk Times Plan in Appendix B, page 243, to use for planning and keeping a record of your Talk Times. You may want to include these plans in a pronunciation journal. Look at the Sample Talk Times Plan, page 244, for ideas. Watch your comfort level increase as you complete more Talk Times.

Practice Tips for the Audio Tapes

Practicing with the audio tapes for this book is an integral part of making your new pronunciation a habit. Look at suggestions 1–7. Save the remainder of the tips until later. They will be helpful after you have established a regular practice schedule.

1. **Practice every day for 10–20 minutes.** This is better than practicing once a week for an hour or more. The more frequently you practice for brief periods, the quicker you will progress. Keep a record of your practice times until you establish a regular schedule.

2. **Practice in a quiet environment.** Practice in a place where you will have few or no interruptions so you can concentrate on the tape and on imitating what you hear.

3. **Do a lot of listening.** Replay the tape and go over the parts that need extra work as you proceed through each chapter. Listen to each exercise several times before you attempt to repeat what you have heard. Look away from your book so you can concentrate on listening.

4. **Use the pause button.** Put your tape recorder on pause if you need more time to repeat what you hear.

5. **Self-monitor.** Stay alert and focused as you practice. Improving your ability to hear yourself clearly and to discover your own errors is an important part of your progress.

6. **Practice the same exercises in each chapter many times during the week.** This kind of repetition is needed to train your speech muscles and improve your listening skills.

7. **Move with the rhythm of the speech.** As you listen, tap your finger or hand on the desk, tap your foot on the floor, nod your head, or move your arms to reinforce the rhythm.

Save These Tips for Later

Vary the ways you practice.
Try different things. Find the ways that work best for you.

1. **Just listen.** Concentrate on what you hear on the tape without speaking. Replay each paragraph or dialogue many times. You are more likely to repeat something more accurately after you have done a lot of listening.

2. **Listen and repeat while using the book.** Listen to the whole paragraph or dialogue as you look at the book. Replay the tape and repeat one sentence at a time, putting your tape recorder on pause and looking away from your book. Continue repeating one sentence at a time until you are familiar with the whole exercise. Monitor your speech to match the speaker as closely as you can.

3. **Close the book.** After you are familiar with an exercise, listen and repeat what you hear on the tapes without using the book. This will strengthen your auditory skills. Put your tape recorder on pause to give yourself enough time to repeat what you heard and monitor.

4. **Memorize short segments of speech.** Replay short sections of the tape until you can repeat what you heard without looking at your book.

5. **Use slow speech.** Listen to a word or a phrase to practice. Put your tape recorder on pause. Close your eyes and say the word or phrase very slowly. Concentrate on your speech.

6. **Feel the speech.** Close your eyes. Whisper or silently say a word or chunk of speech. Move very slowly and concentrate on what your mouth and tongue feel like as they form the words.

7. **Say a phrase or sentence along with the tape.** Concentrate on speaking along with the speaker. Replay the tape and try this again. This kind of simultaneous speech can be an effective way of learning the intonation patterns, especially for longer sentences. It requires more than one try.

8. **Practice using "backward build-up."** For extra practice, after you have listened to a phrase or sentence, start by saying the last word in a sentence. Then say the last two words. Then "back-up" and say the last three words. Keep going backwards until you have said the whole sentence.

9. **Practice without the tape.** After you are extremely familiar with the sound of a paragraph or dialogue from your book, practice without listening to the tape. Self-monitor your speech. Afterwards, play the tape and check yourself.

2

Stressing Syllables and Speaking Clearly

Most English words have one strongly stressed syllable that sounds longer, louder, and higher in pitch than the other syllables. Speech can be hard to understand when the strongly stressed syllable is not clear or the wrong syllable is stressed.

 Listen to the following sentences. The meaning changes when you change the stress.

Look at the **DE**sert.

Look at the des**SERT**.

He gave me a **MES**sage.

He gave me a mas**SAGE**.

What did you think of the **CO**medy?

What did you think of the com**MIT**tee?

He lives in a **JEEP** now.

He lives in **E**gypt now.

I'm taking an **AR**abic class.

I'm taking an ae**RO**bics class.

My aunt lives in **MIS**ery.

My aunt lives in Mis**SOU**ri.

Word Stress

a. Two-syllable Words

Listen and tap the rhythm of the stressed and unstressed syllables. Then sing the melody using "da." Trace the pattern as you say the word in the box. (To trace is to follow the line and the dots with your finger.) The line is long and high because the stressed syllable sounds long and the pitch is high. Touch the dot lightly and quickly as you say the unstressed syllable. Lower the pitch.

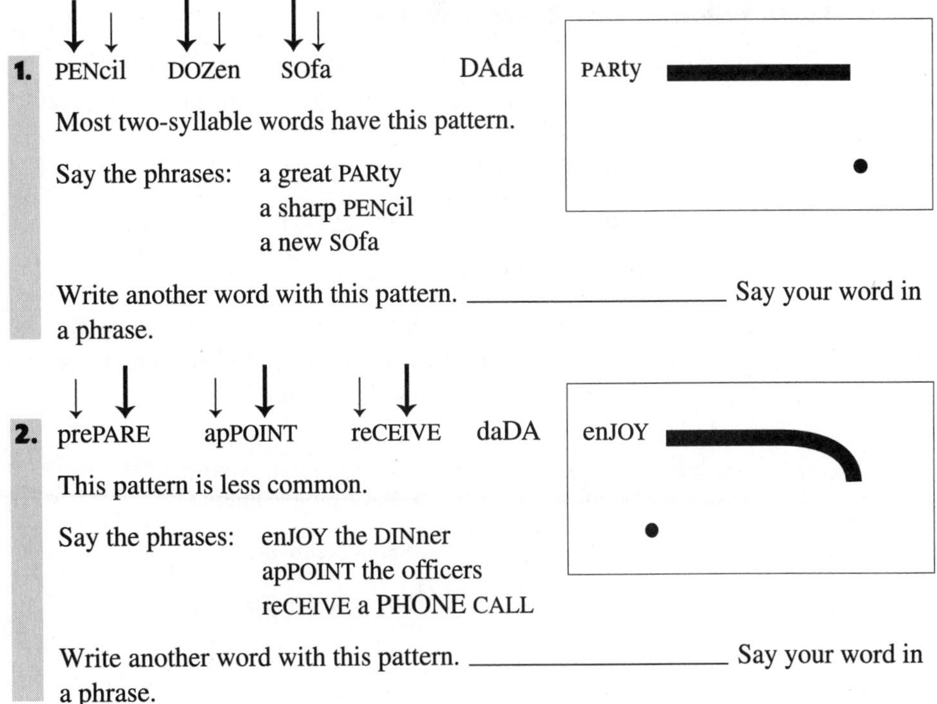

1. PENcil DOZen SOfa DAda

PARty

Most two-syllable words have this pattern.

Say the phrases: a great PARty
a sharp PENcil
a new SOfa

Write another word with this pattern. ____________ Say your word in a phrase.

2. prePARE apPOINT reCEIVE daDA

enJOY

This pattern is less common.

Say the phrases: enJOY the DINner
apPOINT the officers
reCEIVE a PHONE CALL

Write another word with this pattern. ____________ Say your word in a phrase.

b. Nouns

Most two-syllable nouns have stress on the first syllable. Draw a dot over the stressed syllable. Add to the lists.

Examples basket Alice

Names of Things	**Names of People**
table	Robert
number	Betty
auto	Gary
window	Linda Taylor
office	David Miller
__________	__________
__________	__________
__________	__________

A few two-syllable names have stress on the second syllable, such as ELAINE, SuZANNE, and EuGENE.

Unstressed Syllables and Schwa Vowels

Unstressed syllables sound weaker than stressed syllables. They are lower in pitch, shorter, and harder to hear clearly than the vowels in stressed syllables. The vowel sound that native speakers say in most weak syllables is called *schwa.* Any vowel letter in a weak syllable can sound like schwa. The symbol for schwa is ə.

Examples PENcil DOzen aBOUT (ə over the crossed-out vowel in each)

To make a schwa

Keep your mouth relaxed. Let your tongue rest gently behind your lower teeth. Open your lips a little and say "uh." The sound is short and low. You will learn more about the ə sound in Chapter 5.

Practice these words and sentences.

PROblem (ə)	What's the PROblem?
MOment (ə)	Wait a MOment.
SEATed (ə)	Please be SEATed.
ROses (ə)	I bought a DOzen ROses.

c. Partner Practice: Look-alikes

Some nouns and verbs are spelled alike but are pronounced differently. Exaggerate the stressed syllables to make the verbs sound different from the nouns. The vowels in the unstressed syllables sound unclear and like a schwa in many of these words, especially in rapid informal speech.

Examples PREsent (noun) It's my birthday PREsent.

preSENT (verb) Let's preSENT the idea.

One partner says either (a), the noun, or (b), the verb. The other partner says the matching sentence.

1.	a.	PERmit	You need a PERmit to park here.
	b.	perMIT	Please perMIT me to park here.
2.	a.	INsult	That sounds like an INsult.
	b.	inSULT	Don't inSULT the visitors.
3.	a.	PROduce	They sell PROduce at the market.
	b.	proDUCE	Cars proDUCE a lot of smog.
4.	a.	CONtract	They negotiated a CONtract.
	b.	conTRACT	Your muscles conTRACT when you exercise.
5.	a.	PROgress	He made a lot of PROgress.
	b.	proGRESS	Let's proGRESS to the next item.
6.	a.	OBject	Handle the OBject carefully.
	b.	obJECT	Did his boss obJECT to the change?
7.	a.	INcrease	She got an INcrease in pay.
	b.	inCREASE	They tried to inCREASE their profits.
8.	a.	SURvey	Please answer the questions on the SURvey.
	b.	surVEY	Let's surVEY the situation before we decide.
9.	a.	PROject	We completed the project.
	b.	proJECT	Project the slides onto the wall.
10.	a.	CONduct	The crowd's CONDduct was disorderly.
	b.	conDUCT	We are planning to conDUCT an experiment.

d. Partner Practice: "What am I?"

The suffixes "er" and "or" are not stressed in English.

Examples BETter BIGger MAJor FAVor

1. Listen to your instructor and repeat the two-syllable names and occupations. Say the stressed syllables longer and higher in pitch.

JAson LIsa RObert KATHy ALlen NANcy MARshall Alice RICHard HANnah

ARTist AUthor BUILDer DOCtor FARMer LAWyer MAYor PLUMBer SAILor TEACHer

2. Choose an occupation from the above list and write it below next to the appropriate job description.

Name	**Job Description**	**Occupation**
Jason	writes contracts	___________
Lisa	writes books	___________
Robert	serves in the Navy	___________
Kathy	works at a hospital	___________
Allen	paints pictures	___________
Nancy	builds houses	___________
Marshall	teaches at a kindergarten	___________
Alice	fixes plumbing	___________
Richard	raises chickens and grows corn	___________
Hannah	takes charge of a city	___________

3. Have a conversation with your partner. One partner says a name and a job description from the list and asks the other partner, "What am I?" The other partner responds, then says another name and job description and asks, "What am I?"

Example A: My name is JAson. I write CONtracts. What am I?

B: You're a LAWyer. My name is KATHy. I work at a HOSpital. What am I?

pronunciation tip More than 90 per cent of two-syllable English nouns have stress on the first syllable. More than 60 per cent of the two-syllable verbs have stress on the second syllable.

e. Three-syllable Words

Listen and tap the rhythm of the stressed and unstressed syllables. Then sing the melody using "da." Trace the pattern with your finger as you say the word in the box. The line is long and high because the stressed syllable sounds longer and higher in pitch. Touch the dot lightly and quickly as you say the unstressed syllables. Lower the pitch.

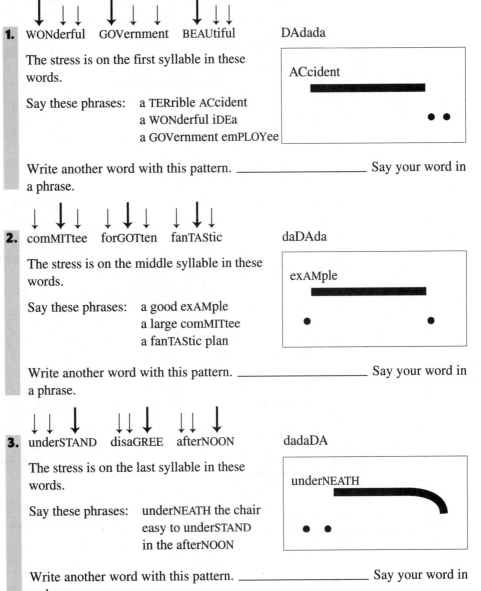

1. WONderful GOVernment BEAUtiful DAdada

The stress is on the first syllable in these words.

ACcident

Say these phrases: a TERrible ACcident
a WONderful iDEa
a GOVernment emPLOYee

Write another word with this pattern. ________________ Say your word in a phrase.

2. comMITtee forGOTten fanTAStic daDAda

The stress is on the middle syllable in these words.

exAMple

Say these phrases: a good exAMple
a large comMITtee
a fanTAStic plan

Write another word with this pattern. ________________ Say your word in a phrase.

3. underSTAND disaGREE afterNOON dadaDA

The stress is on the last syllable in these words.

underNEATH

Say these phrases: underNEATH the chair
easy to underSTAND
in the afterNOON

Write another word with this pattern. ________________ Say your word in a phrase.

f. Four-syllable Words

Listen and tap the rhythm of the stressed and unstressed syllables. Then sing the melody using "da." Trace the pattern with your finger and say the word in the box as you did for the two- and three-syllable words.

1. occuPAtion explaNAtion acaDEmic dadaDAda

The stress is before the "tion" and the "ic" suffixes in these words.

sympaTHEtic

Say these phrases: a sympaTHEtic friend
a new occuPAtion
a good explaNAtion

Write another word with this pattern. ____________ Say your word in a phrase.

2. preOCcupy aNALysis asTROLogy daDAdada

The stress is after the first syllable in these words.

psyCHOLogy

Say these phrases: a psyCHOLogy class
the asTROLogy chart
a careful aNALysis

Write another word with this pattern. ____________ Say your word in a phrase.

3. SECretary MEdiator EStimating DAdadada

The stress is on the first syllable in these words.

APpetizer

Say these phrases: a delicious APpetizer
a careful SECretary
a good MEdiator

Write another word with this pattern. ____________ Say your word in a phrase.

g. Same or Different?

You will hear two words. Listen for the stressed syllables. Is the stress on the same syllable or a different syllable? Put a check (✓) under S (same) or D (different).

			S	D
Example	busy	bigger	✓	___
	appeal	apple	___	___
	appetite	animal	___	___
	exercise	excuses	___	___
	atlas	at last	___	___
	possible	possession	___	___

h. Which Sentence Do You Hear?

Listen to a sentence from either column 1 or column 2. Check (✓) the sentence you hear.

Example ___ moved over ✓ move it over

	1	2
1.	___ Look at the rows of bushes.	___ Look at the rose bushes.
2.	___ It's an integrated school.	___ It's in a great school.
3.	___ Is it Colorado?	___ Is color added?
4.	___ The corporation was helpful.	___ The cooperation was helpful.
5.	___ She speaks her original language.	___ She speaks her regional language.
6.	___ It's in numerical order.	___ It's a miracle order.

pronunciation tip To signal the stressed syllable: 1. lengthen it. (Take your time!) 2. raise the pitch. (Think high and lift your head!) 3. emphasize it. (Make it strong!)

End-of-the-sentence Intonation: Steps and glides

The ends of the sentences are important in English.

- Frequently, the focus word, the most emphasized word, is near the end of the sentence.
- Most sentences end with a downward pitch line, or melody, that lets your listener know that you are finished with the sentence. This downward pitch line is called *falling intonation.* The melody either glides or steps down. (To glide is to move smoothly and effortlessly.) Occasionally the intonation rises, for example on "yes-no" questions. You will learn more about end-of-the-sentence intonation in Chapter 8, "The Melody of Speech."

Listen to the humming followed by the words and sentences. Replay the tape and repeat what you hear.

(To hum is to sing the melody saying *hmmm.*)

Glides The pitch on the last stressed syllable jumps up before it glides down.

aGAIN	I heard it a**GAIN**.
MATH	I teach **MATH**.

Steps If the stressed syllable is not last, the pitch goes up on the stressed syllable and then steps down.

RAINbow	I can see a **RAIN**bow.
proFESsor	I'm a pro**FES**sor.

Sometimes the most important word or focus word is not the last word in the sentence. The melody will step down like this.

Glad to **MEET** you.

Let's **EAT** now.

guideline **If the last syllable is stressed, the melody glides down. If the last syllable is unstressed, the melody steps down.**

i. Check Your Listening: Steps and glides

Listen to the speaker hum these sentences. Does the sentence end with a step or a glide? Check (✓) the column that describes the ending. Replay the tape to make sure.

Example I bought a com**PU**ter. _✓_ Steps Down

I bought a **CAR**. _✓_ Glides Down

Sentence	Steps Down	Glides Down
1. I bought some equipment.	___	___
2. I need a new pen.	___	___
3. Close your books.	___	___
4. I lost my passport.	___	___
5. It can't compare.	___	___
6. Please pass the sugar.	___	___
7. No smoking allowed.	___	___
8. We need to buy spaghetti.	___	___

j. The Echo Game

Many words in English have the same pattern as short phrases.

repuTAtion	See you LAter.	Glad to MEET you.	How's your FAMily?
compreHEND	in the END	Make a FRIEND.	Pay the BILL.

1. Divide into two groups. One group are speakers. The other group is the echo. (An "echo" is something that is repeated or imitated.) The echo responds with a phrase that has the same intonation pattern as the word the speakers just said. Work with your group until you sound like a chorus speaking in unison. To speak in *unison* means to speak or sing exactly at the same time and with the same melody.

Example Speaker: fanTAStic. Echo: It's **PLAS**tic.

Speaker: acQUAINTed Echo: He **FAINT**ed.

Speaker: underSTAND Echo: Hold my **HAND**.

2. Add movement to the echo game. Tap your hands lightly on the unstressed syllables and raise your hands or arms on the stressed syllable. Listen and watch the speaker. Echo the intonation and copy the hand movements.*

Speaker: conTENTed Echo: He SENT it. Movement:

Speaker: interACT Echo: It's a FACT. Movement:

Speaker: apPROpriate Echo: I NOticed it. Movement:

*Movement figures were designed by Cathy Davies, Davies Associates.

3. Alternate between Groups A and B. Group A are the speakers. Group B is the echo.

Example Speakers: SatisFACtion Echo: It's the BLACK one.

Speakers: SatisFACtion Echo: a reACtion

Speakers: SatisFACtion Echo: after TAXes

4. Switch speaker and echo roles after each set of three words.

Speaker	**Echo**	**Movement**
comMITtee comMITtee comMITtee	the CIty She's PREtty. He's WITty.	
interRUPtion interRUPtion interRUPtion	Let's have LUNCH now. He's my UNcle. in the MIDdle	
accommoDAtion accommoDAtion accommoDAtion	I'm on vaCAtion. They're not reLAted. an obliGAtion	
identifiCAtion identifiCAtion identifiCAtion	He went on vaCAtion. Prescribe mediCAtion. I made the arRANGEments.	
inapPROpriate inapPROpriate inapPROpriate	I can HOPE for it. You can Open it. It's not Over yet.	
comPLEXion comPLEXion comPLEXion	You GUESSED it. He CHECKS it. an EXtra	
aRITHmetic aRITHmetic aRITHmetic	a CHRISTmas gift I LOOKED at it. He LIFTed it.	
interACT interACT interACT	It's a FACT. Don't reACT. Here's your HAT	
macaROni macaROni macaROni	dozen DOnuts broken RECord slice of PIZza	
contraDICtion contraDICtion contraDICtion	Pass the CHICKen. Here's the WINner. science FICtion	

Dropping Unstressed Syllables

The weak syllable is often dropped in certain common words. For example, FAMily ⟶ FAM-ly. Listen to your instructor say these words. Draw an "X" through the dropped letter. Then say the words and phrases.

Examples SEVeral ASpirin VEGetable

1.	SALary	a good salary	5. SCENery	the scenery along the coast
2.	CHOColate	chocolate ice cream	6. BUSiness	a family business
3.	CAMera	an expensive camera	7. INteresting	an interesting book
4.	FAVorite	What's your favorite name?	8. AVerage	an average amount

k. Small Group Survey: Which one do you prefer?

Work in groups of three or four. One person in each group asks everyone in the group the first survey question and records the results. A second person asks the second survey question and records the results, and so on until everyone has a turn. Report the results of your group survey for a class tally. Monitor your speech and the speech of the others in your group.

- Signal the stressed syllable. Shorten the middle weak syllable in the underlined words.
- Step or glide down in pitch at the end of each sentence. Follow the pitch lines.

Example A: Which do you prefer, chocolate ice cream or chocolate cake?

B: I prefer chocolate cake.

Results: chocolate cake 1 person

To prepare for the survey, listen and repeat the questions on the following survey. Follow the pitch lines that give your listener a choice.

Survey

1. Which do you prefer, chocolate ice cream or chocolate cake?

   Results: chocolate ice cream ____ chocolate cake ____

2. Which would you rather have, an interesting job or a good salary?

   Results: an interesting job ____ a good salary ____

3. Which would you rather photograph with your new camera, interesting scenery or a beautiful family?

   Results: interesting scenery ____ a beautiful family ____

4. Which is better when you have a cold, several aspirin or homemade vegetable soup?

   Results: several aspirin ____ homemade vegetable soup ____

l. Limerick

Listen to the limerick. Lengthen the stressed syllables. Tap the desk to emphasize the rhythm.

A GLAmorous INternet User

Got MAIL from an OBvious LOser.

Then SHE, in a DASH,*

DUMPed his NOTE in the TRASH

In SPITE of the FACT it aMUSED her.

m. Role Play: "What's in the bag?"

1. Prepare for the role play.

Listen and repeat each item on the list. Tap the desk for each syllable. Write the number of syllables next to the word, and draw a dot over the stressed syllable.

Example ba•nanas 3

milk	___	butter	___
detergent	___	oranges	___
cranberry juice	___	tuna fish	___
pepper	___	salami	___
mustard	___	shampoo	___

Make a shopping list. Count the syllables in each item. Draw a dot over the stressed syllable. When you finish your list, see if you and your partner agree about the stressed syllables on both your lists.

Example •cereal 3

Shopping List	**How many syllables?**
________________	___
________________	___
________________	___
________________	___
________________	___
________________	___
________________	___
________________	___

*To move in a dash means to move quickly.

2. Role play with a partner. Plan a shopping trip. Talk about the things you need to buy. Monitor your own and your partner's speech. Pay attention to lengthening the stressed syllable and end-of-the-sentence intonation. Listen to the sample conversation.

A: We're out of butter and bread for sandwiches. Can you think of anything else we need?

B: Yes, we need some fruit. Bananas, apples, and oranges would be good.

A: Did you notice if we had any pasta?

B: I didn't see any. Would you rather have angel-hair pasta or spaghetti?

Predicting Stress: Which syllable should I stress?

There is no perfect way to know which syllable to stress when you see a new word. Although there are no clear rules, there are guidelines. The next section will help you figure out some of the guidelines.

n. Two-syllable Words

1. Most two-syllable words have stress on the first syllable. Listen to your instructor and repeat the words and phrases.

STORy PICture ARTist FUNny PRETty FAmous

Phrases: a FUNny STORy a PRETty PICture a FAmous ARTist

2. Figure out the guideline. What parts of speech are the above words? (nouns, verbs, pronouns, etc.)

Guideline Stress the first syllable in most two-syllable __________ and __________.
(fill in the parts of speech)

3. Figure out the guideline. The next pattern is less common. The stress is on the second syllable. What part of speech are these words?

apPLY anNOUNCE deNY rePEAT preFER alLOW

Guideline Stress the second syllable in many two-syllable __________.
(part of speech)

Other two-syllable words with this pattern are adverbs such as:

behind below ahead above

4. Review the look-alike words on page 25. Then read the following sentences and predict the stress in the underlined words. Are they nouns or verbs? Decide which syllable gets the stress and say the sentences.

1. The convict is guilty. The jury voted to convict him.
2. She became a rebel against the government. She decided to rebel.
3. He was the prime suspect in the crime. I suspect that he is guilty.
4. She is a convert to the religion. Let's convert the bedroom into an office.
5. That's an interesting subject. Don't subject me to your criticism.

Dictionaries and Pronunciation

The most accurate way to find the stressed syllable is to use a dictionary. Since dictionaries vary in the ways they show pronunciation, learn about your dictionary.

Stress Figure out how your dictionary shows word stress and the number of syllables. Remember to exaggerate the strongly stressed syllable by lengthening it and raising the pitch. Here are ways that four different dictionaries show the stressed syllable. All other examples in this exercise are from *The American Heritage* ***ESL*** *Dictionary*, published by Houghton Mifflin (1998).

1. Look up the word *banana* in your dictionary and write it below. Compare your dictionary to the other dictionaries.

bə nan´ə bə **nan´**ə bə'nan ə bə.NAN.ə Your dictionary: __________

Light Stress Some dictionaries use an additional stress mark to show secondary stress or light stress in some longer words. This can vary from dictionary to dictionary. The pronunciation of light stress can also vary with different English dialects. However, the lightly stressed syllable always sounds lower in pitch than the strongly stressed one. Look for the lightly stressed syllable in *appreciate* and *patriotic*.

(appreciate) ə **prē´** shē āt´ (patriotic) pat´ri **ot´**tik

2. Look up these words with light stress in your dictionary. Write how your dictionary shows stress for these words.

international ____________________ antibiotic ____________________

Unstress Unstressed syllables are not specifically marked. Dictionaries often show a schwa vowel ə in many of the unstressed syllables. These syllables sound shorter and lower in pitch than stressed syllables. Look for the ə in the unstressed syllable in *about* and *absent*. ə **bout´** **ab´** sənt

Sounds Dictionaries vary considerably in the ways they show vowel and consonant sounds. Many use a combination of phonetic symbols and letters. The only symbol to learn now is the *schwa*, or ə.

3. Copy the way your dictionary shows pronunciation for these words and write it on the chart on page 37:

allow legal application department consonant exceptional guarantee companion

4. Look at the words you wrote and learn how your dictionary shows strong and light stress. Your dictionary also shows many symbols for vowel and consonant sounds. It is not necessary for you to learn these symbols at this time, but it is important to realize that they are different from letters. Locate the pronunciation key that explains your dictionary's symbol system.

Write the word. Draw a dot over the stressed syllable.	**Copy the way your dictionary shows pronunciation for this word.**
Example pajȧmas	pə **jä´**məz
1.	
2.	
3.	
4.	
5.	
6.	
7.	
8.	

pronunciation guideline There are three levels of stress shown in most English dictionaries: strong stress, light stress, and unstress.

pronunciation tip The most important thing you can learn from a dictionary about pronouncing English words is which syllable to stress strongly.

o. Longer Words: Prefixes and suffixes

Some English words fall into patterns. Learning the intonation of these patterns can help you predict stress when you find a similar word. The following examples show some of the common prefixes that come before words and suffixes that come at the end of words.

1. Listen to the words on each list. Replay the tape several times.

2. Practice saying each group of words. Tap the desk for each syllable. Think of other words with the same prefix or suffix. Say each word in a sentence.

1. Suffixes: *-tion-sion* The stress is on the syllable just before the suffix

↓↓↓	↓↓↓ ↓	↓↓↓↓ ↓
deCIsion	satisFACtion	magnifiCAtion
inFLAtion	prepoSItion	simplifiCAtion

2. Suffixes: *-ic-ical-tal* The stressed syllable is before the suffix.

MAGic AtLANtic iDENtical developMENtal acciDENtal

Practice these related words.

SYMPtom-symptoMAtic ALcohol-alcoHOLic ATHlete-athLETic eCONomy-ecoNOMical

3. Suffixes: *-logy-ity* Stress the syllable before the suffix. The "y" ending is unstressed.

biOlogy eCOlogy reALity

Practice these related words.

ACtive-acTIVity POSsible-possiBILity NAtional-nationALity psyCHOlogy-psychoLOGical

4. Suffixes: *-ese-eer-ee* The stress is on the last syllable.

JapanESE auctionEER trusTEE

5. Suffix: *-ian* The stress is before the suffix.

CamBOdian INdian CoLOMbian CaNAdian

6. Prefixes: *-a-in-un* The prefix is unstressed. The syllable after the prefix is often stressed.

aWAKE inTOLerant unHEALthy

---

pronunciation tip Prefixes and suffixes are usually not stressed in English.

---

p. Partner Practice: Predict the stress

1. Look at the preceding lists to predict the pronunciation of these words with prefixes and suffixes. Draw a dot over the stressed syllable. Compare answers with your partner. Use a dictionary to make sure.

Example identification

atomic geology employee administration indifferent pioneer popularity

Scandinavian unlawful indicate monetary untruthful attack inactive

2. For more challenge, select a reading of at least six paragraphs from one of your English textbooks or use a reading that the instructor selects. Look for words with prefixes and suffixes such as you see on the preceding lists. Make a list of at least eight of the words and draw a dot over the stressed syllables. Use a dictionary to check the pronunciation. Read your list to your partner.

Finishing Up

REVIEW: WORD STRESS—STEPS AND GLIDES

1. Draw a dot over the stressed syllable and practice these words from the paragraph to follow. Say the stressed syllables longer, louder, and higher in pitch.

Two-syllable Words			Three-syllable Words		Compound Noun
woman	problem	English	forgotten	eleven	supermarket
baby	answered	courage	spaghetti	beautiful	
spoken	ahead	behind			

2. Practice the steps and glides at the end of these phrases from the paragraph.

Glides	Steps
eleven months old	a beautiful baby
place in line	How old is he?
Go right ahead	to get spaghetti
for two days	behind me

3. Practice the paragraph. Monitor for the steps and glides at the ends of sentences.

Small Talk at the Supermarket

[1]The other day when I was at the supermarket I stood behind a woman with a baby. [2]I finally got up the courage to say, "That's a beautiful baby. How old is he?" [3]The woman beamed and said, "He's eleven months old." [4]Then I realized that I had forgotten something. [5]I took a deep breath, smiled, and said to the man behind me, "Would you mind saving my place in line? I forgot to get spaghetti." [6]He answered, "No problem. Go right ahead." [7]I could have just kept quiet, gotten the spaghetti, and lost my place in line. [8]That was more English than I had spoken for two days.

TALK TIMES: MAKE YOUR NEW PRONUNCIATION A HABIT

In-class Preparation: Role play

One partner is shopping at a market. The other partner is the clerk at the market. The shopper asks for help finding items on his or her shopping list. Use the shopping list in "What's in the Bag?", page 34, as a guide.

1. Listen to the sample conversation. The focus words are in bold type.

Shopper: I'm looking for the **CE**real. Do you know where I can **FIND** it?

Clerk: The cereal is on aisle **NINE**.

Shopper: I **LOOKED** on aisle nine, but couldn't find the kind of cereal I **WANT**ed.

Clerk: I'll check to see if we're **OUT** of it. Is there anything **ELSE**?

Shopper: **YES**, I need some **PEP**per. Do you have fresh ground **PEP**per?

2. Role play with your partner. Lengthen the stressed syllable in each word. Step or glide down in pitch at the end of each sentence. Rise in pitch at the end of "yes–no" questions. Switch roles.

Talk Times in Your Daily Life: Shopping at a market

Use what you have learned about word stress in a real-life situation.

1. Make a list of things to buy at a market or other store. Include items with two, three, or more syllables. You can get ideas for your list by reading advertisements or looking at labels. Use a dictionary or ask a native speaker how to pronounce the items on your list. Write the number of syllables next to the word and draw a dot over the stressed syllables.

Examples toothpicks (2 syllables) tomatoes (3 syllables)
avocados (4 syllables)

2. Go to a market or other store. Ask for help finding the items on your list. Choose three to five items to ask about each time you go. When you locate the item, check the spelling on your list.

3. Self-monitor. Pay close attention to your speech during Talk Times. Target word stress. Lengthen the stressed syllables and change pitch. Use pauses and end-of-the-sentence steps and glides to make your speech easy to understand.

ON YOUR OWN

1. Practice with the audio tapes for this chapter for 10–20 minutes each day. This is better than practicing once a week for an hour or more. Keep a list of your practice times until you establish a regular schedule. Work in a quiet environment so that you can listen carefully to the tapes and can self-monitor.

2. Complete the following word stress charts. They show common stress patterns for two-, three- and four-syllable words. Each word has one strongly stressed syllable. Listen to the words in each group and write them under the correct pattern. Replay the tape and listen again to make sure. Use a dictionary to check your answers. Add words of your own to each pattern.

Two-syllable Words

connect letter receive modem houses compare movie surprise

conNECT the **MO**dem reCEIVE a **LET**ter comPARE the **HOU**ses

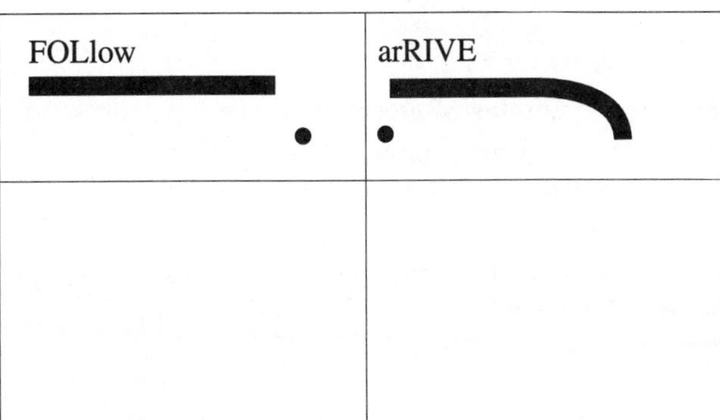

Three-syllable Words

important appointment introduce company engineer visitor
September popular comprehend

an imPORtant ap**POINT**ment a POpular **COM**pany
IntroDUCE the engi**NEER**.

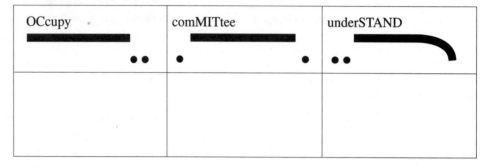

OCcupy	comMITtee	underSTAND

Four-syllable Words

secondary population millennium television enjoyable politician
cemetery entertainment exceptional

the enJOYable enter**TAIN**ment the new mil**LEN**nium
EStimating the popu**LA**tion

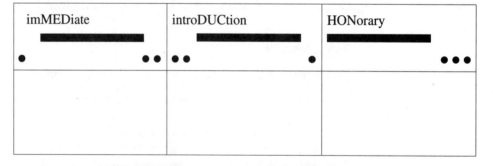

imMEDiate	introDUCtion	HONorary

3. **For more examples of words and stress patterns, see Appendix B, Common Word Stress Patterns, page 245.** For more practice, complete the word stress chart, page 246.

4. **Record the following sentences and review paragraph.** Listen to your tape and monitor for word stress. Exaggerate the stressed syllables. Monitor for falling pitch at the end of each sentence. The pitch should step or glide downward.

1. Sentences. Exaggerate the step or glide at end of each sentence.

a. I heard it again.
b. I teach math.
c. I can see a rainbow.
d. I'm a professor.
e. I bought some equipment.
f. I need a new pen.
g. Close your books.
h. It can't compare.
i. Please pass the sugar.
j. No smoking allowed.

2. Sentences with longer words. Use your dictionary to figure out the stressed syllable on the underlined words. Emphasize the stressed syllable. Fall in pitch at the end of each sentence. Listen to your tape and check your pronunciation.

   a. The company has a good reputation.

   b. The restaurant was advertised in a magazine.

   c. The station has problems with reception.

   d. They speculated in the stock market.

   e. The activity is good for the economy.

---

pronunciation tip Listening to your speech on tape will help you to identify your pronunciation targets and to become more comfortable with the sound of your own voice speaking English.

---

5. Begin your personal glossary. (See Appendix B, page 247, for a glossary form to copy and use.) Keep a list of words from your everyday life that you want to learn to pronounce. Use your dictionary to check the syllable stress and the spelling. Draw the pattern and trace it as you say the word. You may need help at first drawing the pattern, but soon you will be able to draw these patterns on your own.

6. Make small talk. Look for opportunities to make brief conversations in English everyday—at school, at a shopping mall, in the cafeteria, or wherever you happen to be. Get to know people in this class so you can talk about pronunciation. People who converse in English make more progress with their pronunciation and become more comfortable when speaking.

---

a helpful hint Become your own best teacher. Take responsibility for your own pronunciation training by deciding what parts of your accent you need to target.

3

Pronunciation Basics

Clear pronunciation depends upon good intonation. Intonation is the musical part of speech, and every language has its own distinct melody and speech rhythm. Even when you can't understand the words, you can often recognize a language by the intonation. It provides important information that is not provided by the words alone.

"Do-you-know-who-I-am-I-am-a-pow-er-ful-ro-bot." This robotic intonation is very different from English intonation which is full of contrasts. Listen to the same phrase with these changes in the melody and the rhythm. "Do you KNOW who **I** am? (pause) I'm a POWerful **RO**bot."

You can hear English intonation most easily when you listen to a whole phrase or thought group. These thought groups become like little songs with their own melody, rhythm, and focus word.

In this chapter, you can start practicing the music of English speech with these basics.

- linking
- finishing words and syllables
- thought groups
- steps and glides (end-of-the-sentence intonation)
- focus words

Linking

The words in phrases or thought groups are usually linked together. The consonant that finishes one word connects to the sound at the beginning of the next word. "Missed her" sounds like "Mister." "Spear it" sounds like "spirit." When listening to conversations, it is not always clear where one word stops and the next word starts. "Sue's in love" sounds like "Susan Love." A phrase can sound like one long word, and this can be confusing. "There is a bus coming" sounds like "therzaBUScoming." In order to understand spoken English, you have to recognize when words are linked together.

Listen and repeat the following phrases. Hold the last sound of one word until you say the first sound of the next word. Use slow speech to feel the linking. ⟶ means "sounds like."

1. turn around ⟶ tur-naround
2. turns around ⟶ turn-zaround
3. look alike ⟶ loo-kalike
4. looks away ⟶ look-saway
5. jumps up ⟶ jum-psup
6. jumped up ⟶ jump-tup
7. call after ⟶ cal-lafter
8. called after ⟶ call-dafter
9. pulled out ⟶ pull-dout
10. bakes it ⟶ bake-sit

Finishing Words and Syllables

a. Partner Practice: Finish the link

Some people mispronounce English words by leaving off final consonants. If your native language does not end syllables with consonants, you need to pay special attention to this, especially when you are linking words into phrases or sentences. Missing sounds can change the meaning. "The pla . . . arrived" sounds as if you are talking about the theater. "The plane arrived" is about an airplane.

1. Sentence (a) in the following example does not make sense because the underlined word is missing an ending sound. Change the word by adding a final sound and write the correct word on the line.

2. After you finish, compare answers. Take turns saying sentence (b) correctly. Link the ending sound to the next word. Monitor your speech and the speech of your partner.

Example a. His fee are big.

b. His feet are big.

1a. It was A hours long.

b. It was ____________________ hours long.

2a. The foe is ringing.

b. The ____________________ is ringing.

3a. The row is closed for repairs.

b. The ____________________ is closed for repairs.

4a. Turn rye at the corner.

b. Turn ____________________ at the corner.

5a. I her him laugh.

b. I ____________________ him laugh.

6a. I knee a ride.

b. I ____________________ a ride.

7a. Please moo your car.

b. Please ____________________ your car.

8a. Do you have fie dollars?

b. Do you have ____________________ dollars?

b. Improve Your Monitoring: Missing sounds

When sounds are missing, often the words do not make sense. Monitor the next speaker by listening for missing sounds at the ends of words. Learning to monitor for specific pronunciation targets such as missing sounds will help you to speak English clearly.

1. Listen to each sentence. Decide if the speaker says the underlined word or a similar word that does not make sense in that sentence. Check (✓) the word you hear. Replay the tape to make sure.

Example	The phone is not installed yet.	___ phone	_✓_ foe
1.	I need a car wash.	___ need	___ knee
2.	The hike was fun.	___ hike	___ hi
3.	I got a bank loan to buy my car.	___ loan	___ low
4.	The plane takes off at noon.	___ plane	___ play
5.	Take a bite of the cookie.	___ bite	___ buy
6.	I have to move in January.	___ move	___ moo
7.	Jeffrey got lost on his way to the highway.	___ lost	___ law
8.	There was a long line at the Post Office.	___ line	___ lie

2. Practice saying the sentences correctly. Link the underlined word to the next word. Self-monitor. Pay attention to the ending sounds and the linking.

Thought Groups

Native speakers divide longer sentences into thought groups to make them easier to understand. A thought group is a phrase or short sentence that is spoken. You can recognize a thought group when you hear a sweep of melody and a focus word. The speaker pauses at the end of each thought group.

Listen to part of a poem by Edward Lear. Trace the lines with your finger as you listen to the thought groups. The stressed words are shown in capital letters. The focus words are in bold. To learn the rest of this rhythmic poem, go to the Targeting Pronunciation Web page.

The OWL and the **PUS**sy-CAT / WENT to **SEA** / in a **BEAUT**iful / PEA-GREEN **BOAT.** /

They TOOK some **HON**ey / and PLENty of **MO**ney / WRAPPED **UP** / in a FIVE-POUND **NOTE.** /

Steps and Glides

c. Chunks of Speech: Reductions

Some thought groups are repeated so often that they become familiar chunks of speech. (A *chunk* is something that is in one thick piece, like a block of wood.) The words in a chunk of speech are linked together and flow like the melody of a song. The unstressed words often sound shortened and changed. These shortened words are called *reductions.* Step or glide in pitch at the end of each chunk.

Listen and repeat the following chunks of speech. Start by singing "duh" instead of saying the words. Follow the melody line for each sentence. A falling pitch makes the speaker sound finished. The last chunk rises in pitch because it is a "yes-no" question.

DUH duh duh **DUH**	What do you **WANT**?
DUH duh duh **DUH**	Give it a **TRY**.
duh DUH **DUH**	I don't **KNOW**.
DUH duh **DUH**	Take a **CHANCE**.
DUH duh duh **DUH**	Give me a **BREAK**.
duh duh **DUH**	Are you **SURE**?

d. Join the Chorus

Listen first. The words in each chunk are linked together. Then divide into groups A and B. Practice with your group to sound like a chorus singing in unison. Follow the melody line that you hear at the end of each chunk. Tap your desk as you say the focus words to keep up with the rhythm. Switch groups.

IdonNO

1. A: What do you **WANT**? (WHATdya**WANT**?)

   B: a cup of **COF**fee (aCUPa**COF**fee)

   A: a can of **COKE** (acanna**COKE**)

   B: a piece of **CAN**dy (aPIECa**CAN**dy)

   A: What do you **WANT**? (WHATdya**WANT**?)

   B: I don't **KNOW**, I REALly don't **KNOW**. (idon**NO**. iREALlydon**NO.**)

2. A: What did he **SAY**? (WHADdiddy**SAY**?)
   B: Don't ask **ME**! (DONAS**ME**.)
   A: Beats **ME**!* (beats**ME**)
   B: I wish I **KNEW**. (iWISHi**NEW.**)
   A: What did he **SAY**? (WHADdiddy**SAY**?)
   B: I don't **KNOW**. Let's GIVE him a **CALL**. (I don**NO**. let'sGIVima**CALL.**)

3. A: What do you **THINK**? (WHADdaya**THINK?**)
   B: Give it a **TRY**. (GIViddа**try.**)
   A: Give me a **BREAK**.[†] (GIMmya**BREAK.**)
   B: Take a **CHANCE**. (TAKa**CHANCE.**)
   A: What do you **THINK**? (WHADdaya**THINK?**)
   B: I don't **KNOW**. Keep CHANGing my **MIND**.[††]
   (Idon**NO**. keepCHANGingmy**MIND**.)

Focus Words

Every language has a way of showing what is important. In English it is the focus word. One word in each thought group is strongly stressed and easier to hear than the other stressed words. The melody steps or glides down in pitch on the focus words at the ends of these sentences. Follow the pitch line as you listen to your instructor and repeat what you hear.

Here's a glass of **WAT**er.	It's time to **GO**.
It's a piece of **CAKE**.	I'll see you **LAT**er.
I like it a **LOT**.	I need some **HELP**.
She wants to **SEE** you.	He forgot to **BRING** it.

e. Descriptive Phrases

Listen and underline the focus word in each phrase.

Example some cold water

walking slowly	a famous man	the last chance
an electric light	loves music	a messy paper

***beats me:** Puzzles me
[†]**give me a break:** Stop trying to fool or bother me.
[††]**change my mind:** Change my opinion.

f. Partner Practice: New information–old information

The focus word shows what's important by emphasizing new information. As the conversation proceeds, new information in one sentence may become old information in the next sentence.

1. Listen to the dialogues and underline the focus words.

Example A: I lost my **BOOK**. ("book" is new information)

B: **WHICH** book? ("book" is now old information)

A: My **HIStory** book. ("history" is new information)

1. A: I found my book.

   B: Which book? Your history book?

   A: No, my math book.

2. A: That must be his house.

   B: The white house?

   A: No. The gray one with the car in front.

   B: Is that Tom's car?

   A: It looks like his father's car.

2. Compare your answers and practice the dialogues with a partner.

g. Finishing Numbers and Linking

Say the last sound of each number. Close your eyes and slowly whisper ***nine***. Feel your tongue touch the gum ridge for n at the beginning and again at the end of the word.

Whisper these phrases and link the last part of the number to the next word. Feel the linking.

one o'clock five eggs eight oranges nine apples ten hours later

ninety-five elephants

h. Phone Numbers and Addresses

1. Divide long numbers into thought groups to make your speech easier to understand. Focus on the last number in each group. Then pause. Listen and draw a slash (/) where you hear a pause.

Example My **PHONE** NUMber is: / Area code / 3 1 **0** / 8 2 **9** / 9 2 4 **5**/

My address is: 1 5 3 1 3 rd Avenue

My credit card number is: MasterCard 4 3 3 1 5 7 9 2 6 7 1 9

The website address is: http://www.gorilla.org

2. Listen to the operator's phone message and draw a slash (/) where you hear a pause.

The number you have dialed 3 1 0 4 5 8 8 0 9 7 has been changed. The new number is 2 1 3 5 8 9 7 8 6 2. Please make a note of this.

i. Partner Practice: Dictate the numbers

1. Write down imaginary numbers to dictate to your partner. Say each number clearly, but focus on the last number in each group. Then pause.

My phone number is _ _ _ _ _ _ _ _ _ _.

My credit card is ______________________________
(card name)

_ _ _ _ _ _ _ _ _ _ _ _ _ _ _ _.
(card number)

The expiration date is: _ _ _ .

2. Record your partner's dictation. Find out if your numbers were clear. Exchange suggestions.

My phone number is _ _ _ _ _ _ _ _ _ _

My credit card is ______________________________
(card name)

_ _ _ _ _ _ _ _ _ _ _ _ _ _ _ _
(card number)

The expiration date is: _ _ _

Practice Pronunciation Basics

j. Partner Practice: Two dialogues

1. Listen to the dialogues. Each short sentence is one thought group. Pay attention to the focus words. Step or glide at the end of each sentence.

Dialogue 1

Where's the **GATE**?

A: I'm wondering where to catch my **PLANE**.

B: Let's see your **TICK**et. You need to go to Gate 70-**A**. It's **THAT** way.

A: **THANK** you.

A: Ex**CUSE** me. I can't find Gate 70-**A**. Can you **HELP** me?

B: Gate 70-**A**? There **IS**n't a Gate 70-**A**. Where are you **GO**ing?

A: To Van**COU**ver.

B: You need to go to Gate **78** (seventy-eight). It's in the other di**REC**tion.

Dialogue 2

Time to **GO**

A: Hurry **UP**! It's time to **GO**.

B: We don't have to go **YET**. It's too **EAR**ly.

A: **NO**, it's **NOT** too early! It's five o'**CLOCK**. The movie starts at five-**THIR**ty.

B: You're **RIGHT**. We'd better **HUR**ry.

A: That's what I've been trying to **TELL** you!

2. Practice with a partner. Listen and repeat one line at a time before saying the whole dialogue. Glide or step down in pitch at the end of each sentence. Switch roles.

---

pronunciation tip Pay attention to the ends of words and sentences. The endings of words and sentences are important in English.

---

k. Check Your Listening: Dictation

Listen to each sentence and write what you hear. You will hear the sentence two times.

1. ______________________________
2. ______________________________
3. ______________________________
4. ______________________________
5. ______________________________

l. Role Play: Planning a party

Partners A and B are giving a party for a friend who just got a great new job. They are both busy and wish to take care of as much as possible in advance. They divide the responsibilities and make a list.

1. Discuss the list with your partner. The list is not in order. Talk about which things can be done in advance (i.e., one or two weeks before), which things a day or two ahead, and which things the day of the party.

Example A: When should we borrow some dishes?

B: Let's do it a day or two ahead.

2. Lengthen the focus word at the end of each phrase. The focus word is in bold type. The pitch lines either glide or step down at the end of the phrase.

"to do" list	in advance	a day or two ahead	the day of the party
make a list of the **GUESTS**	____	____	____
address the invi**TA**tions	____	____	____
borrow some **CHAIRS**	____	____	____
arrange the **FLOW**ers	____	____	____
set the **TA**ble	____	____	____
clean the a**PART**ment	____	____	____
buy the **FOOD**	____	____	____
plan the **ME**nu	____	____	____
mail the invi**TA**tions	____	____	____
prepare the **FOOD**	____	____	____

m. Song: "Getting to Know You"

Listen to this song from *The King and I* by Richard Rodgers and Oscar Hammerstein. The music echoes the flow of conversational speech. The focus word in each line sounds longer and slower than the other words. Emphasize to make the meaning clearer.

1. Fill in the missing focus words. They are listed here in alphabetical order.

all breezy day easy know know learning like me new nicely noticed precisely say tea way

Getting to ________________ you.
Getting to know ________________ about you.
Getting to ________________ you,
Getting to hope you like ________________.
    Getting to know you
    Putting it my ________________, but ________________,
    You are ________________
    My cup of ________________.
Getting to ________________ you,
Getting to feel free and ________________,
When I am with you
Getting to know what to ________________.
    Haven't you ________________.
    Suddenly I'm bright and ________________
    Because of all the beautiful and ________________
    Things I'm ________________ about you
    Day by ________________.

2. Compare answers with a partner.

3. Discuss the meaning of these expressions.

You are my cup of tea.   free and easy   bright and breezy

n. Song Exercises

Complete the following exercises. Discuss your answers with a partner.

1. Word stress. Most of the words in the song have one syllable.

Examples know you like

Write the two- and three-syllable words below under the correct pattern on the chart. Trace the pattern as you say the word. The long line shows the stressed syllable. Say it longer and higher in pitch.

getting putting haven't noticed because suddenly breezy

beautiful precisely

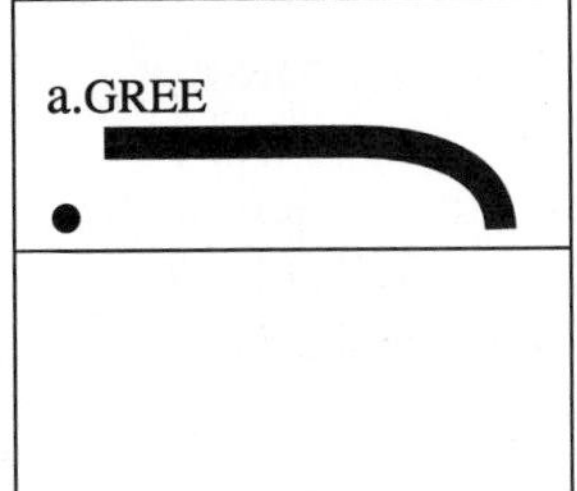

2. Focus Words. Underline the focus word in these lyrics from the song. Slash marks show thought groups for the longer sentences. Each phrase or thought group has its own focus word. Lengthen the focus words and change pitch at the end of each line.

Getting to know you . . .*

Getting to like you . . .

Getting to feel free and easy . . .

Getting to know what to say . . .

You are precisely / my cup of tea . . .

Haven't you noticed? . . .

Suddenly I'm bright and breezy . . .

Because of all the beautiful and new . . .

Things I'm learning about you . . .

Day by day . . .

3. Finishing Words and Linking. Say the phrase in one chunk. Hold the final sound of one word until you are ready to say the next word. Make the focus word easier to hear.

CUP of **TEA**

the BEAUtiful and **NEW**

FREE and **EAS**y (free'n easy)

BRIGHT and **BREE**zy (bright'nbreezy)

WHAT to **SAY**

beCAUSE of **ALL**

* The subject of the sentences starting with "getting" is "I."
Example: (I'm) getting to know you.

4. **Contrastive Focus.** Listen to these phrases. The words are the same, but the focus is different. Which focus do you hear in the song?

1. I hope you **LIKE** me.
2. I hope **YOU** like **ME**.
   Usually small words like "you" or "me" are not stressed. Sometimes they are stressed to emphasize new information or to show contrast.

5. **Thought Groups and End-of-the-sentence Intonation.** The lyrics for "Getting To Know You" translate easily into conversational speech. Practice saying the verses of the song using a conversational style. Pay attention to the focus words, finishing syllables, linking, and word stress. Fall in pitch at the end of each sentence.

o. Talk: Getting to know your partner

1. Interview your partner and introduce him or her to the class. Find out your partner's name and native country. Tell at least three important things about your partner. Talk from notes. Emphasize the focus words. Fall in pitch and pause at the end of each sentence.

2. Word stress. Write three words with more than one syllable that you will say when you introduce your partner. Draw a dot over the stressed syllables. Lengthen them and raise the pitch.

Finishing Up

REVIEW THE BASICS: MAKE A LIST

Look over the chapter. List four important things you learned about English pronunciation. Compare your list with your partner's list. You may want to add something to your list.

1. ______________________________
2. ______________________________
3. ______________________________
4. ______________________________

TALK TIMES

In-class Preparation

1. **Write a message for your answering machine.** Decide what you want people to hear when you are not able to answer your phone. Give any information you think is important. Divide your message into thought groups. Choose a focus word in each thought group to emphasize.

Example You have **REACHED** / 31**0**/ 87**5**/ 282**9**. / Janet and **I** / are not a**VAIL**able / to answer the **PHONE** right now. / We want to **TALK** to you, / so leave us a **MES**sage / and we'll return your **CALL** / as soon as **POS**sible. / Start **TALK**ing / when you hear the **BEEP** / and speak **SLOW**ly. /

____

____

____

____

2. **Write a message to leave on a friend's machine.** Decide what information you want to give. Possible ideas: A party is taking place next weekend; you are going out of town; you want your friend to go to a movie; the meeting you were going to was cancelled; you want to talk about a class assignment. Include your name, the reason for your call, your phone number, and the best time to reach you. Use pauses and pitch changes to make your message as clear as possible.

Example This is your old friend **RO**bert. / I've been trying to reach you for **DAYS**. / What's going **ON**?/ I need to find out about the **MATH** assignment. / Please call me either to**NIGHT** / or to**MOR**row night / at 31**0** / 82**9** / 463**8**. / I'll be home after six o'**CLOCK**. /

____

____

____

____

3. **Practice with your partner.** Say the answering machine message and the caller message you wrote. Fall in pitch and pause at the end of every sentence. Speak slowly. Find out if your messages were clear and if your partner has suggestions.

Talk Times in Your Daily Life: The message machine

1. **Leave at least three messages on answering machine tapes.** The machine could belong to a friend or a business. Plan ahead. Think about how to leave a clear message. Use a tape recorder to practice. When the person calls you back, ask if your message was clear. Keep a record of your calls and what happened.
2. **Re-tape the message on your own answering machine.** Listen to the message and decide if it is as clear as you would like it to be. Pay attention to the targets for this chapter.

ON YOUR OWN

1. **Practice with the audio tapes for this chapter.** It is better to practice daily for 10–20 minutes than for an hour once a week. Find a time and a place where you will have few or no interruptions so that you can concentrate on self-monitoring.

   Suggestion: Keep a daily record of your practice times. Write on your calendar whether or not you practiced and for how long. Do this until you establish a schedule.
2. **Record one of these dialogues:** Where's the Gate?, page 52, or Time To Go, page 52. Record the conversations in Exercise f, page 50, contrasting old information with new information. Listen to your speech. Is there anything you want to change? Make another recording, listen, and notice the improvements.
3. **Add to your personal glossary.** Keep collecting words from your everyday life that you want to pronounce correctly. Use a dictionary to find the stressed syllable. Use each word in a sentence.
4. **Make small talk.** Have short casual conversations in English as often as possible. You can do this anywhere you happen to be where English is spoken. The more you converse in English the more comfortable you will become.
5. **Call one person from this class to have a "phone meeting."** It could be the partner you interviewed for the "Getting To Know Your Partner Talk." Talk about the class.

   Write the name and number of someone to call:

   ______________________ ______________________
   name phone number

---

a helpful hint Use a tape recorder to become more comfortable with your own voice speaking English. Listening to your speech on tape gives you a chance to hear things about your pronunciation that you did not hear at first.

4

Speech Rhythm: Stress and Unstress

When you listen to the music of a language you hear both melody and rhythm. The rhythm variations in English words and sentences are more exaggerated than most other languages.

Words

The syllables in an English word are never all the same length. The stressed syllables are held longer and the weak syllables go by more quickly than you might expect from your original language. Stressed syllables are higher in pitch and sound louder. Unstressed syllables are shorter and lower in pitch.

The most important thing to remember about pronouncing English words clearly is to emphasize the stressed syllable. Review word stress in Chapter 2.

Sentences

Sentence Stress: Content words and focus words

The stressed words in English sentences are important. They tell most of the meaning and stand out like headlines in a newspaper. **"STOCK MARKET SOARS" "BOMB SUSPECT CONFESSES."**

1. Tap the desk as you say each stressed syllable.

I FOUND a DOLlar in my **POCKet**.

- FOUND DOLlar **POCKet** are all content words. They tell the main meaning.
- **POCKet** gets the strongest stress. It is the focus word.

2. Look at the following drawing. Tap the elephants as you say each stressed syllable.

I FOUND a DOLlar in my **POCKet**.

3. Tap the desk as you say each stressed syllable in this sentence.

I forGOT to SET the **aLARM**.

- forGOT SET aLARM are content words.
- ____________________ gets the strongest stress. It is the focus word.

4. Look at the following drawing. Tap the elephants as you say each stressed syllable.

I forGOT to SET the **aLARM**.

The most important thing to remember about pronouncing English sentences clearly is to emphasize the focus words.

Figure Out the Guideline.

Which parts of speech are the following content words:

FOUND DOLlar **POCKet** forGOT SET **aLARM**

Are they nouns, pronouns, verbs, articles, adjectives, or other?

Guideline: Content words are often ______________, ______________, or adjectives.
(fill in the parts of speech)

Unstress: Structure words

The unstressed words in between the content words are called *structure words*. They are important to the grammatical structure of the sentence. Structure words can be hard to hear clearly because the vowels are weak and short.

Look for the structure words in these sentences and write them below.

I am PLANning to TAKE a **TRIP**. She LIKES SALT and PEPper on her **EGGS**.

Structure words: ______________________________

Tap the Rhythm

Tap the desk for each stressed word as you say the sentences with your instructor.

BEAT 1 (tap)		BEAT 2 (tap)		BEAT 3 (tap)
DOGS		CHASE		**CATS**.
The DOGS		CHASE	the	**CATS**.
The DOGS	are	CHASing	the	**CATS**.
PEOple		PLANT		**TREES**
The PEOple	are	PLANTing		**TREES**.
The PEOple	have	PLANTed	some	**TREES**.
The PEOple	should have	PLANTed	some more	**TREES**.

a. Partner Practice: Where's Bob?

Sentences with the same number of words can have a different rhythm. Pay attention to the stressed syllables shown on the following page with capital letters. They get the beat.

Listen first and tap the desk for the focus words. Then work with a partner to count the words, syllables, and beats. Practice the dialogue.

Where's Bob?	**Words**	**Syllables**	**Beats**
1. A: GO FIND **BOB.**	3	___	___
2. B: I **FOUND** him.	3	___	___
3. A: WHAT'S he **DO**ing?	3	___	___
4.5 B: **LOOK** at him!	3	___	___
He's READing the **ADS.**	4	___	___
6. A: WHAT'S he **LOOK**ing for?	4	___	___
7. B: A BEAUtiful a**PART**ment with CHEAP **RENT** that inCLUDES u**TIL**ities in a GOOD lo**CA**tion that's NEAR **t**ranspor**TA**tion.	16	___	___
8. A: I HOPE he **FINDS** one.	5	___	___

b. Rhymes and Limericks

Most English-speaking children learn Mother Goose rhymes at an early age. Although these children don't always understand or say the words correctly, they learn the rhythm.

Linking The words in the rhyme are linked together. Phrases sound like one long word. "Jack and Jill" sounds like "JACK'n**JILL**." "Could eat no fat" sounds like "c'dEATno-**FAT**."

Listen to the rhymes and limerick until you can say them along with the speaker. Tap the desk for the focus words and move your head to keep up with the rhythm.

Two Mother Goose rhymes

JACK and **JILL**
went UP a **HILL,**
to FETCH a PAIL of **WA**ter.
JACK fell **DOWN**
and BROKE his **CROWN,**
and JILL came TUMBling **AF**ter.

JACK **SPRAT**
could EAT no **FAT.**
His WIFE could EAT no **LEAN,**
and SO be**TWIXT**
the **TWO** of them
they LICKED the PLATter **CLEAN.**

Limerick

Tap the desk for each stressed word as you listen to a limerick by a famous nineteenth-century nonsense poet. Replay the tape and say the limerick with the speaker.

There ONCE was a MAN so su**BLIME,**

Who MARried three WIVES at a **TIME.**

When **ASKED** "Why a **THIRD**?"

He re**PLIED,** "One's ab**SURD**!

"And BIgamy, SIR, is a **CRIME.**"

—Edward Lear

Predicting Stress

You can predict stress and unstress in sentences by looking at the parts of speech. Study the examples and add more examples to the categories.

Stress: Content Words and Focus Words

Nouns	Main Verbs	Adjectives	Adverbs	Question Words	Numbers and Negatives
phone, paper	call, walk	happy, large	slowly, fast	what, when	don't, won't, ten
__________	__________	__________	__________	__________	__________
__________	__________	__________	__________	__________	__________
__________	__________	__________	__________	__________	__________

Unstress: Structure Words

Pronouns	Helping Verbs	Articles	"To Be" Verbs	Prepositions	Conjunctions
he, her, it	will, have	the, a, an	is, were	on, of, to	and
__________	__________	(There are	__________	__________	but
__________	__________	only three	__________	__________	if
__________	__________	articles.)	__________	__________	because

c. Partner Practice: Identifying content words

1. Listen to each sentence. Underline the content words.

Example I <u>put</u> my <u>foot</u> on the <u>brakes</u>.

1. What would you like for dessert?
2. I haven't received the bill yet.
3. Our professional staff will be happy to assist you.
4. He planted a variety of vegetables in his garden.
5. Ethnic foods such as bagels and pizza are popular.

2. Compare answers. Use the previous chart. Discuss the parts of speech of the words you underlined.

3. Practice saying the sentences.

d. Partner Practice: Structure words

1. Add structure words to the following sentences. There may be several good choices.

Example I CALLED you on the **TEL**EPHONE.

1. WHAT ____ ____ THINK ____ ____ **MO**VIE?
2. ____ CAR ____ ____ FLAT **TIRE**.
3. ____ BOUGHT ____ BOX ____ **CAN**DY.
4. ____ SAILED ____ BOAT ____ ____ LAKE ____ ____ **MOON**LIGHT.
5. ____ ____ FIND ____ SHORTCUT ____ ____ **AIR**PORT?
6. ____ ____ ____ BIG DENT ____ ____DOOR ____ ____ NEW **CAR**.
7. ____ STOPPED HOME ____ ____ WAY ____ ____ **LI**BRARY.
8. ____ LISTENS ____ ____ PHONE MESSAGES ____ ____ **MORN**ING.

2. Compare answers with your partner and practice the sentences. Emphasize the content words. Say the structure words softly. Lower the pitch. Glide or step down in pitch at the end of the sentence.

practice tip Whisper the structure words to yourself and say the content words out loud. This will highlight the contrast between the stressed and unstressed words.

Focus Words: The basic stress pattern

English speakers use speech rhythm and intonation to show what's important. It would be confusing if all the content words were stressed equally. The focus words call attention to what is most important.

 **Guidelines for Focus Words.** Listen and repeat some examples for each guideline. Tap the desk as you say the focus words.

---

guideline 1 The focus word is usually the last content word in each thought group or short sentence.

---

in the **DARK**

at the **MO**vies

I SAT in the LAST **ROW**.

She WORKS at the **BANK**.

---

guideline 2 If there are several content words in a row, the last one usually gets the focus.

---

a BUsy **SCHED**ule

reCOvered **QUICK**ly

It STOPPED **SNOW**ing.

the LAST YELlow **BUS**

---

guideline 3 The focus word is usually an important part of speech.

Add your own focus word in the sentences to follow.

The focus word is a:			
	Noun	JIM is a GOOD **TEACH**er.	TOM is a YOUNG ________.
	Verb	It's TIME to **EAT**.	It's TIME to ________.
	Adjective	The FLOWer is DELicate and **BEAUtiful.**	The TREE is ________.
	Adverb	She FINished **QUICKly**.	She SINGS ________.

guideline 4 Adverbs at the end of the sentence that answer the questions "where" and "when" are usually unstressed and fall in pitch.

I'm planning to **LEAVE** now.

I've never **BEEN** there.

There are a lot of **TREES** here.

We're expecting **RAIN** today.

guideline 5 Structure words at the ends of sentences in the basic pattern are unstressed and fall in pitch.

I'll **WAIT** for you.

What **BANK** is it in?

There's a lot of **CREAM** in it.

We bought **FOUR** of them.

guideline 6 In longer sentences there is a focus word in each thought group.

Some credit card companies offer low **IN**terest / but they charge an annual **FEE**. /

If you're interested in becoming a **DOC**tor / it's helpful to have experience in a **HOS**pital./

e. Partner Practice: The basic pattern

Write a focus word to finish each sentence and take turns saying your sentences. Monitor your speech and your partner's speech for focus words and falling pitch.

1. I forgot to call my __________.
2. The concert starts at __________.
3. We plan to __________.
4. My friend works at a __________.
5. Tell me the answer __________ly.
6. He told me about the__________.
7. She just learned how to __________.
8. The movie was very __________.

f. Partner Practice: Dialogue

1. Listen and underline the focus word in each sentence in the dialogue.

Fix the Roof

A: What's the matter?

B: My roof is leaking.

A: Why don't you fix it?

B: It's raining. I don't want to get wet.

A: You could wait until the rain stops.

B: Then I won't have to fix the roof.

2. Compare answers and practice saying the dialogue with a partner.

g. Join the Chorus

1. Listen to two poems. Then divide into Groups A and B. Replay the tape. Listen and repeat each poem with your group. Tap the desk as you say each focus word. Switch groups.

Happy Thought

Group A: The world is so **FULL** / of a number of **THINGS,** /

Group B: I'm sure we should **ALL** / be as happy as **KINGS.** /

Rain

Group A: The rain is raining all a**ROUND,** /
It falls on field and **TREE,** /

Group B: It rains on the um**BREL**las here, /
And on the ships at **SEA.** /

—Robert Louis Stevenson

2. Work with a small group to learn one of the poems. Practice until you sound like a chorus speaking in unison.* Present your poem to the class.

* **unison:** the same note at the same time, as if with one voice

h. Partner Practice: Focus words

1. Listen and underline the focus words in these short conversations. Notice whether or not the focus word is at the end of the sentence.

1. A: I got a call from Jennifer.
   B: Really? I wonder how her father is.
2. A: I'd like to find out about the college.
   B: Here's some information for you.
3. A: John isn't feeling well.
   B: What's the matter with him?
4. A: How long have you been here?
   B: About an hour.
5. A: Peter finally arrived.
   B: Good. We've been waiting for him.
6. A: Did you remember to cash the check?
   B: No. I forgot about it.

2. After you listen several times, say the dialogues with a partner. Switch roles.

3. Review the guidelines on page 66. Then underline the focus words and compare answers with your partner. Practice saying the short conversations.

1. A: We're expecting visitors today.
   B: I would like to meet them.
2. A: Why did your friend decide to go to Guatemala?
   B: Because he's never been there.
3. A: Do you have any information about skiing in Utah?
   B: Yes. Here are some brochures for you.
4. A: I hope you've considered all the possibilities.
   B: I've considered all of them.
5. A: We are not quite prepared for the meeting today.
   B: Perhaps we should cancel it.
6. A: We have to install a new phone line here.
   B: I hope we won't have to wait a long time for it.

i. Join the Chorus

Listen first. Then divide into Groups A and B. Replay the tape and practice one line at a time until your group sounds like one voice. Tap the desk as you say the focus words to keep up the rhythm. Although other content words may receive stress, the focus word gets the most emphasis. Switch groups.

What's Happening?

A: How are you **DO**ing today, **ANNE**?

B: I'm doing **FINE**, and **YOU**?

A: Nothing much is **HAP**pening,

B: Nothing much is **NEW**.

A: I **THINK** I'm ready for a **CHANGE**.
I'd like a new rou**TINE**.

B: I've been working **HARD** these days,
The busiest I've ever **BEEN**.

A: Things have been going **SMOOTH**ly,
Time has been flying **BY**.

B: I'm feeling on top of the **WORLD**.*
And I don't know exactly **WHY**.

A: What's going **ON** these days? What's **NEW**?
How are things working **OUT**?†

B: This has been a fantastic **YEAR**.
It's **GREAT**, without a **DOUBT**.

A: Oh, I'm **BU**sy, I'm **DIZ**zy,
Everything's in a **SPIN**.

B: My schedule's over**LOAD**ed
My patience is wearing **THIN**.

A: Well, I've been very **HAP**py.
Things have been going **WELL**.

B: I'm delighted to **HEAR** that.
I can **LOOK** at you and **TELL**.

A: How are you **FEEL**ing today, **PAUL**?

B: How about **YOU**—what's **UP**?

A: There's a **LOT** that's going **ON**,

B: There's a **LOT** that's shaping **UP**.††

*__on top of the world:__ Feeling very happy, delighted.
†__working out:__ Progressing, turning out.
††__shaping up:__ Developing, taking shape.

j. Partner Practice: The weather report

1. Read the weather report and underline the focus words. The longer sentences will have more than one focus word. Use the parts of speech to help predict the stress.

> Good afternoon. Here is the latest weather news on this wet Tuesday. Heavy rain is falling throughout the Southland. Cloudy skies and showers will continue until Friday. The low yesterday was fifty-six. The high was sixty-eight. Temperatures in the same range are expected today and for the next few days. Keep your umbrellas handy. You'll need them.

2. Listen to the report to see if you and your partner predicted correctly. Discuss your answers.

3. Practice saying the weather report. Use the basic stress pattern for sentences. Lengthen the focus words and step or glide down in pitch at the end of each sentence.

k. Role Play: A TV weather reporter

You are a TV weather reporter. Prepare a short weather report for the class. Write out the report and underline the content words. Start by announcing your name, the day, the time, the TV station, etc. Lengthen the focus words. Change pitch and pause at the end of each sentence.

Example And now for the 11 o'CLOCK WEAther rePORT. This is Jody **CHAN** with the CHANnel **4** NEWS and **WEA**ther. I'm BRINGing you the LAtest **WEA**ther rePORT for **TUES**day, April **SE**cond. You can expect SUNSHINE to**DAY** and the REST of the **WEEK**. The TEMperature conTINues to **RISE**.

____

____

____

____

____

____

pronunciation tip

To decide which words in a sentence receive stress, look at:

- the stressed syllable in the individual words.
- the parts of speech.

Changes in Focus: New information

As conversation proceeds, the speaker uses focus to respond appropriately to the previous statement or question. New information is highlighted. The speaker may stress words that would not normally receive strong stress at the beginning of the conversation. Listen to the examples.

Use focus to answer a question. Stress the word that answers the question.

1. A. Jerry lost his **BOOK**. (basic pattern)

   B. **WHO** lost his book? ("book" is old information)

   A. **JER**ry lost his book. (answers the question "who")

2. A. Jerry lost a **BOOK**. (basic pattern)

   B. **WHOSE** book? ("book" is old information)

   A. He lost **HIS** book. (answers the question "whose book")

Use focus to disagree. Stress the word that highlights the disagreement.

1. A: I think that the movie ends at NINE-**THIR**ty. (basic pattern)

   B: I read that the movie is supposed to end at **TEN**-THIRty.

2. A: Ann is going to win the gold medal for **SWIM**ming.

   B: I think that **JANE** is going to win the gold medal for swimming.

   A: I don't a**GREE**. **I** think Jane is going to win the **SIL**ver medal.

Use focus to show enthusiastic agreement. Stress the helping verb to show enthusiastic agreement with the previous statement.

1. A: That was a marvelous **FILM.**

   B: That **WAS** a marvelous film.

2. A: That sounds like a great i**DE**a.

   B: That **DOES** sound like a great idea.

Use focus to highlight new information. Stress the word that gives the new information.

1. A: I need to borrow some **MO**ney. ("money" is new information)

   B: How **MUCH** money? ("money" is now old information)

   A: Well, not **TOO** much money. ("much" and "money" are both old information)

   B: I have about ten **DOL**lars. ("dollars" is new information)

   A: I was hoping to borrow **TWEN**ty dollars. ("dollars" is now old information)

I. Partner Practice: Finish the conversation

Partner A uses the basic focus pattern. Partner B uses focus to show disagreement and enthusiastic agreement. Complete Partner B's part of the conversation and underline the focus words. Practice the short connections.

Show disagreement in these conversations. Stress the word that highlights the disagreement.

Example A: The book costs eLEven **DOL**lars.

B: With the tax it's closer to **TWELVE** DOLlars.

1. A: The next town is about FIVE **MILES** from here.

   B: I thought the next town ______________________

2. A: There were four people **WAIT**ing.

   B: Are you sure? I thought ______________________

3. A: Excuse me, do you know what **TIME** it is? I'm exPECting my **FRIEND**.

   B: It's EIGHT o'**CLOCK**.

   A: **REAL**ly? I thought it was about ______________________

4. A: How much are the tickets for the **BAS**ketball GAME?

   B: I think they're about $25 a**PIECE**.

   A: That sounds ex**PEN**sive. I thought they cost about ______________________

Show enthusiastic agreement in these conversations.

Example A: My mother is a great **COOK**.

B: She **IS** a great cook.

1. A: That was a long **WALK**.

   B: ______________________

2. A: Mark has been a loyal **FRIEND**.

   B: ______________________

3. A: That new schedule is a real im**PROVE**ment.

   B: ______________________

4. A: We've been waiting here a long **TIME**.

   B: ______________________

5. A: That was an exciting soccer game.

   B: ______________________

m. Partner Practice: New information

Listen and underline the focus words in the following dialogues. The focus words emphasize the new information. Then replay the tape to check your answers. Practice the dialogues with a partner.

Where Are You Going?

A. Where are you going?

B. To buy a car.

A. What kind of car?

B. A used car. A cheap used car. Where are you going?

A. I'm going to a meeting.

B. The staff meeting?

A. No, the director's meeting.

A Fearful Shopper

A. I'd like to look at a printer, a laser printer.

B. Do you want a color printer or a black and white printer?

A. I don't care about the color. I'd like to see that one, the laser printer with the carrying case. It looks like a portable laser printer.

B. I'm sorry, but that's not a portable printer. It's a laptop computer. Would you like to look at a laptop computer? They're great for airplanes.

A. I'm sure they are great for airplanes. Thank you, but not today. I'm still afraid to fly.

n. Partner Practice: Stressing structure words

One partner says sentence A. The focus word is underlined. Listen to the focus shift to the structure word in sentence B and underline the focus words you hear. Discuss your reasons. Practice the short conversations.

Example A: What's your favorite <u>color</u>? ("color" is new information and the last content word)

B: Purple. What's <u>your</u> favorite color? (the phrase "favorite color" is old information)

Discussion When you repeat the question that someone just asked you, shift the focus word to the pronoun.

1. A: How's your family?

   B: Fine, thank you. How's your family?

2. A: What do you want?

   B: An apple. What do you want?

3. A: Who's your favorite actor?

   B: I don't know. Who's your favorite actor?

Discussion When someone gives you a choice, answer by picking one thing, or pick them both by stressing the structure word.

4. A: Do you want cake or ice cream?

   B: I want cake and ice cream. I want them both.

5. A: I'm hoping we can have dinner and see a movie.

   B: We have time to have dinner or see a movie, but not both.

6. A: Would you like meat or fish?

   B: I'd like fish.

7. A: Should we go by plane, or drive the car?

   B: I don't want to go by plane or drive the car.

o. Partner Practice: Answering questions

First listen to the short conversations, then practice saying them. One partner asks a question. The other partner uses focus to answer the question and contrast new information. The focus words in the question are underlined. Underline the focus words you hear in the answers. Discuss your reasons with your partner.

Example A: Who has a degree in physics? ("physics" is new information)

B: John has a degree in physics. ("physics" is old information. "John" answers the question)

Discussion Speaker A used the basic focus pattern. The focus was on "physics," the last content word. Speaker B shifted the focus word to "John." This answered A's question about "who."

1. A: How many languages does your friend's father speak?

   B: My friend's father speaks three languages.

2. A: Are you planning to buy a car?

   B: No, I'm planning to rent a car.

3. A: How many cities is Nancy planning to visit on her trip to China?

   B: She told me she was planning to visit three cities on her trip to China.

4. A: Is <u>John</u> planning to go on <u>vacation</u> before he finishes the <u>project</u>?

   B: As far as I know, John is going on vacation after he finishes the project.

5. A: Would you like a <u>coupon</u> to save <u>$1.00</u> on a <u>carwash</u>?

   B: Thank you, but I already have a coupon to save $1.00 on a carwash.

6. A: Would your <u>family</u> like <u>tickets</u> for the <u>baseball game</u>?

   B: Thank you, but my family has tickets for the baseball game.

p. Partner Practice: Finish the dialogues

Partner B's responses below change the focus from the basic pattern. Write a sentence for Partner A. Compare your answers with your partner's and practice the short dialogues. There may be more than one possible answer.

Example A. *Let's visit my grandmother before dinner.*

B. I'd rather visit your grandmother **AF**ter dinner.

1. A. ______________________________

   B. I'd rather eat **AF**ter the movie.

2. A. ______________________________

   B. I ordered a **CHEESE** sandwich and a salad.

3. A. ______________________________

   B. I think that this ad is **MORE** interesting.

4. A. ______________________________

   B. I thought we **MAILED** them the request on Thursday.

5. A. ______________________________

   B. I'm going to be away on Friday **AND** Monday, so can we set up the meeting for Tuesday?

6. A. ______________________________

   B. Let's **WALK** to the meeting and take a **CAB** home.

q. Talk: You're the expert

Tell the class how to do something that you know very well. Pick something with about ten steps. Start with an introduction and end with a conclusion. Use a conversational style to make your talk interesting.

Sample topics

How to take a good picture; how to wash your car; how to cook your favorite dinner recipe; how to program your VCR; how to plan a trip; how to be a good shopper.

1. Prepare your talk.

- Write the steps in your talk.
- Make a list of the longer words and draw a dot over the stressed syllables.
- Underline the focus word in each phrase or sentence. (See sample below.)
- Use a tape recorder to practice your talk. Listen to your recording and self-monitor.

Sample introduction and steps

"How to make a pot of tea"

Drinking tea with a <u>friend</u> is one of my favorite ways to <u>relax</u>. Here's how I like to <u>make</u> it.

First step: Decide how many cups of <u>tea</u> you want to <u>make</u>.

Last step: Serve with <u>milk</u> or <u>lemon</u> or <u>sugar</u>, along with your favorite <u>cookie</u> or <u>cake</u>.

Word stress: relax decide lemon sugar favorite cookie

2. When giving your talk, speak from memory or from notes. If you need to look at your paper, look at your audience before you speak. Monitor for focus words and end-of-the-sentence intonation.

r. Role Play: Interview your partner

You are helping with a survey of international students from various campuses and departments. You plan to interview several students from your campus. Start by interviewing your partner.

1. Prepare for the role play.

- Make sure that you can pronounce the name of the school you attend, your major, other schools in your area, and other majors. Find out from your instructor how to pronounce these correctly. Make up some sentences about this information and emphasize the focus words.

______________________	______________________
(your school)	(your major)

- List other schools in your area.

______________________ ______________________

______________________ ______________________

- Practice the pronunciation of these majors. Draw a dot over the stressed syllables.

English Business Engineering Computer Science Education

Psychology Other: ______________________

- Practice saying the questions on the survey with your partner. Help each other with the pronunciation. Wh-questions fall in pitch.

Question 1: What school are you attending and what is your major?

Question 2: What are you planning to do after you leave this school?

Question 3: Where do you plan to live in the future?

Question 4: What kind of work do you plan to do?

2. Change partners for the role play. Interview your new partner. Take turns asking each other the survey questions. Monitor for focus words and end-of-the-sentence intonation. Emphasize one important word in each thought group and fall in pitch.

Finishing Up

REVIEW

Predict Stress and Unstress: The basic pattern

Underline the content words and circle the focus word in each sentence. Practice the sentences.

The shoes are old but good.

I bought some popcorn at the movies.

I can go to Toronto on Monday.

Predict the Focus: New information

Underline the focus word in each line of the dialogue. The last sentence is longer and has two focus words.

Which Bus?

A: When is the next bus?

B: Which bus?

A: The bus to the shopping mall.

B: There are two shopping malls.

A: Well, I want to go to the best one.

B: The bus to that shopping mall should be here soon.

There are three levels of stress in English sentences.

- **strong stress (focus words)**
- **stress (content words)**
- **unstress (structure words)**

TALK TIMES: MAKE YOUR NEW PRONUNCIATION A HABIT

In-class Preparation: Role play

Your friend has recommended a restaurant. You want to find out more about it before you take your guest for dinner. One partner is the customer. The other partner answers the phone at the restaurant.

1. Plan a conversation with your partner about calling the restaurant for information. Write the questions you will ask. Possible topics:

- the price range of the entrees
- what is included (salad, dessert, etc.)
- the dress, formal or informal
- the appropriateness for children
- the location (include cross streets)
- the parking (street parking or parking lot)
- reservations needed

2. Role play the conversation. Monitor for word stress, focus words, end-of-the-sentence intonation.

Talk Times in Your Daily Life: Choosing a restaurant

Call or visit at least three different restaurants for information.

1. Choose two or three things to ask about during each call. Write down the questions you plan to ask, and practice these before you make the call. Decide what targets you are going to monitor.

2. Make notes about what happened and how well you monitored for your targets. Rate your comfort level. Plan your next call.

ON YOUR OWN

1. **Practice with the audio tapes.** Repeat the same exercises on several different days during the week. Replay small sections of the tape several times, especially the parts that need work. Listen and repeat one line at a time by putting your tape recorder on pause. All this listening will improve your ability to hear English clearly.

2. **Record the sentences in exercise c, page 64, and the Dialogues in exercise n, page 73.** Listen and compare your recording to the speaker on the audio tapes. Improve your pronunciation and re-tape your speech.

3. **Record the paragraph "Grandparenting" on the Targeting Pronunciation Web page.** Follow the directions for paragraphs.

4. **Notice words that you want to pronounce more clearly and add them to your personal glossary.** Use your dictionary or ask a native speaker how to say them. Most nonnative speakers have to exaggerate the stressed syllable by lengthening it and changing pitch more than usual.

5. **Make small talk.** Conversing frequently in English will give you more confidence.

---

a helpful hint

Improve your listening by recording your favorite TV program on video so that you can listen again. The more familiar you are with the content, the easier it is to hear the pronunciation. Don't skip the commercials! They can be good for hearing natural pronunciation.

---

another helpful hint

Keep congratulating yourself. It takes courage and effort to change the way you speak. Many people feel self-conscious when they try talking differently. This probably means that their pronunciation is improving. Your efforts and successes, large and small, are all important.

Vowels and Speech Rhythm

English has at least fifteen different vowel sounds, although there are only five vowel letters. Most other languages have between five and eight vowels. It is often difficult for nonnative speakers to identify or pronounce all these vowels. The most important thing about pronouncing English vowels is to lengthen the stressed ones. The vowels in unstressed syllables are shortened and unclear. As you learned in Chapter 2, these unclear, unstressed vowels are sometimes known as *schwa.*

Clear

Clear vowels
Stressed syllables

Unclear

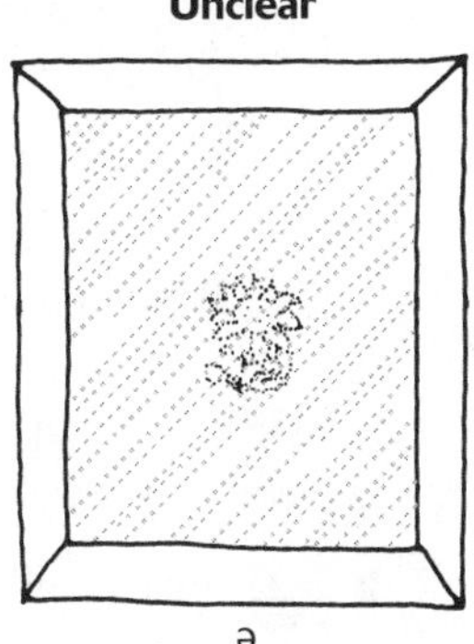

ə
Most unstressed syllables

Review how to say ə

Let your whole face, lips, and tongue relax.

Open your mouth just a little and let your tongue rest gently behind your lower teeth.

Say a quick "uh." Make it lower in pitch and quieter than the stressed syllable.

Unstress: Shortening the vowels in weak syllables

The most common sound in English is the schwa. Any unstressed vowel can be reduced to ə, and most of them are, especially in informal rapid speech. All unstressed schwas may not sound exactly alike. They are hard to hear clearly and are often called "unclear vowels." However, all unstressed schwas are very short and low in pitch.

a. Two-syllable Words: Which syllable has the ə?

1. Listen to the words and sentences. Trace the word pattern. Touch the dot lightly and quickly for the unstressed syllable with the schwa vowel.

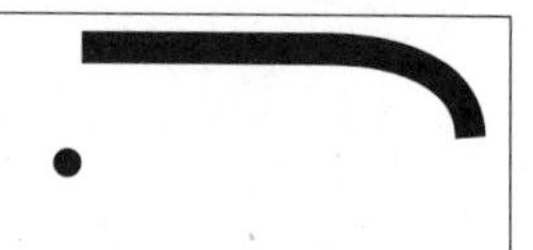

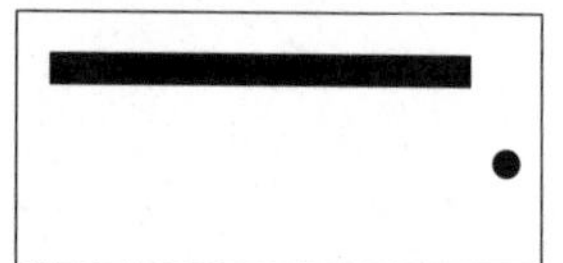

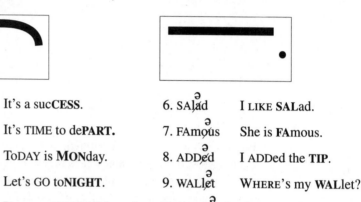

1.	s~~u~~cCESS	It's a suc**CESS**.	6.	SAL~~a~~d	I LIKE **SAL**ad.
2.	d~~e~~PART	It's TIME to de**PART.**	7.	FAm~~o~~us	She is **FA**mous.
3.	t~~o~~DAY	ToDAY is **MON**day.	8.	ADD~~e~~d	I ADDed the **TIP**.
4.	t~~o~~NIGHT	Let's GO to**NIGHT**.	9.	WALl~~e~~t	WHERE's my **WAL**let?
5.	~~a~~GREE	Do you a**GREE** with me?	10.	HUSb~~a~~nd	Her HUSband is at **WORK**.

2. Replay the tape. Look away from the book as you say the words and sentences with the speaker. Make the stressed syllables sound much longer than the unstressed syllables.

b. Partner Practice: Compare clear vowels and reduced vowels.

1. Say "pen." It has a clear vowel. Say "HAPp~~e~~n." The vowel in the syllable "pen" is reduced to schwa.

2. Listen and repeat the words on the following chart. Exaggerate the difference between the stressed and the unstressed syllables.

Clear Vowels	Reduced Vowels	Clear Vowels	Reduced Vowels
1. man	WOm~~a~~n	6. fin	MUFf~~i~~n
2. fast	BREAKf~~a~~st	7. age	HOSt~~a~~ge
3. sip	GOSs~~i~~p	8. den	d~~e~~NI~~a~~l
4. mass	m~~a~~sSAGE	9. pro	pr~~o~~DUCtive
5. ad	~~a~~dVICE	10. no	INn~~o~~c~~e~~nt

3. Practice the words in your own sentences. One partner says the one-syllable word with the clear vowel, the two-syllable word with the unclear vowel, and a short sentence. The other partner does the same with the next pair of words. Take turns.

Example Partner A: man WOman The woman stood in line.

Partner B: fast BREAKfast Do you want some breakfast?

c. Partner Practice: Countries and names

Most two- and three-syllable names in English have at least one unstressed schwa vowel. To prepare for the following role play, listen to your instructor and repeat these names.

JaPAN KoREa GERmany CHIna FINland MoROCco POLand ITaly

ALice NORman MARsha KARen ALlen Ethan ReBECca KENneth

Role play. You and your partner are in charge of hosting a reception. Discuss your plans. You each have a chart telling who in your group is going to greet students from different countries. Ask each other questions so that you both have all the information. Use the unstressed schwa in the names. Lengthen the stressed syllables.

Example

A: Who is going to greet the student from Finland?

B: I believe it's Alice. Who is going to host the student from Morocco?

A: Karen doesn't have anyone to greet. Let's ask her to host the student from Morocco.

Partner A's List		**Partner B's List**	
Greeter	**Country**	**Greeter**	**Country**
	Finland	Alice	Finland
Karen			Morocco
Marsha		Marsha	Germany
Ethan	Poland	Ethan	
	Italy	Kenneth	
Allen	China	Allen	
Norman		Norman	Japan
Rebecca	Korea	Rebecca	

Questions and Answers

1. Do native speakers always say a schwa vowel in the same words?
Not necessarily. When native speakers talk more slowly or more formally, they may use fewer schwa vowels. Also, in some words the unstressed vowel can sound closer to I than ə.

2. How do I know when to use a schwa vowel?
As you hear English speech more clearly you will begin to recognize the sound of a schwa. Then you can begin to self-monitor and use it in your own speech. Most English dictionaries show a ə or an unstressed I when they are commonly used in unstressed syllables.*

3. Do I always have to say a schwa vowel to sound effective in English?
No. You need to shorten the unstressed syllables and lower the pitch.

4. Do I have to say a schwa frequently in unstressed syllables to sound like a native speaker?
Yes.

Reductions

When native speakers converse, they shorten many unstressed structure words used in everyday speech. They may omit certain consonants. The vowels in these shortened, or reduced, words often sound like a schwa. The same word said alone has a full clear vowel.

d. Reducing Structure Words

Listen and compare some structure words said alone and in phrases or sentences. Replay the tape and look away from your book to hear the sound of the reductions. After you have listened several times, say each phrase with the reduced structure words.

Structure Words

1. your	WHAT'S your (ə) FAVorite **STORy**?
2. you	Are you (ə) **REAdy**?
3. and	FUN and (ə) **GAMES**
4. are, than	ComPUters are (ə) FASter than (ə) **EVer.**
5. an	I WANT an (ə) **ORange.**
6. a, of	HAVE a (ə) GLASS of (ə) **JUICE.**
7. at	Let's LEAVE at (ə) **NOON.**
8. to, the	They WENT to (ə) the (ə) **MOVies.**
9. from, to	It's from (ə) FOUR to (ə) **FIVE.**

* In addition, the *Houghton Mifflin AHESL Dictionary* (1998) gives two pronunciations, a regular and a reduced, for the most common structure words.

e. Listening for Reductions

It's important to listen for these reductions even if you don't always say them. Reductions were introduced on page 48.

Listen to the sentence. Decide if the speaker uses native-like speech with reduced structure words or the speaker says all clear vowels. Check (✓) the appropriate answer.

		Reduced Structure Words	All Clear Vowels
Example	Does the bus go to the beach?	✓	____
	Does the bus go to the beach?	____	✓
1.	You have to sit down.	____	____
2.	He said that he was sorry.	____	____
3.	I can tell that you want to go.	____	____
4.	Please pass the sugar and cream.	____	____
5.	Put them down.	____	____
6.	Would you like to read the paper?	____	____
7.	He was interested in everything.	____	____
8.	Do you think so?	____	____

f. Can and Can't: What's the difference?

Even native speakers get confused at times and need to ask for clarification. Lengthen the vowel and raise the pitch for "can't" because negative words are stressed in English. Lower the pitch and reduce the vowel in "can." Practice humming the melody and saying the sentences.

can ⟷ **Reduced, Unstressed, Lower Pitch**	**CAN'T** ⟵⟶ **Not Reduced, Stressed, Higher Pitch**
Adam can **GO** with us.	Adam CAN'T **GO** with us.
I can TELL the **DIF**ference.	I CAN'T TELL the **DIF**ference.
Melinda can **ANS**wer now.	Melinda CAN'T **ANS**wer now.
She can SPEAK **SPAN**ish.	She CAN'T SPEAK **SPAN**ish.

g. Group Dictation

1. Work in groups of three or four. Each person takes a turn dictating five sentences to the group. Say either "can" and "can't" in each sentence. Check (✓) the word you say, but don't let your group see the word you check.

2. Listeners write down the word you hear. Compare answers after each speaker finishes the dictation.

Speaker 1:	1. I ________ go tomorrow.	____ can	____ can't
	2. You ________ borrow my car.	____ can	____ can't
	3. I ________ leave now.	____ can	____ can't
	4. I ________ meet you later.	____ can	____ can't
	5. We ________ be there at 5 PM.	____ can	____ can't
Speaker 2:	1. ________ you come earlier?	____ Can	____ Can't
	2. She ________ tell the difference	____ can	____ can't
	3. I ________ fix it by noon.	____ can	____ can't
	4. My friend ________ come at six.	____ can	____ can't
	5. I ________ loan you the money.	____ can	____ can't
Speaker 3:	1. Why ________ that happen?	____ can	____ can't
	2. I ________ believe it!	____ can	____ can't
	3. It ________ be done that way.	____ can	____ can't
	4. I ________ hear the neighbor's radio.	____ can	____ can't
	5. You ________ buy it at a supermarket.	____ can	____ can't

h. Partner Practice: Dialogue

Listen and underline the focus words. Replay the tape and listen for the reduced "can". Practice the dialogue with a partner.

Phone Confusion

A: Can you hear me?

B: Yes, I can hear you. Can you hear me?

A: We must have a bad connection. I can't hear you at all.

B: Well I can hear you! You're the one who can't hear.

A: What did you say? I guess you can't hear me either.

B: I can hear you. Listen, I'm hanging up. I'll call you back on another line.

Clear Vowels and Unclear Vowels

Clear vowels are not reduced. Most clear vowels are in stressed syllables. Native English speakers from different countries and with different dialects can vary in the way they pronounce individual vowel sounds, but all native speakers emphasize stressed syllables. Unstressed schwa vowels are unclear and reduced. This exercise gives you a chance to hear the fifteen vowel sounds in words with American English pronunciation. For more practice with vowels, see Appendix D.

---

pronunciation tip **There are three ways to signal the stressed syllable. Lengthen it. Say it louder. Raise the pitch. Exaggerating the stressed syllable is one of the most important things you can do to speak English clearly and effectively.**

Listen and repeat the sentences in the following chart. The underlined words are examples of the fifteen clear vowel sounds shown in grey boxes before the sentences. The vowels are divided into long vowels and short vowels.

Long Vowels

These vowels sound	ey	CHANGE the DATE to the **EIGHTH**.
longer than the short	iy	LEAVE the KEYS on the **SEAT**.
vowels. The tongue	ay	MIKE would LIKE some **RICE**.
glides* from one place	ow	He TOLD me an OLD **JOKE**.
to another as you say	uw	The NEW SHOES are **HUGE**.
them. Listen for "a"	aw	I FOUND the TOWN in an **HOUR**.
"e" "i" "o" and "u."	əy	The BOY enJOYS his **TOY**.

Short Vowels

The tongue does not	a	My FAther GOT the **JOB**.
move from one place	ə	Can you COME for LUNCH on **SUN**day?
to another when you	I	GIVE him a SIP of **MILK**.
say the short vowels.	æ	I was MAD at the MAN in the **CAB**.
	E	The GUESTS LEFT at **SE**ven.
	U	LOOK! I TOOK a **COOK**ie!
	ɔ	I BOUGHT some COFfee at the **MALL**.
	ər	SIR, can you LEARN the **WORK**?

***glide**: To move smoothly and without effort.

Contrast Two Short Clear Vowels

Shut ə (stressed)	**Shot a**
• Rest the tongue tip behind the lower front teeth.	• Rest the tongue tip behind the lower front teeth.
• Let the mouth drop open gently.	• Open the mouth wider than for schwa.
• Say "uh" without moving or tensing any part of your mouth.	• Lower the tongue and say "ah" as if the doctor wants to look at your throat.
• This is the most relaxed of all the vowels.	• The jaw is lower than for any other vowels.
He shut the door with his hand.	He shot the door with a gun.

Listen and repeat the phrases. Emphasize the focus words.

ə	COME for **LUNCH**	my MOther **COUNTry**	ONCE a **MONTH**
a	LOCK the **BOX**	STOP the **CLOCK**	a POPular **TOpic**

pronunciation tip **Practice with the stressed schwa can help you to learn the sound of the unstressed schwa. The unstressed schwa goes by quickly, but has the same sound.**

i. Partner Practice: ə and a

Listen to your instructor say the sentences contrasting two clear vowels.

1.	a.	You look good in that color.	Good! I like red.
	b.	You look good in that collar.	It feels a bit tight.
2.	a.	I was wondering about the city.	Would you like some information?
	b.	I was wandering about the city.	Were you lost?
3.	a.	Is your luck good?	Yes, I got a good job and a big apartment.
	b.	Is your lock good?	Yes, but I lost the key.
4.	a.	I hear a loud pop.	Is it a balloon bursting?
	b.	I hear a loud pup.	Has he been barking long?
5.	a.	He's in the bucks.	When did he get all the money?
	b.	He's in the box.	What's he doing in a carton?

2. One partner says either sentence (a) or (b). The other partner says the appropriate answer.

Example		
	a. This <u>cut</u> is uncomfortable.	a. Would you like a bandage?
	b. **This <u>cot</u> is uncomfortable.**	b. **Would you rather sleep on a futon?**

Unstressed Syllables with Clear Vowels: Two-syllable words

Not all the unstressed vowels are reduced to schwa. You can hear an unstressed clear vowel in some words, but it will be quieter and lower in pitch. Listen and compare.

	Unstressed Schwa	**Unstressed Clear Vowel**
1.	COMmøn (ə)	COMment
2.	MANa̸ge (ə)	MANdate
3.	BAcøn (ə)	BAKing
4.	PROfi̸t (ə)	PROgress
5.	BANdi̸t (ə)	BANjo
6.	cønCLUDE (ə)	conCRETE

j. Check Your Listening: Listen for schwa

Most unstressed syllables have schwa vowels, especially in rapid conversation. Listen for the unstressed syllable in these two-syllable words. Decide if you hear a schwa. Check (✓) the correct column.

Example COOKie ____ unstressed schwa vowel _✓_ unstressed clear vowel

		Unstressed Schwa	**Unstressed Clear Vowel**
1.	hoTEL	____	____
2.	camPAIGN	____	____
3.	PEAnut	____	____
4.	URban	____	____
5.	WAITed	____	____
6.	transMIT	____	____
7.	ELbow	____	____
8.	colLECT	____	____

k. Partner Practice: Story

1. Listen to the story.

Breakfast Conversation

[1]The man and the **WO**man were having **BREAK**fast. [2]"I hope we can finish breakfast **FAST** because I don't want to be late for **WORK**." [3]The man started to eat his bacon **OM**elet. The woman took a bite of her **MUF**fin, but got dis**TRAC**ted. [4]They began to **GOS**sip about the woman's **BOSS**. [5]"Can you i**MA**gine? He has a lot of ad**VICE** about being pro**DUC**Tive and making a **PRO**fit. Then he leaves **EAR**ly on **FRI**day before things are **FIN**ished." [6]"Well, I can be**LIEVE** it! He never seems to work very **HARD**." [7]"And did you notice his **SHOES** at the Open **HOUSE**? . . . Ex**PEN**sive, but not **PO**lished." [8]"**NO**. I didn't **NO**tice." [9]**MEAN**while, the omelet was getting **COLD** and the minutes were ticking a**WAY**.

2. Practice these words from the story. In rapid casual conversation unstressed syllables are more likely to be reduced to a schwa. These reduced vowels are marked with a ə.

WOm~~a~~n BREAKf~~a~~st FIN~~i~~sh START~~e~~d MUFf~~i~~n BAC~~o~~n
OMEl~~e~~t disTRACT~~e~~d iMAG~~i~~ne ~~a~~dVICE pr~~o~~DUCtive
PROf~~i~~t NOt~~i~~ce POl~~i~~shed MIN~~u~~tes ~~a~~WAY

3. Alternate reading the lines from the story. Pay attention to shortening the unstressed vowels and lengthening the stressed ones.

l. Proverbs

Listen and fill in the missing structure words. Replay the tape and repeat each proverb one at a time. Discuss the meaning of each proverb.

1. ____ bird ____ ____ hand / ____ worth two ____ ____ bush./
2. ____ stitch ____ time / saves nine./
3. Don't put all ____ eggs / ____ one basket./
4. Necessity / ____ ____ mother ____ invention./
5. Money ____ ____ root / ____ all evil./
6. Grab ____ bull / ____ ____ horns. /
7. Rome ____ built / ____ ____ day./
8. ____ err ____ human; / ____ forgive ____ divine./
9. ____ apple doesn't fall far / ____ ____ tree./
10. ____ grass ____ always greener / ____ ____ other side ____ ____ fence./

m. Partner Practice: Scrambled thought groups

The proverbs are divided into two thought groups. One partner says the first part from column A. The other partner looks for the answer in column B and finishes the proverb. Emphasize the focus words at the end of each thought group. Step or glide down in pitch at the end of the sentence.

A	B
1. A bird in the **HAND**	saves **NINE.**
2. A stitch in **TIME**	is the mother of in**VEN**tion.
3. Don't put all your **EGGS**	of all **E**vil.
4. Ne**CES**sity	in one **BAS**ket.
5. Money is the **ROOT**	is worth two in the **BUSH.**

More Proverbs	**Group 2**
1. Grab the **BULL**	to forgive is di**VINE.**
2. Rome wasn't **BUILT**	on the other side of the **FENCE.**
3. To err is **HU**man;	by the **HORNS.**
4. An apple doesn't fall **FAR**	from the **TREE.**
5. The grass is always **GREEN**er	in a **DAY.**

n. Talk about a Proverb

1. Give a short talk (9–12 sentences) about one of the proverbs. Start your talk by saying the proverb and explaining it in your own words. You might compare the proverb to a similar proverb in your language.

2. Plan your talk, but don't read it. Talk from notes. Target stress and unstress, thought groups, and focus words.

o. Partner Practice: How many syllables?

Say "blow" (one syllable). Blow the **HORN**. Say "bəLOW" (two syllables).

It's bəLOW the **WIN**dow.

1. Listen to your instructor and repeat the sentences. Pay attention to the syllables in the underlined words. Do you hear a schwa vowel?

1.	a.	Do you have an I.D.?	I have my driver's license.
	b.	Do you have an idea?	I'm thinking about life on Mars.
2.	a.	The thief was rested this morning.	He got a good night's sleep.
	b.	The thief was arrested this morning.	The police took him to jail.
3.	a.	It's cute.	You mean her puppy?
	b.	It's acute.	You mean her illness?
4.	a.	His estate is large.	He has a lot of money.
	b.	His state is large.	He's from Texas.
5.	a.	It's not fair.	It's not "just" or "impartial."
	b.	It's not a fair.	It's not a trade exhibit or a carnival.
6.	a.	I've been learning about signs.	Are you talking about billboards?
	b.	I've been learning about science.	Physics and chemistry?
7.	a.	Use "surfs" in a sentence.	He surfs the Internet daily.
	b.	Use "surface" in a sentence.	The surface of the desk needs cleaning.

2. One partner says either sentence A or B. The other partner responds.

Example A: Do you have an I.D.? B: I have my driver's license.

p. Partner Practice: Finish the sentences

Figure out which words go in the blanks. One partner says the word pairs. The other partner says the sentence.

Example A: I.D. idea B: I haven't any idea what happened to my I.D.

1.	I. D.	idea	1. I haven't any ________ what happened to my ________ .
2.	state	estate	1. The ________ is in the ________ of Washington.
3.	sport	support	2. The ________ fans enthusiastically ________ the team.
4.	steam	esteem	3. His self-________ lost some of its ________ when he failed the exam.
5.	rested	arrested	4. John ________ after the thief got ________.
6.	signs	science	5. The ________ in front of the ________ building are green.
7.	surfs	surface	6. He ________ on the ________ of the waves.

q. Partner Practice: Dialogue

1. Listen to the dialogue. Underline the focus words. The focus words in line one are already underlined. Compare your answers with your partner.

The Optical Shop

A: I need new contact lenses and glasses.

B: I know a couple of good optical shops that are not far from here.

A: What are their names?

B: I think one is "I-Care Optical," and the other one is called "Eye-Care Optical."

A: What are you talking about? Both those names sound alike to me.

B: They may sound alike, but they're not spelled alike. That makes them different,* don't you think?

A: That's possible, but what about their prices? I want to know if they're expensive.

2. List two-syllable words from the dialogue. Figure out which ones have schwa in one syllable and which ones have two clear vowels. Check (✓) the chart. Discuss your answers with your partner.

Two-syllable Words		Schwa Syllable	Two Clear Vowels
Example	contact	___	✓
	different	✓	___
1.	__________	___	___
2.	__________	___	___
3.	__________	___	___
4.	__________	___	___
5.	__________	___	___
6.	__________	___	___

* *different* is usually said as a two-syllable word in informal conversation.

3. Find two words from the dialogue with three syllables. Mark the unstressed syllables where native speakers say a schwa.

Example optical ________________ ________________

4. Practice the dialogue with a partner. Switch roles.

Longer Words: Light stress

In some words you may hear a syllable with light stress in addition to the strongly stressed syllable. The lightly stressed syllable has a clear vowel and is lower in pitch than the strongly stressed syllable.

Four-syllable words:	eCOnoMIZE	CONfiDENtial
	COMpeTItion	phoTOGraPHY
Five-syllable words:	HIPpoPOtamus	MULtiNAtional
	acCOMmoDAtion	INcomPATible

r. Partner Practice: Look alikes

These nouns and verbs are spelled the same but pronounced differently. The difference is in the last syllable. What is the difference between these pairs of words that look alike?

DUplicate (noun) I need a duplicate of my birth certificate.

DUpliCATE (verb) Can you duplicate this report?

Before you practice, listen to the following words and sentences. Then one partner says either the noun, the adjective, or the verb. The other partner says the matching sentence. Take turns.

1.	GRAduate (noun)	She's a college graduate.
	GRAduATE (verb)	When will you graduate?
2.	EStimate (noun)	Here is an estimate of the costs.
	EStiMATE (verb)	Can you estimate the cost per square foot?
3.	apPROXimate (adjective)	That's an approximate amount.
	apPROXiMATE (verb)	Let's approximate the costs.
4.	ADvocate (noun)	She's a Women's Rights advocate.
	ADvoCATE (verb)	We advocate a change in the law.
5.	asSOciate (noun)	He is an associate in the law firm.
	asSOciATE (verb)	We associate sun bathing with the beach.

Some "ate" words are used as adjectives. For example:

a SEParate piece   a DUplicate copy   an asSOciate professor

s. Role Play: Planning a move

Imagine that you and your partner are roommates. You are both planning to move at the end of the month. Both have exciting jobs in another city. You are busy and want to divide the responsibilities.

1. To prepare for the role play, review the things to do before you move. Find at least one word in each item on the "to do" list that has an unstressed schwa vowel. There may be more than one, but you only need to find one. Mark the schwa vowel and practice the word in the phrase.

Example NOtify the **GAS** COMpany

2. Discuss the "to do" list with your partner. Put initials next to the task to show who is doing what: in advance, a day before the move, the day of the move. What should you do? Monitor for word stress. Make the stressed vowels sound much longer than the unstressed vowels. Stress the focus words in each sentence.

"To Do" List	In Advance	The Day Before	The Day of the Move
notify the electric company	____	____	____
cancel the newspaper	____	____	____
contact the phone company	____	____	____
notify the apartment manager	____	____	____
mail change of address cards	____	____	____
have a garage sale	____	____	____
collect extra boxes	____	____	____
throw stuff away	____	____	____
clean the apartment	____	____	____
compare prices (hiring a mover, renting a truck)	____	____	____

Finishing Up

REVIEW

Check Your Listening: Dictation

Write the sentences you hear. You will hear each sentence two times. Correct your own dictation by listening to the tape again.

1. ______________________________
2. ______________________________
3. ______________________________
4. ______________________________
5. ______________________________

Study the Chart: The basics about vowels and speech rhythm

1. ←——→ Strongly stressed syllables all have clear vowels.

	Clear strongly stressed vowels
BAcon	• sound like one of the 15 clear vowels on the chart.
reVIEW	• have a higher pitch and sound longer than unstressed vowels.

2. ←→ Unstressed syllables have a mixture of clear and unclear vowels.

aBANdon	• The vowels in most unstressed syllables sound like a ə or a short I. They are low in pitch. They go by quickly and are hard to hear clearly, so they are called "unclear."
camPAIGN PROgram	• The vowels in some unstressed syllables sound like one of the 15 clear vowels. They are low in pitch and sound short.

3. ←——→ Lightly stressed syllables have clear vowels that are low in pitch.

SATisFACtion inVEStiGATE	Some longer words have another stressed syllable that is lower in pitch and shorter than the strongly stressed syllable.

---

pronunciation guidelines

Native speakers often use schwa vowels in:
- unstressed syllables.
- reductions, especially in informal conversation.

The most important thing about vowels is to make the stressed syllables sound much longer than the unstressed syllables even if you don't say a native-like schwa.

TALK TIMES: "USE IT OR LOSE IT"

In-class Preparation: Role play

1. One partner is the customer who needs information about moving. The other partner works for either a moving company or for a truck rental agency. Both of you need information from the other partner, and both have information that the other partner needs. What do you need to find out? Write a list of questions that the customer and either the mover or the truck-rental agency might ask.

Possible topics for questions:

Information the moving company needs

- the number of rooms to move
- what is being moved (furniture, belongings)
- the distance of the move
- who will pack (need help or do it yourself)
- supplies needed (boxes, tape, etc.)

Information the customer needs

- cost (hourly rate, estimate of total costs)
- availability on a certain date
- experience of the moving company
- insurance to protect against loss or damage

2. Practice the sample dialogue with your partner.

A: Good afternoon, Peacock Van and Storage. How can I help you?

B: I'm planning to move at the end of the month. How much do you charge?

A: That depends. How far are you moving?

B: To another city—about 350 miles from here.

A: How many rooms in your apartment?

B: One bedroom, a living room, and a dining room.

A: Do you need help packing?

B: I can pack my own things. So how much do you think the move will cost?

A: We can come over tomorrow and give you an estimate.

3. **Role play a conversation with your partner about calling a moving company or calling a truck rental agency.** What do you need to find out? Make the stressed syllables sound much longer and higher in pitch than the unstressed ones even if you do not always reduce the unstressed vowels to schwa. Monitor your own and your partner's speech. Switch roles.

Talk Times in Your Daily Life: Calling about moving

Pretend you are moving from your one-bedroom apartment to a city 350 miles away. Make three calls to decide between using a mover or renting a truck. Get information and compare prices. Choose one or two things to ask about during each call. Write your questions and practice saying them before calling. Mark the stressed syllables and the focus words.

ON YOUR OWN

1. Practice regularly with the audio tapes for short periods of time. This is important to your progress. Practice only as long as you can concentrate and self-monitor. Read *Practice Tips for the Audio Tapes,* page 20, for ideas about how to vary your practicing.

2. Record the dialogue, The Optical Shop, page 93.

3. Record the following paragraph.

- Listen first and then read the paragraph silently to become familiar with the content. Then cover the paragraph with a piece of paper and listen.
- Replay the tape. Listen and repeat one line at a time, looking away from your book. Record your speech and listen to your recording. Decide what you want to improve, and record the paragraph again.

The Photographer

[1]Anything is possible. [2]My brother Adam just won a North American photography competition. [3]He specializes in taking pictures of desert animals. [4]He exhibited his photographs in communities across the United States and Canada. [5]After some local television appearances, he immediately sold some of his photographs for exceptionally good prices. [6]Until a few years ago, Adam didn't even own a camera.*

4. Keep writing words in your glossary that you want to pronounce more clearly. Use your dictionary to find the stressed syllable. Include names and places in your community in your glossary. Get help with the pronunciation from a native speaker.

5. Continue to make small conversations in English each day. This will increase your self-confidence and your comfort level.

---

a helpful hint

Tape record your speech to become more comfortable with your own voice and to monitor your pronunciation. Read silently a short paragraph from a newspaper or a magazine. Then record the paragraph. Listen to the recording several times to hear things that you did not hear at first. Decide what you want to change, and then record the same paragraph again.

---

try this

Close your eyes. Visualize a TV screen and a channel changer. Switch the channel to English. You are now an English-speaking actor in an English program. Breathe English. Move English. Use the English channel when you are doing Talk Times. Later, switch back to your native language channel for speaking your original language.

---

* Notice how frequently this speaker uses stressed and unstressed schwa vowels. The schwa in "just" and "won" is stressed.

6

The Speech Pathway—What's Happening Where?

Talking is so automatic that we usually don't think about how it happens. Babies cry and babble. Eventually they learn to talk. At a young age we listen and learn to repeat the words and intonation of our native language. The sounds we make, baby sounds or talking, start with the air we breathe. There is a pathway for speech that starts at the lungs and ends with the mouth and nose where the air comes out.

Follow the Speech Pathway

Explore the pathway for the speech sounds of English. Walk your finger along the drawing of the head to the various numbered locations as you practice saying the sounds that you make there.

Lungs: Location 1 on the pathway

Take in a deep breath (inhale). Say "ah" as you breathe out (exhale). The energy for saying "ah" and all speech comes from the air we breathe. Put your hand near your mouth and say "hat." Feel the air.

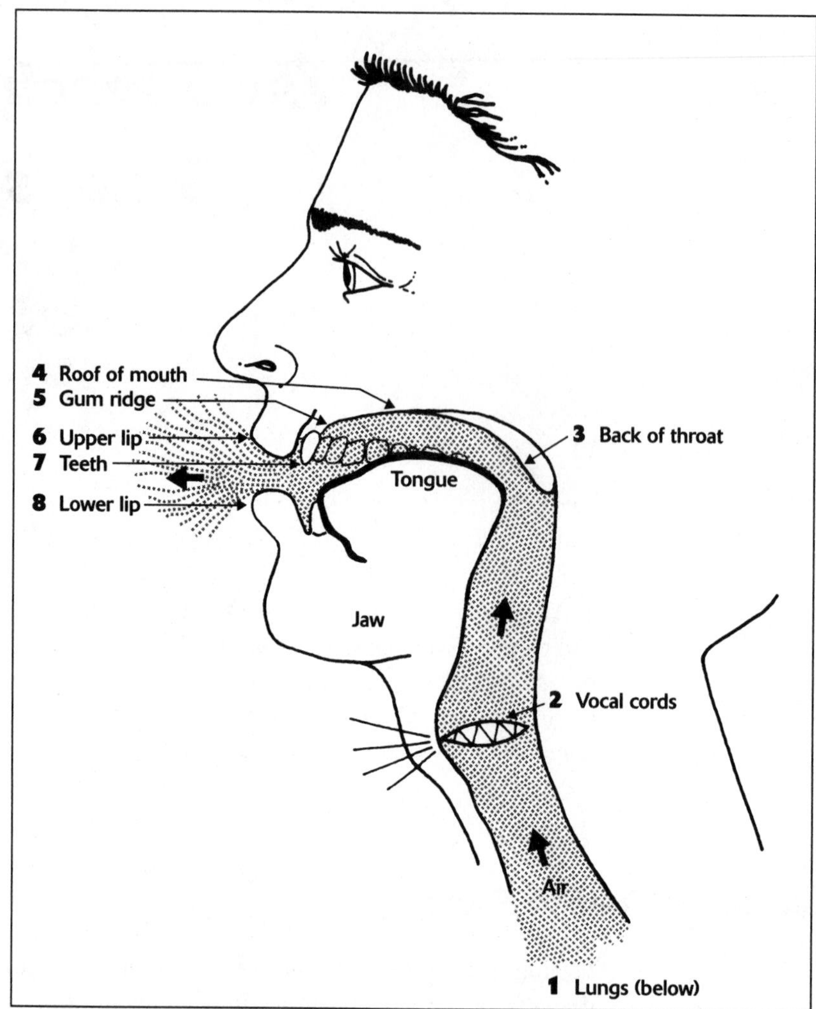

Vocal Cords and Voicing: Location 2 on the pathway

What is voicing?

After the air leaves the lungs, it goes through the vocal cords. Sometimes the vocal cords vibrate. The vibration is called *voicing*. Find the vocal cords on the drawing of the speech pathway.

1. Put your hand gently on your throat. Say "aaah," then "mmm." Feel the vibration.
2. Say "ssss." Do you feel any vibration on your throat? Alternate between "ssss" and "zzzz." The vibration turns on and off. The consonant sounds written in grey boxes with a squiggly underline are voiced. The consonant sounds written in plain grey boxes are voiceless.

Examples s (voiceless) z (voiced) f (voiceless) v (voiced)

What sounds are voiced?

- All vowels are voiced.
- Some consonants are voiced and some are not.

Stops: The air stops along the speech pathway

To make speech sounds, the air from the lungs either briefly stops along the pathway or continues out without stopping. Look at the picture of the closed window to see the sounds called *stops*. The picture of the open window shows examples of sounds called *continuants*. The air for these sounds continues out the pathway without stopping.

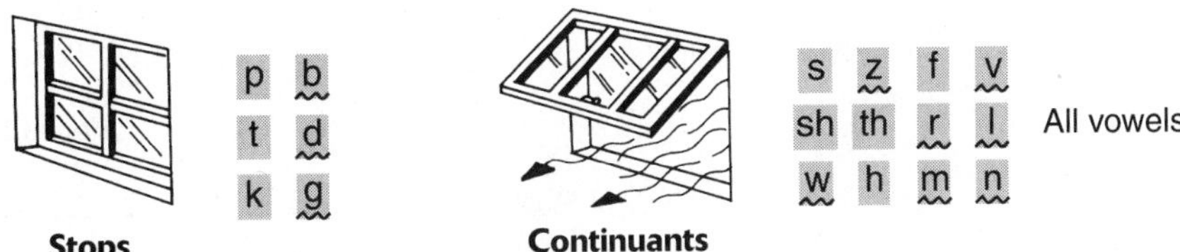

Practice saying the consonant stops in the following exercises. There are three places where you stop the air to make these sounds. Check locations 3 (back of throat), 5 (gum ridge), and 6 and 8 (lips) on the drawing, page 100

Back of the Throat: Location 3 on the pathway

k

1. Take a breath and start to say "key." Squeeze the k sound tightly in the back of your throat to stop the air and build up air pressure. Then release the air and finish saying "key."

2. Say the words and phrases **k**iss sac**k** ba**k**ing bac**k** away ta**k**e a walk pic**k** a number

3. Write a word that starts with k. ________________
Write a word that ends with k. ________________
Say each word in a sentence.

g

1. Start to say "go." Squeeze the g in the back of your throat. Finish saying "go." Next, slowly run your tongue tip from behind your front teeth along the bony roof of your mouth. Move back toward your throat until you get to the soft part where you stopped the air for k and g.

2. Say the words and phrases. **g**ame bi**g** bi**gg**er ba**g** of gum e**gg** and toast bi**g** apple

3. Write a word that starts with g. ________________
Write a word that ends with g. ________________
Say each word in a sentence.

4. Put your hand on your throat and say k – g. Which is voiced, k or g? ____
Which is voiceless? ____ Contrast voicing. **K**ate–**g**ate **c**old–**g**old

Gum Ridge: Location 5 on the pathway

t

1. Lift your tongue to touch the roof of your mouth just behind your top teeth. Take a breath and hold your tongue on your gum ridge. Let the air build up by preventing it from coming out either your mouth or your nose. Whisper t as you release the air in a puff.
2. Say the words and phrases. **t**iger a**t** a**tt**emp**t** I los**t** it.
   He kep**t** it all day. Put sal**t** on it.
3. Write a word that starts with t. ____________________
   Write a word that ends with t. ____________________
   Say each word in a sentence.

d

1. Feel the same bony gum ridge behind your top teeth. This gum ridge is an important place for English speech. You put your tongue on your gum ridge when you say the past tense ("ed").
2. Say the words and phrases. **d**ay E**d** rea**d**y re**d** apple Sli**de** over
   adde**d** a dollar staye**d** all day.
3. Write a word that starts with d. ____________________
   Write a word that ends with d. ____________________
   Say each word in a sentence.
4. Put your hand on your throat and say t – d. Which is voiced, t or d? ____
   Which is voiceless? ____ Contrast voicing. **t**ie–**d**ie **t**ime–**d**ime

Lips: Locations 6 and 8 on the pathway

p

1. Whisper p. Take a breath and start to say the word "pop." Hold your lips closed for the p. Let the air build up. Where do you feel the sound? Finish saying "pop."
2. Say the words and phrases. **p**ay u**p** ha**pp**y Si**p** it slowly.
   Sto**p** it! Ho**p** along.
3. Write a word that starts with p. ____________________
   Write a word that ends with p. ____________________
   Say each word in a sentence.

b

1. Take a breath and close your lips to stop the air. Then say "**b**a**b**y." Feel your lips close two times.

2. Say the words and phrases. **b**ee tu**b** ru**bb**er Ru**b** it off. Gra**b** a sweater.

3. Write a word that starts with b. __________
Write a word that ends with b. __________
Say each word in a sentence.

4. Put your hand on your throat and say p and b. Which is voiced, p or b? ____
Which is voiceless? ____ Contrast voicing. **p**ay–**b**ay **p**ill–**b**ill

a. Watch the Air Release: Voiceless stops

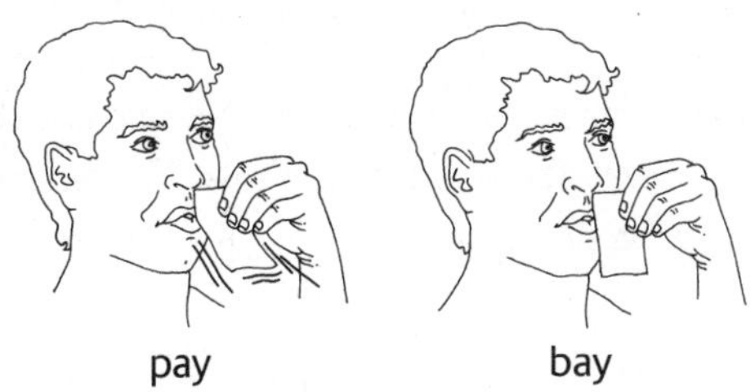

1. With one hand, hold a narrow strip of paper about 1 × 3 inches long in front of your mouth.

2. Say "pay." The paper moves as you release the puff. Say "bay." The paper doesn't move. There are three places along the pathway where the air releases in a puff at the beginning of words. Watch the air blow the strip of paper as you say the voiceless stops. p t k

3. Tongue exercise for voiceless stops.

- Slowly whisper "PUH-TUH-KUH" several times. Feel the places in your mouth where the air stops.
- Say "**PUH**-tuh-kuh, **PUH**-tuh-kuh, **PUH**-tuh-kuh." See how quickly you can repeat this sequence and still keep up the rhythm.

b. Holding Final Stops

Often native speakers of North American English do not finish saying the stop sounds at the ends of sentences. Hold the final stop by leaving your tongue where it is. Let the air build up, but do not release the air in a puff at the end of these sentences. *Turn on the ligh**t**.* *Take a brea**k**.*

1. Listen and repeat the following words and sentences. Hold your tongue or lips in place and feel the final stop.

2. Underline the place in your mouth where the air stops.

Example I tied a KNOT. lips - gum ridge - throat

1.	CAT	Where's the CAT?	lips - gum ridge - throat
2.	BAC**K**	She's hiding in BAC**K**.	lips - gum ridge - throat
3.	BO**B**	What happened to BO**B**?	lips - gum ridge - throat
4.	TE**D**	He's waiting for TE**D**.	lips - gum ridge - throat
5.	MA**P**	Where's the MA**P?**	lips - gum ridge - throat
6.	BA**G**	It's under the BA**G.**	lips - gum ridge - throat

3. Practice these sentences as three dialogues.

---

pronunciation tip

When speakers hold the final stop, you can tell the difference between two similar words by the length of the vowel. The vowel before the final voiceless stop sounds shorter.

⟷ (voiceless final stop) ⟷ (voiced final stop)

mo**p**	mo**b**
righ**t**	ri**d**e
pic**k**	pi**g**

---

c. A Flap (or tapped "t")

Not all "t's" are the same. Sometimes a "t" sounds similar to a "d." The tongue lightly taps or flaps against the gum ridge without building up or releasing a puff of air, and this is called *a flap.*

Listen to the following examples of a flap. Put your tape recorder on pause after each line and practice.

Before unstressed "er" or "or": LAter BETter WAter MOTor TRAITor

Before "ing" and "ed": SHOUTing SHOUTed WAITing WAITed

Before an unstressed vowel: CIty FORty PAtio CItizen PHOtograph

Linking words: right‿aCROSS wait‿aROUND washed‿it sliced‿it

d. Partner Practice: What's happening today?

1. Partner A looks at one of the charts with the pictures of people doing things. Partner B looks at the other chart. Some of the names on both charts are missing pictures. Find out if your partner knows what these people are doing. Take turns asking and answering questions.

2. First, practice the flap. Listen to your instructor say the names on the charts and the "ing" verbs describing what these people are doing. Repeat what you hear.

Betty Dotty Eddy Katie Marty Matty Otto Peter Rita Teddy

batting cutting eating fighting knitting painting

planting skating voting writing

Sample conversation

A: What's happening today? Is Peter batting a baseball?

B: No, Peter is skating on the lake. What's Rita doing today?

A: Rita is painting a picture. Do you know what Teddy is doing today?

Partner A's information

Marty 	Eddy 	Rita 	Dotty 	Matty 
Peter	Betty	Katie	Teddy	Otto

Partner B's information

Marty	Eddy	Rita	Dotty	Matty
Peter 	Betty 	Katie 	Teddy 	Otto 

e. The Syllabic "n"

The unstressed syllables in words such as MOUNtain or PARdon have a sound called a syllabic "n."

1. Shake your head to mean "no" and say "nnh-nnh" (lips slightly open). This "no" sound is a syllabic n̩. Your tongue stays on your gum ridge.

2. Say the first syllable of "BUTton" and hold your tongue against your gum ridge for the second syllable. Instead of saying "ton," make a quick n̩ sound in your throat. There is no vowel in the second syllable. Say "BUT'n."

3. Listen to your instructor and repeat these groups of words with the syllabic "n."

Nouns: COTton CARton KITten NEWton DAYton BRItain

Verbs: WRITten forGOTten EAten FATten STRAIGHten

Adjectives and Adverbs: CERtain HIDden ROTten SUDdenly CERtainly

Contractions of "not": SHOULDn't DIDn't WOULDn't HADn't COULDn't

f. Partner Practice

1. Listen to the paragraph. Then silently read the paragraph and underline the words you think have the syllabic n̩. See the first sentence as an example. Listen to the paragraph again to make sure, and check your answers with the instructor.

A Family Mystery

[1]Peter Wharton had certainly tried to trace his grandparents. [2]His parents had moved from Dayton, Ohio, to Fort Morton, Colorado, east of the Rocky Mountains. [3]He knew that one of his grandmothers was from Great Britain, but he hadn't been able to locate her. [4]Suddenly, when he didn't expect it, a letter arrived from Great Britain. [5]It was written by a woman named Katie Newton who claimed to be his aunt. [6]Katie Newton sent a picture that she had found at the bottom of an old carton. [7]It was taken a long time ago of a little girl that Katie said was her mother. [8]The girl, wearing a cotton dress with buttons down the front, was holding a kitten. [9]On the back of the picture was written "Dotty Burton, 1936". [10]Peter had forgotten until now that his grandmother's name was Dotty Burton. [11]Apparently Katie Newton who sent the picture was his mother's sister. [12]He couldn't believe that he hadn't heard of her before. [13]Peter Wharton was eager to straighten out the family mystery.

2. Replay the tape and practice the paragraph one line at a time, alternating lines with your partner.

3. Discuss the family mystery. Monitor for the syllabic n.

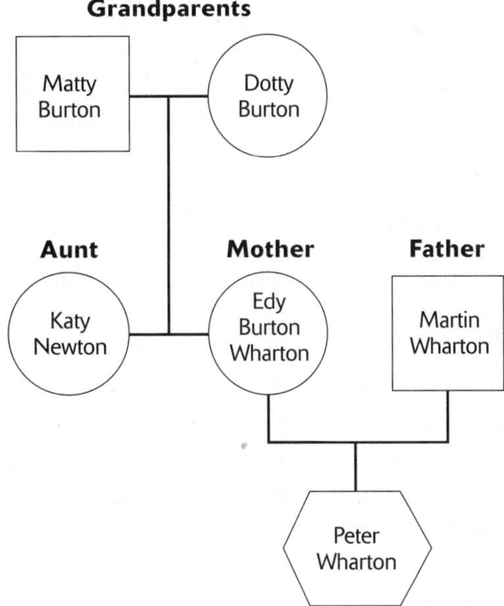

Continuants: The air flows out the pathway

All sounds that are not stops are called *continuants*. The air from the lungs continues up the pathway and flows out the mouth or the nose without stopping until the air is gone.

Take a breath. Say "ah" as long as you can. How many times can you tap your finger before you run out of air? Say "ssss" as you tap your finger until you run out of air. Most English consonants are continuants. Look at the window drawings, page 101, to see some examples.

f *and* v *: Locations 7 and 8 on the pathway*

Look at the lips and the teeth in the following pictures.

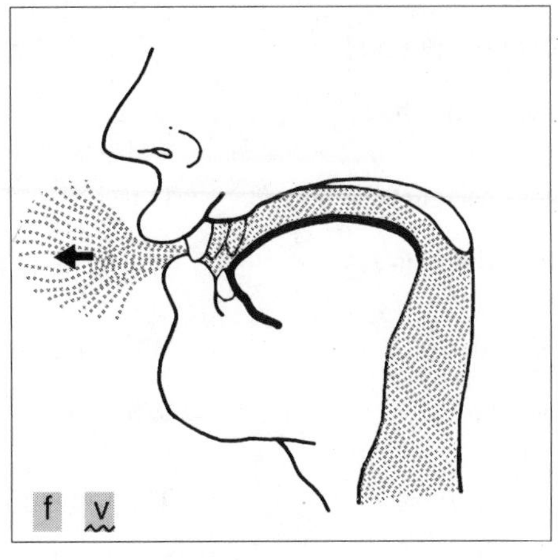

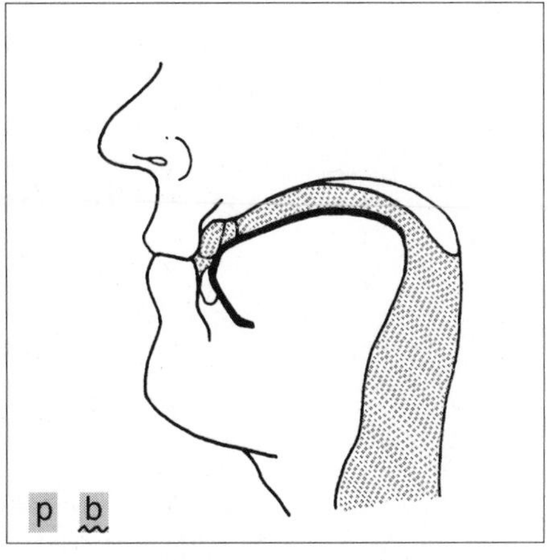

feel – very

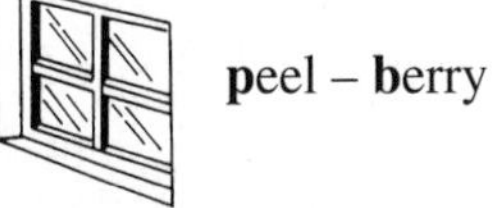

peel – berry

1. Say a long slow f. Make sure that your top teeth are resting gently inside your lower lip. Keep your lips open and don't stop the air. Say "fan." Feel the difference as you say "fan–pan–fan–pan."

2. Put your hand on your throat and say f. Then say v. Keep your lips open. Which is voiced, f or v? ____ Which is voiceless? ____

3. Listen and repeat the words and phrases for f (voiceless) and v (voiced).

face **f**orward   loa**f** of bread   hal**f** a muffin   sta**ff** assistant   rou**gh** edges

very hea**v**y   abo**v**e all   li**v**e alone   ha**v**e everything

microwa**v**e oven   dri**v**e around

4. Write a word that starts with f. ____________
Write a word that ends with f. ____________
Write a word that starts with v. ____________
Write a word that ends with v. ____________
Say your words in a sentence.

g. Partner Practice: Contrast b and v

1. Practice these word pairs. Both sounds are voiced. Open your lips for v.

bet–**v**et   **b**an–**v**an   **b**oat–**v**ote   cur**b**–cur**v**e   **b**ail–**v**eil   **b**ase–**v**ase

2. One partner says either sentence (a) or (b). Hide your mouth with a piece of paper. The other partner answers. Take turns.

Example a. I chose that bet for my horse. — Did your horse win the race?

b. I chose that vet for my horse. — **Was your horse sick?**

1. a. Tell me about the **b**an. — There's no smoking on airplanes.
   b. Tell me about the **v**an. — It's large and comfortable.

2. a. The president wants my **v**ote. — When is the election?
   b. The president wants my **b**oat. — Your sailboat or your motor boat?

3. a. There's a car near the cur**b**. — Is it parked?
   b. There's a car near the cur**v**e. — Is it coming toward us?

4. a. She needs the **b**ail now. — Who's in jail?
   b. She needs the **v**eil now. — When is the wedding?

5. a. The **b**ase is made of glass. — The top is made of metal.
   b. The **v**ase is made of glass. — It's filled with flowers.

h. Partner Practice: Contrast p and f

1. Practice saying the word pairs. Both sounds are voiceless. Open your lips for **f**.

pear–**f**air **p**an–**f**an la**p**–lau**gh** **p**ace–**f**ace **p**ast–**f**ast

2. One partner says either sentence (a) or (b). Hide your mouth with a piece of paper. The other partner answers. Take turns.

Example	a. What did you see at the port?	Ships and water.
	b. What did you see at the fort?	**Soldiers and guns.**
1.	a. Enjoy the **p**ear.	Is it ripe?
	b. Enjoy the **f**air.	Is there a merry-go-round?
2.	a. What's the **p**an for?	Cooking eggs.
	b. What's the **f**an for?	Keeping cool.
3.	a. How do you spell "la**p**"?	l-a-p
	b. How do you spell "lau**gh**"?	l-a-u-g-h
4.	a. What do you think of his **p**ace?	He's going too fast.
	b. What do you think of his **f**ace?	He's quite handsome.
5.	a. Don't drive **p**ast her.	She's waiting at the corner.
	b. Don't drive **f**aster.	I'm driving below the speed limit.

The Voiced and Voiceless th *Sounds: Location 7 on the pathway*

1. Open your mouth slightly so that your teeth are parted. Put your tongue gently behind your top teeth, but don't touch anything or bite down. Keep your tongue inside your mouth as you blow air gently out over your tongue and whisper "thank."

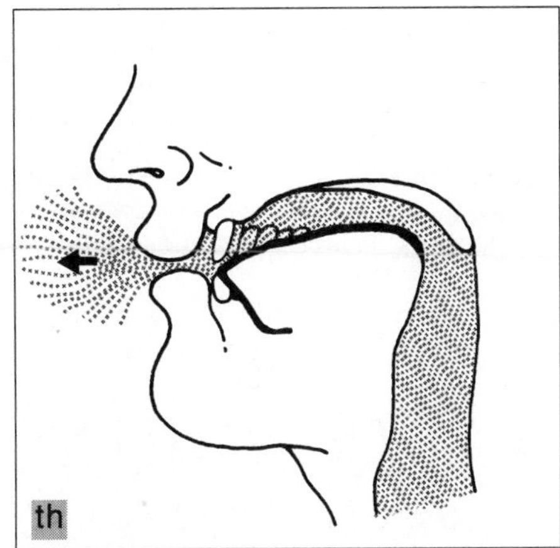

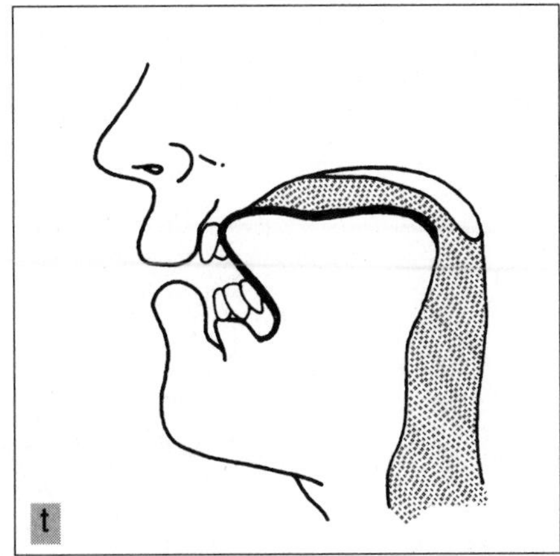

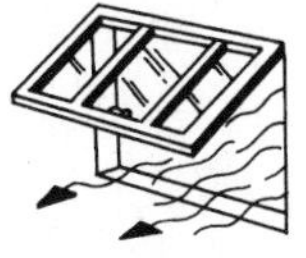

thank

tank

2. Say the words and phrases with "th."

Voiced th: **the** **this** fa**th**er mo**th**er brea**the** easy ba**the** often
soo**the** over

Voiceless th: **th**ink no**th**ing me**th**od four**th** of October
Nin**th** Avenue mo**th**-eaten sweater

i. Partner Practice: Contrast th and t.

boa**t**–bo**th** **h**igh–**t**ie **th**anks–**t**anks **th**ought–**t**aught
deb**t**–dea**th** boo**t**–boo**th** mi**tt**–my**th**

One partner says either sentence (a) or (b). The other partner answers. Take turns.

Example	a. How do you spell "boat"?	b - o - a - t
	b. How do you spell "both"?	**b - o - t - h**

1.	a.	I spilled coffee on my **th**igh.	Did you get burned?
	b.	I spilled coffee on my **t**ie.	Did the coffee stain it?
2.	a.	I'm sending you **t**anks.	Are there soldiers driving them?
	b.	I'm sending you **th**anks.	You're welcome!
3.	a.	I **th**ought about the Civil War.	What did you think?
	b.	I **t**aught about the Civil War.	What did your students learn?
4.	a.	He's depressed about his father's dea**th**.	Did his father die recently?
	b.	He's depressed about his father's deb**t**.	Did he owe a lot of money?
5.	a.	What's in his boo**t**?	His foot.
	b.	What's in his boo**th**?	A table, a chair, and some books.
6.	a.	Which is your favorite my**th**?	The story of Zeus.
	b.	Which is your favorite mi**tt**?	The leather one.

Look at the window openings. Which sound has the most airflow? Which sound stops the air?

th thank

s sank

t tank

j. Partner Practice: Contrast th and s

thank–**s**ank **th**eme–**s**eam **th**igh–**s**igh **th**ick–**s**ick

ten**th**–ten**s**e mou**th**–mou**s**e fa**c**e–fai**th**

One partner says either sentence (a) or (b). The other partner answers. Take turns.

Example	a. How do you spell "thank"?	"Thank" is spelled t-h-a-n-k.
	b. How do you spell "sank"?	**"Sank" is spelled s-a-n-k.**
1.	a. The **th**eme is obvious.	She's a careful writer.
	b. The **s**eam is obvious.	She's not a careful seamstress. (A "seamstress" is a woman who sews.)
2.	a. His **th**igh is painful.	Are you saying "thigh" spelled t-h-i-g-h?
	b. His **s**igh is painful.	Are you saying "sigh" spelled s-i-g-h?
3.	a. It's very **th**ick.	Are you saying "thick" spelled t-h-i-c-k?
	b. It's very **s**ick.	Are you saying "sick" spelled s-i-c-k?
4.	a. There's a mou**th** in the picture.	Is it open or shut?
	b. There's a mou**s**e in the picture.	Can you see the tail?
5.	a. Jim is the ten**s**e person in line.	Is he always this nervous?
	b. Jim is the ten**th** person in line.	I thought he was ninth.
6.	a. Her fa**c**e is strong.	She looks like her mother.
	b. Her fai**th** is strong.	She is very religious.

k. Partner Practice: Conversation with "th"

Listen first. Then practice saying the dialogue. Monitor for "th." Switch roles.

Shopping

A: I need a present and a birthday card for my brother. His birthday is tomorrow. Do you like this card or that one?

B: Both are nice. But I guess I like this one better than that one.

A: My brother mentioned that he needs a sweater. I wonder where the men's clothing is.

B: Next to the bathing suits. I think that's on the third floor.

A: Look over there! There are some things on sale.

B: That sounds interesting. Let's take a look. Then you'll get the gift for your brother!

l. Partner Practice: Linking

The endings of words in English often provide grammatical information, such as past tenses. You can recognize the past tense when you hear a flap linked to the next word. Listen first. Then one partner says the present tense linking the continuant and the other partner says the past tense linking the flap.

	Present Tense (Linking a continuant)	Past Tense (Linking a flap)
n	Let's clean it up.	He cleaned it up.
m	Don't slam on the brakes.	He slammed on the brakes.
w	Sew it up.	It's all sewed up.
f	Puff on the pipe.	He puffed on the pipe.
v	I have an apple.	I had an apple.
sh	Push it open	I pushed it open.
z	She has an idea.	She had an idea.
th	Breathe easy.	We breathed easy.
l	Pull over.	I pulled over.

m. Check Your Listening: Past or present?

Listen to either the past or the present tense. Check (✓) the tense you hear. Then practice both choices.

Example (**row** rowed) across the lake ____ Past __✓__ Present

	Past	Present
1. (show-showed) up	____	____
2. (hiked-hike) over the hill	____	____
3. (play-played) the flute	____	____
4. (grab-grabbed) it	____	____
5. (jump-jumped) around	____	____
6. (stay-stayed) all day	____	____
7. (tie-tied) a knot	____	____
8. (move-moved) in October	____	____
9. (share-shared) our dinner	____	____
10. (figure-figured) it out	____	____

Are You Ready for "r" and "l"?

Look at the following drawings. See the tongue curl for r. The tongue tip is not touching the top of the mouth. See the tongue touch the top of the mouth for l. The air flows out over the sides of the tongue.

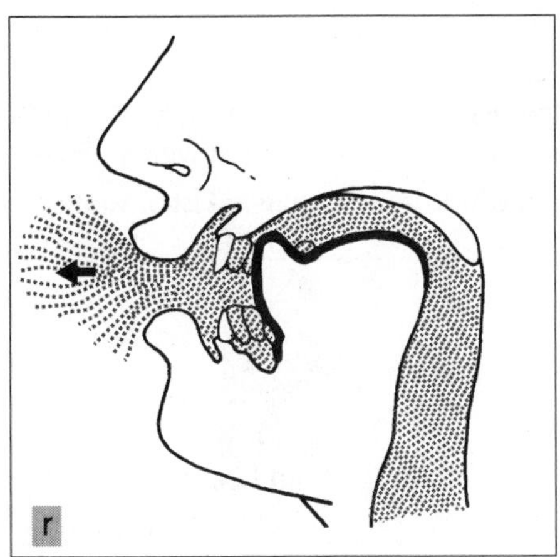

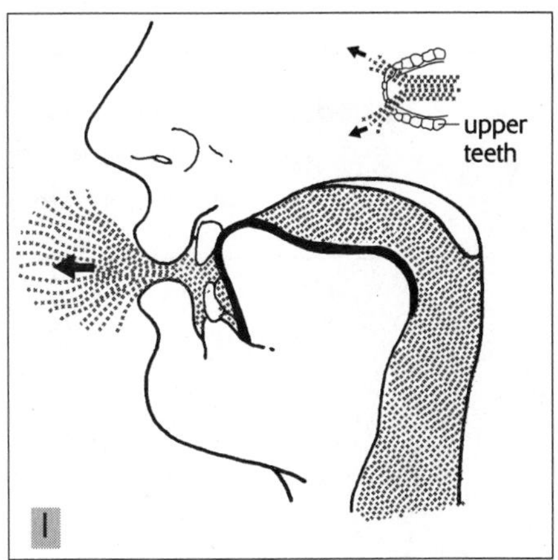

How to Say r

1. Open your mouth slightly. Squeeze the sides of your tongue against your upper and lower molars and keep it there. Tighten and roll the tip of your tongue backward. The tip of the tongue doesn't touch any part of your mouth. Keep curling your tongue tighter as you say "rrrrr." Release your tightly rolled tongue into the r words.

2. Listen first. Then say these words and phrases. Concentrate on what you hear and what it feels like.

red **r**ain **R**on **r**ow **r**adio **r**ent **r**ush a**r**ound **r**ight **r**eason **r**eady to **r**est

---

pronunciation tip

Use your hands to help you say r. Curl your fingers and make a tight fist as you curl your tongue tightly and say "rrrrr." Release your fingers and open your palms quickly as you release your tongue and say "ray."

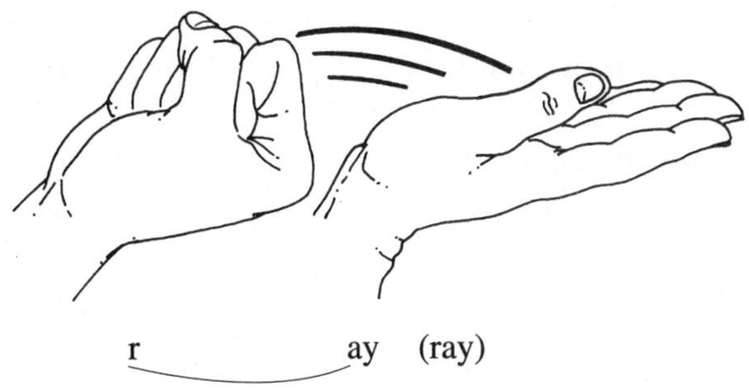

r ay (ray)

3. Make a tight fist with your hands and release your fist as you say each of these words.

rush rope run rent right round

---

another tip

Use your ears to hear your best r. Sometimes people have an easier time saying r in one word than in another. When you hear a word with your best r, hold the position and concentrate on feeling where your tongue is. Listen some more as you try it again.

How to say l

1. Keep your mouth relaxed. An l should be comfortable. Press the front part of your tongue gently up on the roof of your mouth, either behind your top teeth or further back. The exact place may vary. It is easier if you touch the front of your tongue softly, rather than point the tip sharply. As you keep the front of your tongue on the roof of your mouth, lower the rest of your tongue and pull the sides toward the center so that the air can flow out.

2. Listen first. Then say these words and phrases.

lay lamp allow alike July fall off sell everything circle around

---

pronunciation tip

Find the easiest way to say l. The exact place for making an l can change according to the sound that comes before or after the l. Touch the top of your mouth with the most comfortable part of your tongue. The important thing is to let the air flow out the sides.

---

n. Partner Practice: Contrast r and l

One partner says either sentence (a) or (b). The other partner answers. Take turns.

Example a. Is the pipe red? — No, it's black.

b. Is the pipe lead? — **No, it's copper.**

1. a. Turn toward the **r**ight. — I'd rather turn left.

   b. Turn toward the **l**ight. — It's too bright.

2. a. I tore my w**r**ist. — Does it hurt a lot?

   b. I tore my **l**ist. — Can you still read it?

3. a. Look at the large **cr**owd. They're waiting to get in.
   b. Look at the large **cl**oud. It's blocking the sun.
4. a. How do I **r**ock it? Push it back and forth.
   b. How do I **l**ock it? With a key.
5. a. He wants to p**r**ay. There's a church across the street.
   b. He wants to p**l**ay. Baseball or cards?
6. a. The river f**r**oze. Let's go ice skating.
   b. The river f**l**ows. Let's go swimming.

Common r and l Words

Practice saying some common groups of words with r or l. Monitor your speech.

Colors: red rust brown green gray black blue yellow

Plants: flowers grass trees roses orchids lilies tulips iris

Adjectives: right real raw rusty long low lovely little

Computer words: monitor chooser printer ruler hard drive keyboard spell check scroll bar

Verbs: rent wrap read like leave laugh

Nouns: rope ring rug lamp life load

Names: Randy Ruth Robert Ralph Laurie Larry Lillian Alice

o. Figure Out the Idioms

Work with a partner to match the idiomatic expressions to the definitions. Write the number of the sentence next to the appropriate definition. Say the sentences and monitor for r, l, and th, one sound at a time.

Idioms	**Definitions**
1. She can't go because she's under the weather.	____ a. after something happened, when it's too late
2. Fortunately she's back in the pink.	____ b. ill, not feeling well
3. That idea is behind the times.	____ c. old-fashioned
4. I can't drive because my car is on the blink.	____ d. broken
5. The new vice-president is now in the loop.	____ e. in good health
6. You're on track with that solution.	____ f. part of the group in charge, informed
7. Her offer to help came out of the blue.	____ g. proceeding satisfactorily, reasoning correctly
8. There's no point fixing it after the fact.	____ h. unexpected, without warning

More Idioms	**Definitions**
1. He paid for the favor under the table.	____ a. stop bothering, harassing
2. The new employee has a lot on the ball.	____ b. going out and having a good time
3. I don't like being left in the dark about what happened.	____ c. unconventional, eccentric
4. That guy that came to the door was off the wall.	____ d. in secret, outside the rules or the law
5. Let's celebrate out on the town.	____ e. making a profit
6. The business is finally in the black.	____ f. the central issue or most important idea
7. Let's get to the point right away.	____ g. competent, doing a good job
8. Please get off my back about cleaning up the kitchen.	____ h. in secret, not informed

p. Join the Chorus

Practice the voiced th, r, and l in a chant made up of common idioms. Divide into groups A and B. Work with your group until you can speak in unison. Tap the desk as you say the focus words.

What Did You Say?

A: He's under the **WEA**ther.

B: She's in the **PINK**.

A: It's behind the **TIMES**.

B: It went on the **BLINK**.

A: You're out of the **LOOP**.

B: You're on the right **TRACK**.

A: That's out of the **BLUE**.

B: It's after the **FACT**.

A: It's under the **TA**ble.

B: He's on the **BALL**.

A: I'm in the **DARK**.

B: That's off the **WALL**.

A: We're out on the **TOWN**.

B: 'cause we're back in the **BLACK**.

A-B: Get to the **POINT**.
And get off my **BACK**!

q. Discussion: The world's most common languages

The chart on page 118 lists six of the twelve languages most commonly spoken by native and nonnative speakers around the world.

1. Practice the pronunciation of the countries, languages, and numbers on the chart. Write the missing names of languages and countries of origin. Decide where these remaining six languages should go on the chart.

Spanish Arabic English Japanese French Mandarin

2. Discuss the chart with a partner and explain your choices. You can discuss the language you think is spoken by the most people in the world, and name the country where most of these speakers live. You can compare the total number of speakers of a language to the number of native speakers. Where do most of these people live? For example, do most of the people who speak Portuguese live in Portugal? Do most of the French speakers live in France? Where do most of the people who speak Hindi live?

3. Target word stress and focus words. Choose a consonant sound you want to monitor. After your discussion, check your answers with the instructor and the class.

Language	Country of Origin	Total Speakers	Native Speakers
1.	1.	1,025 billion	863 million
2.	2.	497 million	335 million
3. Hindi	3. India	476 million	357 million
4.	4.	409 million	352 million
5. Russian	5.	279 million	168 million
6.	6. Arabia	235 million	200 million
7. Bengali	7. Bangladesh	207 million	200 million
8. Portuguese	8. Portugal	187 million	173 million
9. Malay-Indonesian	9. Indonesia	170 million	57 million
10.	10.	127 million	75 million
11.	11. Japan	126 million	125 million
12. German	12. Germany	126 million	99 million

Finishing Up

REVIEW THE CHAPTER

List four important things you learned about consonant sounds in this chapter. Compare your list with your partner's. You may want to add something to your list.

1. ______________________________
2. ______________________________
3. ______________________________
4. ______________________________

TALK TIMES

In-class Preparation: Role play

One partner is considering a trip and calls an airline to gather information about flights. The other partner works for the airline.

1. **Write questions that you could ask the airline.** Use destinations that start with sounds that you find difficult such as th, f, or v. Underline the focus words and circle your difficult sounds.

Example I'm going from Vancouver to Boston. Do you have any nonstop flights?

Possible topics for questions:

- flight information (times, destinations, available seats)
- the cost, lowest fare, any restrictions
- nonstop flight or stopovers
- the meals (special, vegetarian, etc.)
- the movie

2. Practice your questions with your partner. Monitor your own and your partner's pronunciation for focus words and difficult consonants.

3. Role play the conversation about calling the airline. Switch roles.

Talk Times in Your Daily Life: Planning a trip

Call an airline for flight information about a possible trip. Use the questions in the role play in the previous exercise as a guide. Add questions of your own. You can make this call on different days to different airlines. Practice your questions before you make the call. Take notes on what happened or tape your part of the conversation so you can plan your next call. Target "th" and other difficult sounds. Pay attention to linking final sounds.

ON YOUR OWN

1. Practice regularly with the audio tapes. Replay the sections of the tape with sounds that are difficult for you. Whenever possible, look away from your book as you speak. Pay attention to the intonation as well as to the sounds when you are repeating phrases and sentences.

2. Record any two exercises from the chapter that will help you practice difficult consonant sounds.

3. Look in Appendix C for more practice with consonants that you find difficult.

4. Add to your personal glossary. Include the names of streets and places in your community. Ask a native speaker how to say them. Exaggerate the stressed syllable by lengthening it and raising the pitch.

5. **Look for opportunities to make small talk in English.** Conversing frequently in English helps build your confidence. Have a "phone meeting" with someone from this class to talk about pronunciation.

---

a helpful hint

Tape record your part of a phone conversation. Keep the tape recorder going in the room as you speak on the phone to a friend or business. You will not be recording the other person's part of the conversation. Listen later to discover things about your pronunciation you did not hear when you were talking.

7

More about Vowels and Consonants

Pronouncing English vowels can be confusing. A slight shift in the position of your tongue can change the way a vowel sounds. Fortunately, speaking clearly in English depends more upon lengthening and shortening the vowels than it does upon their exact pronunciation. Consonants can be especially challenging to pronounce when they are grouped together into clusters.

More about Vowels

Voicing and Vowel Length

The vowel before a voiceless consonant sounds shorter. The vowel before a voiced consonant sounds longer.

←→	←——→		
boo**t**	booe**d**	Put on the boot.	The crowd booed.
hal**f**	ha**v**e	I want half of it.	I want to have it.

a. Partner Practice

One partner says either a word in column A or a word in column B. The other partner says the appropriate sentence. Take turns.

Example First partner: la**b** Second partner: I work in a lab.

	A (voiceless final stops) ⟷		**B (voiced final stops)** ⟷	
1.	lap	It's on my lap.	lab	I work in a lab.
2.	mop	I need a new mop.	mob	I can hear the mob.
3.	bet	Let's make a bet.	bed	Let's make the bed.
4.	right	That's right.	ride	Let's go for a ride.
5.	think	What do you think?	thing	What is that thing?
6.	pick	Which movie did you pick?	pig	Look at the baby pig.

	A (voiceless final continuants)		**B (voiced final continuants)**	
1.	bus	I can see the bus.	buzz	I can hear the buzz.
2.	price	What's the price?	prize	I won the prize.
3.	peace	Let's hope for peace.	peas	They're eating peas.
4.	rich	She is rich.	ridge	She is on the ridge.
5.	safe	Is the money safe?	save	How much money did you save?

b. Partner Practice

One partner says either sentence (a) or (b). The other partner says the appropriate answer. Glide or step down in pitch at the end of each sentence.

Example:	a. There's a cap at the corner.	a. I wonder who dropped it.
	b. There's a cab at the corner.	**b. Good. I need a ride.**

1.	a.	He found a buck on the sidewalk.	Did he spend it or save it?
	b.	He found a bug on the sidewalk.	Could it fly or crawl?
2.	a.	I got a good price.	How much did you pay?
	b.	I got a good prize.	What did you win?
3.	a.	The seat is hard.	It must be uncomfortable.
	b.	The seed is hard.	It's ready to plant.
4.	a.	Put the groceries in the back.	In the trunk or the back seat?
	b.	Put the groceries in the bag.	Do you want paper or plastic?
5.	a.	What does it mean to proof it?	To review it and make corrections
	b.	What does it mean to prove it?	To give logical arguments
6.	a.	The people are sinking.	Throw them a life raft quickly.
	b.	The people are singing.	Do you know the song?

7.	a.	He fell on his knees.	I hope they're not sore.
	b.	He fell on his niece.	I hope she's not hurt.
8.	a.	Are you planning to write it?	Yes, as soon as I find a pen.
	b.	Are you planning to ride it?	Yes, as soon as I fix the wheels.

c. Improve Your Monitoring

1. Listen to each sentence. Decide if the speaker says the underlined word or a word with a shorter vowel sound that does not make sense in that sentence. Check (✓) the word you hear. Replay the tape to make sure.

Example:	Have you heard the news?	✓ news	___ noose
1.	He is very rude.	___ rude	___ root
2.	The laws are changing.	___ laws	___ loss
3.	She kept her age a secret.	___ age	___ "H"
4.	We try to save money.	___ save	___ safe
5.	I weighed more last year.	___ weighed	___ wait
6.	Did you hear the phone ring?	___ ring	___ rink

2. Say each sentence correctly by lengthening the vowel in the underlined word. Self-monitor.

Grammar and Vowel Length

When nouns and verbs look similar, the part of speech can help you with the pronunciation. The noun sounds shorter because it ends with a voiceless sound. The verb sounds longer because it ends with a voiced sound. Listen to the following examples.

(noun) What's the use? (verb) Can you use it?

⟷ **Nouns**	⟷ **Verbs**	⟷ **Nouns**	⟷ **Verbs**
rice	rise	proof	prove
excuse	excuse	half	have
loose	lose	leaf	leave
advice	advise	relief	relieve

Vowels and Numbers

To make "sixty" and "sixteen" sound different, pay attention to the vowel in the second syllable.

1. The clear vowel in "teen" is lightly stressed. Remember to say the final "n."

THIRTEEN FOURTEEN FIFTEEN SIXTEEN

SIXTEEN **DOL**lars and FOURTEEN **CENTS.**

2. At the end of a sentence "teen" gets more stress. Glide down in pitch.

I moved here at the age of NINE**TEEN.** She's only THIR**TEEN.**

3. The "ty" in SIXty dollars is unstressed and low in pitch. Say a flap.

THIRty FORty FIFty SIXty She's only THIRty. He's turning NINEty.

d. Partner Dictation: "ty" and "teen"

Take turns dictating sentences to your partner. Choose one of the numbers in the parentheses. Your partner writes the number he or she hears. Monitor for "ty" and "teen." Discuss your answers.

1. Mary is (14–40) __________ years **OLD.**
2. They took the elevator up (13–30) __________ **FLOORS** / to the top of a tall **BUILD**ing. /
3. We looked at a **HOUSE** / that was on (216–260) __________ acres of **FARM**LAND. /
4. They were selling the **PRO**perty / for (16–60) __________ percent of its market **VA**lue. /
5. The store sold fresh **EGGS** / for (19–90) __________ cents a half **DO**zen./
6. The chickens were ($2.19–$2.90) __________ cents a **POUND.**
7. I saw an ad for roundtrip **TIC**kets / from New York to **PAR**is / for ($680–$618) __________. /
8. The agency was closing in (15–50) __________ **MIN**utes.

e. Partner Practice: Discuss the calendar

On the next page, one partner looks at the calendar and some facts for October. The other partner looks at the calendar and facts for November. Ask and answer questions about what happens in October and November. Monitor your speech and your partner's speech for "ty," "teen," and th.

- dates that fall on Thursdays
- days of the week that fall on the 15th, 16th, 17th, etc.
- imaginary or real birthdays (mother's, father's, brother's)
- when the rent is due
- whether or not Friday falls on the 13th
- what day is payday
- other

SUN	MON	TUES	WED	THURS	FRI	SAT
					1	2
3	4	5	6	7	8	9
10	11	12	13	14	15	16
17	18	19	20	21	22	23
24	25	26	27	28	29	30
31						

OCTOBER

Facts about October:

October has thirty-one days.

The Canadian Thanksgiving is the second Monday.

October 31st is Halloween.

Columbus Day is the 12th (celebrated on the second Monday).

NOVEMBER

SUN	MON	TUES	WED	THURS	FRI	SAT
	1	2	3	4	5	6
7	8	9	10	11	12	13
14	15	16	17	18	19	20
21	22	23	24	25	26	27
28	29	30				

Facts about November:

November has thirty days.

The U.S. Thanksgiving is the fourth Thursday.

November 11th is Canada's Remembrance Day.

November 11th is the U.S. Veteran's Day.

f. The Long uw Sound: Two pronunciations

Compare the difference in the vowels in these words: boo–you booty–beauty

Beauty ⟶ b^{y}eauty.

1. Listen to more examples. men^{y}u f^{y}uture h^{y}uman conf^{y}use comp^{y}uter

2. "cu" sounds like the name of the letter "q" in these words. Take turns with a partner using the following words in sentences.

c^{y}ute C^{y}uba pec^{y}uliar vac^{y}uum cleaner

calc^{y}ulate calc^{y}ulation circ^{y}ulate circ^{y}ulation chief exec^{y}utive officer

g. Linking Two Vowel Sounds

You can't always tell from looking at a word with two vowel letters if the word is one syllable or two.

1. Listen to your instructor say the following words and write the number of syllables you hear.

ie	piece	1	ui	suit	____	ea	weak	____	ue	true	____
	quiet	2		tuition	____		idea	____		fluent	____

2. Listen for the y sound (like the beginning of "yes") that links the two vowels in the following words.

appreci^y^ate cre^y^ative stere^y^o vide^y^o we^y^all the^y^end

3. Listen for the w sound that links two vowels in the following words.

usu^w^al persu^w^ade casu^w^al go^w^out show^w^up shoe^w^on

h. Partner Practice: Story

Look away from your book and listen to the story. Replay the tape. Then practice with a partner, looking away from each sentence as you say it. Link the words connecting two vowel sounds.

A Cre^y^ative Ide^y^a

I had an ide^y^a . The^y^old lady in our apartment building hadn't been feeling so well. She seemed lonely, and I thought she'd appreci^y^ate some attention. So I pers^w^uaded the neighbors to put in a few dollars to buy her a gift. In the^y^end, we^y^all decided to have a huge potluck dinner. We^y^all cooked our favorite recipes. When we went to deliver the dinner, the^y^old lady was dressed to go^w^out—apparently with a new boyfriend! So we^y^ate the dinner ourselves, and had such a good time that we decided to do it again.

More about Consonants

Consonant Clusters

A cluster is a group of things that are similar, such as a cluster of cherries or a cluster of houses. Sometimes several consonants are grouped together into clusters. Pronouncing consonant clusters can be difficult for people whose native language does not group consonants together.

Practice saying the clusters of consonants in the following words.

Two-consonant beginnings: **tr**ip **st**op **bl**ock **sl**ip **sn**ap **Fr**ed **sp**oon

Three-consonant beginnings: **str**ap **str**ike **str**ong **squ**are **(skw)** **spl**it

Two-consonant beginnings and endings: **trips** **stops** **blocks** **slips** **snaps** **tripped** **stopped** **slipped**

i. Building Longer One-syllable Words

Some syllables are very short: i.de.a (three syllables)

Some syllables are very long: pledged (one syllable)

1. Read the word blocks. Start at the top. These small words get longer as you add consonants.

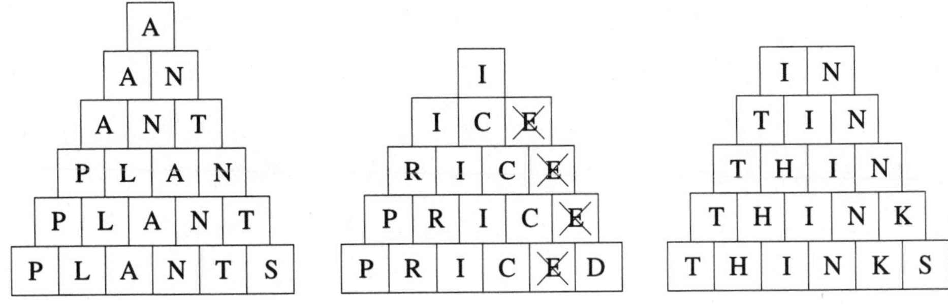

2. Complete the puzzle. Add letters before and after each word at the top of each stack of blocks to build a longer word with one syllable. Figure out where to add the letters below in order to form new words.* Practice saying the words as they get longer. Pay attention to the consonant clusters.

- Start with IT. Add s, p, and l.
- Start with AT. Add f, l, and s.
- Start with TO. Add n, e, and s.
- Start with AM. Add r, t, s, and p.

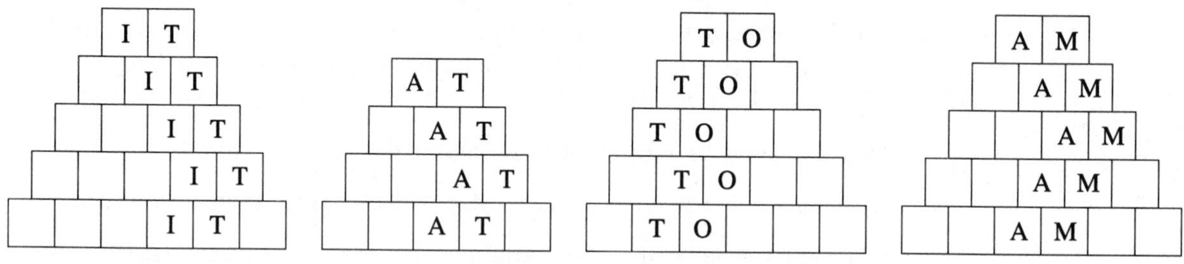

Clusters across Word Boundaries

Linking words in thought groups often requires the blending of consonant sounds into unusual clusters that are not necessarily found within individual words. These are consonant clusters that cross the boundary between two words. The clusters are written in parentheses after the following examples.

vine ripened (nr) stop watch (pw) looks like new (ksl)

What's the problem? (tsth) an action film (nf) tax forms (ksf)

It's a big deal. (gd) plastic bag (kb)

* Some of the letters may be used more than once.

j. Partner Practice: Linked clusters

The following underlined clusters cross word boundaries. Write the clustered consonant sounds (not letters) on the lines. Some of the letters are silent such as the final "e" in "wave." Compare answers with your partner and take turns pronouncing the phrases.

Example waves good-bye _v_ _z_ _g_ (The "s" sounds like a z in this cluster.)

1. science fiction ___ ___ ___
2. likes to talk ___ ___ ___
3. saves time ___ ___ ___
4. That's probably O.K. ___ ___ ___ ___
5. men's department ___ ___ ___
6. plans to quit. ___ ___ ___
7. a word processor ___ ___ ___ ___
8. vice-president ___ ___ ___
9. a Chinese restaurant ___ ___
10. electric stove ___ ___ ___
11. park your car ___ ___ ___
12. cheap shoes ___ ___ ___

Linking the Same Consonant Sound

When you link two sounds that are made in the same place, say the sound once, but hold it longer. The **:** means to hold the sound briefly in place. "Weak: coffee"* should sound different from "we coffee." "Wheat: toast" should sound different from "we toast."

a black: car stop: pushing prevent: disease a wet: diaper

a fine: night mile: long

Simplifying Clusters

Even native speakers have difficulty with some triple consonant clusters and simplify these when speaking rapidly. Three-consonant clusters often lose the middle sound in rapid speech.

s t s	tests → tes:s	The tests are graded.
	tourists → TOURis:s	The tourists are everywhere.
t h s	months → məns	months and months of work
	tenths → tens	nine-tenths of the marbles
s k s	desks → des:s	Fourteen desks were moved.
	asks → as:s	He asks for his change.
c t s	directs → diREX	He directs the traffic.
	facts → fax	The facts are obvious.

* Remember that different letters can have the same sound in English.

Linked Speech

Drop the final t and d in some triple clusters that cross word boundaries. Say a flap when the cluster is linked to a vowel. Listen to the examples.

Linked to a Consonant	Linked to a Vowel
Will you deduct some of the charges?	Will you deduct a dollar from the bill?
We'll adapt some of the customs.	We'll adapt all the customs.
Jim returned late last night.	Jane was the last of the group to return.
Hand me the salt, please.	Hand over your wallet!

---

pronunciation tip

It's more important to think about including all the consonants than to decide which ones can be left out. In English, most consonant clusters are not simplified, especially when they are part of a grammatical ending such as "ed" or final "s."

---

k. Role Play: "Do you know a good . . ."

You and your partner are discussing people whose services you like. One partner needs a good eye doctor. The other partner needs a good plumber. You each have a business card with information about the doctor and plumber you recommend. Tell your partner about your recommendation and how to reach the person on your card. To prepare for the role play, practice pronouncing the information on the cards. Pay attention to consonant clusters and linking. Say any numbers clearly.

Kathleen Lombardo, M.D.
Eye Physician and Surgeon

Clinical Professor
UCLA Department of Ophthalmology
400 UCLA Medical Plaza, Suite 202

Appointments and Messages: 510.849.8205
24-hour emergency number: 510.849.2174

J. F. Gardner Plumbing

Commercial & Residential
Serving all your plumbing needs

repairs ▪ disposals ▪ re-piping ▪ sewer and drain cleaning
remodeling ▪ new construction ▪ water heaters

Family-owned business since 1972
Free estimates. Reasonable rates.

18023 Olympic Blvd. (between Overland and Hill)
24-hour emergency service 818-792-1847

More about r and l

Review the drawings of r and l, page 113.

Vowel + r

There are two r sounds in English. One r comes at the beginning of words: **r**ow **r**ight **r**obin.

The other r comes after a vowel: ca**r** doo**r** pai**r**.* Your tongue has to glide from the vowel to the r.

1. Start by saying the vowel. Your tongue tip is gently behind your lower front teeth.

2. Glide to the r position. Squeeze the sides of your tongue against your upper back teeth. Tighten your tongue tip as you roll it backward. The front of your tongue doesn't touch anything in your mouth. Take your time. Slowly whisper: ah-r-r-r-r-r. Say "are."

3. Listen first. Replay the tape and repeat the following phrases. Practice the phrases with a partner.

near here fair share four more bare floor far star

nearly a year clear air marry Harry warm heart glorious morning

---

pronunciation tip for vowel + r

- Your tongue has to move and tighten. Use your hands to help. Turn up your open palms as you say the vowel before the r. Curl your fingers to make a tight fist as you tighten your tongue and glide from the vowel sound to the r. Take your time.
- Your ear is your best teacher. Experiment with vowel + r sounds until you hear one you like.

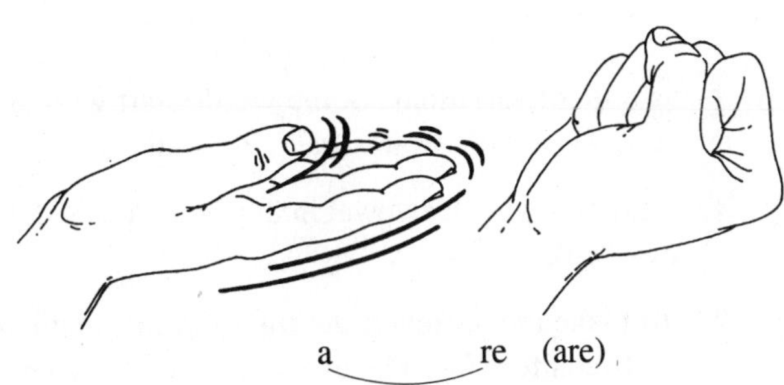

a re (are)

* In some regions, speakers omit many r sounds that follow a vowel. For example, in *park, market,* and *where.*

l. Limerick

1. Listen and tap the desk for the stressed words. Replay the tape and say the limerick with the speaker.

There ONCE was a MAN very **WEIRD**,
Who **SAID**, "It is JUST as I **FEARED**!
"Two OWLS and a **HEN**,
"Four LARKS and a **WREN**
"Have ALL built their NESTS in my **BEARD**."
—Edward Lear

2. Practice the vowel + r words. Use your hands to help.
weird feared larks beard.

m. Partner Practice: Dialogue with r

Listen and then say the dialogue. Work with your partner, pronouncing the r and vowel + r words. Lengthen the focus words and pay attention to the linking.

Needs a Ride

A: Your friend ArLENE / is on the **PHONE**. /

B: Arlene **RO**per,/ my friend from **WORK**? / She's **COM**ing here later. / What does she **WANT**?

A: She needs a **RIDE**. / She's been at the Hare Street **BUS** STOP / for over an **HOUR**./

B: Maybe I should **TELL** her / to call a **TA**xi. / They'll come right a**WAY** / and she'll **BE** here / before you **KNOW** it./

A: I'd rather drive **O**ver / and pick her **UP** / than tell her to call a **TA**xi./

B: That's **GREAT** / because I don't have a **CAR**. /

Vowel + l

l has a lot of variations. Some words start with l. Sometimes the l sound comes after a vowel: tell wall pal ill sail

1. Start by saying the vowel in the word "all." Glide slowly from the vowel to the l. Say "a-ll."

2. To make the l, touch the top of your mouth with any part of your tongue that feels comfortable. The exact place where your tongue touches can vary. Pull the sides of your tongue away from your teeth to let the air escape. Contrast l and d. Feel the difference as you whisper: ed-el ed-el bed-bell

3. Listen first. Replay the tape and repeat the following phrases. Practice the phrases with a partner.

all around   mail it   pull over   sell everything   full of fun   will he   tell him

4. Listen first. Replay the tape and repeat some common words that end with a schwa + l syllable. See the following ways to spell this.

BAgel   FRAgile   AWful   PUZzle   BIble   likable

the FINal SYLlable   a TYPical NOvel   a LOcal CALL

n. Check your Listening: Past or future?

1. You will hear one of the sentences in each pair. Check (✓) past or future.

Example	I'll pour you a drink.	✓ future
	I poured you a drink.	___ past
1.	We'll repair all the cracks.	___ future
	We repaired all the cracks.	___ past
2.	We'll clear away the trash.	___ future
	We cleared away the trash.	___ past
3.	He'll care about the environment.	___ future
	He cared about the environment.	___ past
4.	We'll order it for next year.	___ future
	We ordered it for next year.	___ past
5.	They'll share information.	___ future
	They shared information.	___ past
6.	We'll rehearse every Thursday.	___ future
	We rehearsed every Thursday.	___ past
7.	She'll compare the answers.	___ future
	She compared the answers.	___ past

2. Compare answers with your partner. Then take turns saying the sentences.

o. Role Play: Ordering from Ron's Barbecue

One partner calls to order food by phone. The other partner works at the restaurant.

1. Prepare for the role play by practicing the pronunciation of the sign in the window of the restaurant and the items on the menu. Target the consonant clusters that cross word boundaries. Pay attention to r and l and to saying numbers clearly.

★★★ Ron's Barbecue Take-Out Menu ★★★

"The Price Is Right!"

Main dish price includes two side dishes and buttered French bread.

Main dishes		Any two side dishes	Drinks	
famous "overnight beef"	$5.95	barbecued corn on the cob	club soda	$.99
short ribs	$5.95	fried zucchini sticks	cherry Coke	$.99
marinated chicken wings	$5.50	baked beans	diet Pepsi	$.99
mile long hot dogs	$3.89	french fries	chocolate shake	$2.89
cheeseburgers	$4.79	carrot-raisin salad	**Desserts**	$2.89
mushroom burgers	$4.39	fresh green salad	apricot pie	
		choice of ranch or vinaigrette dressing	chocolate sundae	
			spice cake	

2. Listen to the sample conversation. After you listen, role play your own conversation between a customer and an employee answering the phone at Ron's Barbecue. Switch roles.

R = restaurant employee C = customer

R: Ron's Barbecue. May I help you?

C: I want to order food from your take-out menu.

R: O.K. What would you like?

C: What's your "overnight beef"?

R: Marinated beef that is slowly roasted overnight.

C: I'll have two orders of the overnight beef, barbecued corn on the cob, and the carrot-raisin salad.

R: Any drinks or dessert?

C: Two diet Pepsis and two pieces of spice cake. How soon will it be ready?

R: You can pick it up in thirty minutes.

3. Make up your own conversation between a customer and an employee answering the phone at Ron's Barbecue. Switch roles.

p. Join the Chorus

1. Listen to this poem. Replay the tape and listen again. Then practice saying the poem.

Timothy Boon

1. Timothy **BOON**
Bought a bal**LOON**
Blue as the **SKY**,
Round as the **MOON**.
"Now I will **TRY**
To make it **fly**
UP to the **MOON**,
Higher than **HIGH**!"

2. Timothy **BOON**
Sent his bal**LOON**
Up through the **SKIES**,
Up to the **MOON**.
But a strong **BREEZE**
Stirred in the **TREES**,
Rocked the bright **MOON**,
Tossed the great **SEAS**.
And, with its **MIRTH**,
Shook the whole **EARTH**.

3. Timothy **BOON**
And his bal**LOON**,
Caught by the **BREEZE**
Flew to the **MOON**;
Up past the **TREES**,
Over the **SEAS**,
Up to the **MOON**—
Swift as you **PLEASE**!
And, ere I for**GET**,
They've not come down **YET**!

—Ivy O. Eastwick

2. Write words from the poem with the following vowel sounds. Then say the words.

- ər words. __________ __________ __________
- Long vowel sounds that sound like the names of letters. See the examples.

uw ⟶ "u" *Boon* __________ __________

iy ⟶ "e" *breeze* __________ __________ __________

ay ⟶ "i" *fly* __________ __________ __________

3. Divide into three groups. Work with your group to learn one verse of the poem to say for the class. Practice until you sound like a chorus with one voice. Monitor for focus words and clear vowels. Fall in pitch at the end of each sentence.

Finishing Up

REVIEW

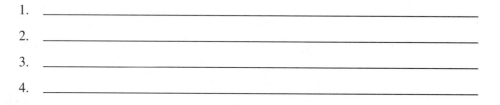

1. Dictation. Write the sentences you hear. You will hear each sentence two times. Check your dictation by listening to the tape again.

1. ______________________________
2. ______________________________
3. ______________________________
4. ______________________________
5. ______________________________

2. Make a List. Look over the chapter. List four things you learned about consonants and vowels in this chapter. Compare your list with your partner's. You may want to add more items to your list.

1. ______________________________
2. ______________________________
3. ______________________________
4. ______________________________

TALK TIMES: MAKE YOUR NEW PRONUNCIATION A HABIT

In-class Preparation: Role play

1. You are expecting out-of-town guests. You do not have room for them to stay with you. Prepare for their visit by contacting several hotels, inns, or bed-and-breakfasts for information. What kind of accommodations would your guests like to have? What will make your guests comfortable? Discuss with your partner the kinds of things you would like to find out. Make a list of questions to ask the hotel or bed-and-breakfast. Possible topics:

- location (near shopping, transportation, etc.)
- rates (daily, weekly, weekend specials)
- description of accommodations (beds, bath, etc.)
- meals, breakfasts provided
- availability and cancellation policy

2. Role play a conversation between someone expecting guests and a clerk at a hotel. Monitor for consonant clusters and r and l. Switch roles.

Talk Times in Your Daily Life: Information about hotels

Call or visit several hotels, inns, or bed-and-breakfasts in your area. Choose two or three things to ask about during each call. Write your questions and practice them. After you complete each call, take notes so that your next call will be more comfortable and successful. Decide what you will monitor each time.

ON YOUR OWN

1. **Try different ways of practicing with the audio tapes.** After you listen to an exercise, replay the tape. Listen to one sentence at a time and put the tape recorder on pause. Look away from the book and repeat the sentence from memory. Read Practice Tips for the Audio Tapes, page 20, for more ideas.

2. **Record the Edward Lear limerick, page 132, or the dialogue "Needs a Ride," Page 132.** Listen to your recording. Decide what you would like to improve. Record the selection again.

Record these sentences. Make the vowel length differences clear.

a. He didn't want to pay the price or spend the prize money.

b. She tried to save time and still drive at a safe speed.

c. I can provide proof that will prove my argument.

3. **Practice vowel sounds in Appendix D.**

4. **Add words to your personal glossary that you want to pronounce more clearly.** Find the correct pronunciation in a dictionary. Practice using your glossary words in a conversation with a friend.

5. **Converse in English as often as possible.** This will build your confidence and make you more comfortable with the language and the pronunciation.

Conversation Strategies

Use your knowledge of the pronunciation targets both to avoid problems and to clear up misunderstandings when you are having a conversation. Here are some conversation strategies:

1. **Use eye contact.** Conversations are easier to understand when you are looking at the other person. Furthermore, to native speakers of English, eye contact establishes trust and confidence. It makes your listener feel that you are interested and attentive.

2. **Look for clues that your listener does not understand what you are saying.** Does your listener look annoyed or impatient, or seem unfriendly? Is your listener responding inappropriately to your questions or comments? It may just be that he or she is having difficulty understanding what you are saying. This may or may not be due to your accent. It could be because you are not using the right words.

3. **Don't be afraid to ask to make sure you are being understood.** You might say, *Can you understand me?* or *Please tell me if I say anything that you don't understand.* This puts everyone at ease. Some people are hesitant to let you know directly when they are having trouble understanding.

4. **When your listener asks *What?*, you probably need to do something more than repeat the word or phrase.** Think about ways you can say it more clearly. Use your knowledge about word stress and focus words to change the way you said it. Frequently, just by lengthening and raising the pitch of the stressed syllable, a word will be easier to understand. Often when you emphasize the focus word more strongly, the phrase or whole sentence will be easier to understand.

5. **Rephrase what you have said using different words.** Explain the meaning of the words, in addition to repeating them. For example, *I work at a Senior Center, a place where older people go.* Substitute other similar words. Use gestures.

6. **Talk more slowly in English than you do in your native language.** This is especially important when you are repeating something, giving unfamiliar information, or introducing new topics. Pause more often. Step and glide in pitch at the ends of sentences more slowly.

7. **Pay attention to specific targets that you know are a problem.** These might be saying final sounds, lengthening stressed syllables in key words, or emphasizing focus words.

8. **Don't worry about your mistakes.** If you hear yourself make a mistake, correct it casually without apologizing, if that seems comfortable. Otherwise, make a mental note of your mistake as you continue with your conversation. Later when you are practicing, say that word or phrase correctly.

---

a helpful hint Improve your listening by monitoring for specific sounds or intonation patterns when you are watching TV. Turn on news programs and the weather report to hear clear pronunciation.

8

Sing Along: The Melody of Speech

All over the world people sing. The songs of a culture can tell you a lot about the intonation of the speech. Speech is another kind of song. Both the speaker's voice and the singer's voice move up and down in pitch to make melody. English speech melody has more high and low notes than most other languages. The intonation of English provides information beyond the meaning of the words themselves.

Songs and Chunks of Speech

a. Song: "Home on the Range"

1. Listen to this traditional cowboy song from around 1880. Fill in the focus words. You may have to listen more than once. Choose from the focus words shown here in alphabetical order.

amazed bright day gazed heard home night ours

play range roam stars word

1. Oh give me a __________,
   Where the buffalo __________,
   And the deer and the antelope __________,
   Where seldom is __________
   a discouraging __________,
   And the skies are not cloudy all __________.

Chorus:

Home, home on the __________,

And the deer and the antelope __________,

Where seldom is __________

A discouraging __________,

And the skies are not cloudy all __________.

2. How often at __________

When the heavens are __________

With the light of the glittering __________

Have I stood there __________

And I asked as I __________

"Does their glory exceed that of __________?"

2. Replay the song. Notice how the pitch changes on each focus word. The melody falls to the lowest pitch at the end of each sentence.

3. Practice saying the words to "Home on the Range," emphasizing the rhythm. Fall in pitch and pause at the end of each sentence.

Common Expressions—Little songs

Native speakers pronounce common phrases in one chunk. Individual words are shortened and linked into familiar melodies. Where did he go? ⟶ Whered'e**GO**? Look away from your book and listen. You will hear the reductions that native speakers use in informal conversation. Replay the tape several times. Concentrate on what you hear.

Common Chunks of Speech	**Reductions**
1. Give me a break. ⟶	GIMme a (ə) **BREAK**
2. That's news to me. ⟶	that's NEWS to (ə) **ME**
3. As a matter of fact . . . ⟶	as (ə) a (ə) MATter of (ə) **FACT**
4. Are you ready? ⟶	are you (ə) **REA**dy (or sometimes, ⟶ 'ya **REA**dy)
5. Is that OK? ⟶	izzat **OK**
6. Let me know. ⟶	LEMme **KNOW**
7. See you tomorrow. ⟶	SEE you (ə) to**MOR**row
8. Don't worry about it. ⟶	don't (t struck out) **WOR**ry about it

9. What in the world is that? ⟶ WHAT in the WORLDizZAT
10. What is your name? ⟶ WHATcher **NAME**
11. Did you hear me? ⟶ didjə **HEAR** me
12. Would you believe it? ⟶ wouldjə beLIEVE it

Rising and Falling Pitch: Four pitch levels

You hear more highs and lows in English than in most other languages. Both male and female speakers use melody variation within their own natural pitch ranges.

Most Speech Flows between Levels 2 and 3

Extra High Level 4	surprise, anger, disbelief, strong emphasis	used to express strong emotions and emphasis
High Level 3	stressed words and syllables, yes/no questions	Most of the time English speech flows between Levels 2 and 3.
Middle-Low Level 2	unstressed words and syllables, reductions	
Extra Low Level 1	glides at the ends of phrases, sentences and wh questions	Most thoughts end with falling pitch in Level 1. The exact pitch varies with the speaker and the situation.

b. How Much Melody Do People Use?

Within levels two and three, people vary in the amount of melody they use. People who use a lot of speech melody in English tend to sound friendly and interested. They also sound more interesting. Too little melody can make the speaker sound distant or disinterested.

Listen to two different speakers talking about winning the lottery. Both their speech melody flows within levels two and three. Which speaker sounds friendlier and more interesting?

Speaker 1. Expressive speech melody

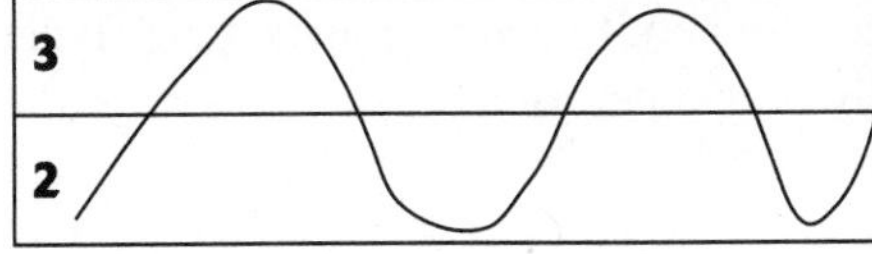

Speaker 2. Very little melody

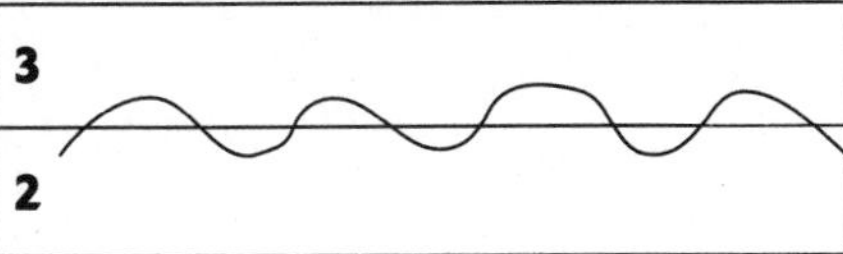

c. Conversation with Melody

Melody can carry meaning, even without words. In this short conversation between neighbors, Neighbor B uses intonation to communicate. Listen several times. Then practice the conversation with a partner.

Neighbor A	Neighbor B		Meaning
1. Have you seen Snowball?	Huh?	1 	lack of understanding
2. My cat! Have you seen my cat?	**Uh**-uh!	2 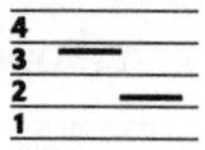	no
3. I can't find her anywhere in the house.	Oh!	3 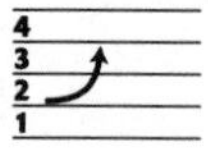	mild surprise
4. She's been missing since yesterday.	Oh!	4 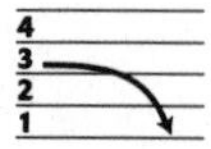	mild pain or discomfort, empathy
5. The cars drive very fast up and down my street.	Uh-**oh!**	5 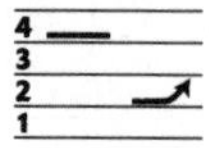	indication of trouble or danger
6. Maybe Snowball was run over by a car.	Oh!	6 	great concern
7. (later in the day) My cat came home this afternoon, safe and sound.	Aahhh!	7 	sigh of pleasure or relief
8. I should probably be more careful about keeping Snowball inside at night.	Mmmm.	8 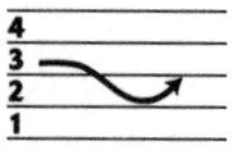	agreement with unexpressed judgment or feeling

The Basic Pattern: Rules and guidelines

The rules for speech melody are not clearly defined. The many variations take time to figure out. Although changing the pitch does not change the definition of a word, it can change the meaning in other ways. The intonation can indicate whether you are finished talking, or you are waiting for a response. Speech melody can make you sound confident or uncertain about what you are saying. It can make you sound sincere or sarcastic, friendly or disinterested.

You will learn the melody of English speech in the same way that you learn the melody of a new song. With time and practice the song becomes automatic. Start by learning some of the basic guidelines.

guideline 1 One stressed word in each thought group or sentence jumps up to the highest pitch. The highest pitch is often on an early content word.

The proFESsor was **LATE**. I SAT on the BLACK **CHAIR**.

guideline 2 The focus word sounds longer, louder, and changes pitch. Often the focus word glides or steps down in pitch at the end of the sentence.

Throw the ball to the **CATCH**er. (step) He's in the **CAR.** (glide)

guideline 3 Falling intonation at the end of a word or phrase indicates that the speaker is finished with a thought, or possibly finished talking altogether.

We waited for the **MAIL**. I forgot my **NOTE**book.

d. Falling Pitch Lines: Practice humming

Listen to the speaker hum the melody of the following sentences. Practice humming before you say each sentence. Glide or step down in pitch at the end of each sentence.

1. The DIRty DOG NEEDS a **BATH.**
2. I THINK it's GOing to **RAIN**.
3. They WENT to the **MOV**ies with us.

4. WHY do you **THINK** so?
5. My PARents live in **MEX**ico.
6. The DRESS was ex**PEN**sive.

Falling Pitch Lines: More guidelines

guideline 4 Strongly falling intonation at the end of a command sounds authoritative.

Close the **DOOR.**

Please wait over **THERE.**

Call after five o'**CLOCK**.

guideline 5 Falling intonation makes the speaker sound confident and certain of the message.

That movie was **EX**cellent.

We're going to make a **PRO**fit.

I'm very happy to **MEET** you.

guideline 6 Wh-questions usually have falling intonation.

Where are you **GO**ing?

Whose **COAT** is this?

What **TIME** is it?

When are the **VIS**itors coming?

Why didn't he **WAIT**?

Which **MO**vie did you see?

e. Level Pitch Lines: Improve your listening

Level pitch lines do not clearly rise or fall. These can give various messages. Level intonation sounds unfinished. The speaker may have more to say. Speakers using level pitch lines express little emotion or opinion. They can sound hesitant, uncertain, or less demanding.

1. Listen to these sentences. One speaker sounds finished and one sounds unfinished.

   For the New Year, I plan to go on a diet . . . ____ finished _✓_ unfinished

   For the New Year, I plan to go on a diet. _✓_ finished ____ unfinished

2. Listen to these commands. One speaker sounds more demanding.

   Please have this ready by Friday. _✓_ less demanding ____ more demanding

   Please have this ready by Friday. ____ less demanding _✓_ more demanding

3. Listen to these sentences. One speaker sounds confident and one sounds hesitant and uncertain.

   The stock market is going up today. ____ confident _✓_ uncertain

   The stock market is going up today. _✓_ confident ____ uncertain

f. Improve Your Monitoring: Finished and unfinished sentences

Level pitch lines or pitch lines that don't fall far enough sound unfinished. Listen to each sentence and the end-of-the-sentence intonation. Decide if the speaker sounds finished or unfinished with each sentence.

Example We're going to London on Saturday. _✓_ finished ____ unfinished

1. I'm planning to leave tomorrow. ____ finished ____ unfinished
2. This is an important article. ____ finished ____ unfinished
3. The winner will be announced. ____ finished ____ unfinished
4. I hope you'll visit the Grand Canyon. ____ finished ____ unfinished
5. John left an important message. ____ finished ____ unfinished
6. The train ride took twenty minutes. ____ finished ____ unfinished

Rising Pitch Lines

guideline 7 "Yes–no" questions usually have rising intonation.

Yes–No Questions

There is a rise to these questions. The speaker shows little emotion, but wants a response.

Are you FINished?

Is it COLD outSIDE?

Would you LIKE to LEAVE a MESsage?

Answering Questions with a Slightly Rising Pitch Line

People who answer questions with a rising intonation sound uncertain and less confident. Self-monitor your intonation at the ends of sentences to make sure you give the message you intend. Listen to each conversation read two ways. Which response sounds more confident?

Conversation 1: A: Where do you work?

B: At a bakery.

A: Where do you work?

B: At a bakery.

Conversation 2: A: Where are you from?

B: From Canada.

A: Where are you from?

B: From Canada.

Intonation Variations

guideline 8 Native speakers use a bigger-than-usual change in pitch to show emphasis or increased emotion, such as great concern, surprise, disapproval, or enthusiastic approval.

More Emotion

Listen and compare different versions of the same statement or question. Notice the changes in meaning.

The Basic Pattern	**Emphasis (more emotion)**
Is he **SICK** again?	Is he sick a**GAIN**? (surprise, concern)
I need to start **STU**dying.	I **NEED** to **START STU**dying! (emphasis)
That was an exciting **GAME**.	That **WAS** an exciting game. (enthusiastic agreement)
They'll return our money in a **MONTH**.	They'll return our money in a **MONTH?** (surprise, disapproval)

Conversations at the Office

Listen to three people who work together in an office.

1. First worker: I came to pick up the report.

   Second worker: Can you come back later? It's not finished. (simple statement)

   First worker: It's not finished? (question/mild surprise) OK, I'll come back later.

   Third worker: It's not finished! (exclamation) I needed it an hour ago!

2. First worker: I'm ready to go to the meeting.

   Second worker: The meeting was canceled.

   First worker: The meeting was canceled? I wonder what happened.

   Third worker: The meeting was canceled! I changed my whole day around because of that meeting.

Beyond the Words

Intonation changes the meaning of these sentences. Listen to each sentence read different ways. Replay the tape and repeat each sentence one line at a time.

Sentence	**Meaning**
1. That new restaurant was pretty **GOOD**.	good (statement, little emotion)
That new restaurant was pretty **GOOD**!	excellent (exclamation, pleasure/surprise)
That new restaurant was **PRET**ty good.	mediocre (statement, little emotion)
That new restaurant was pretty **GOOD**?	not good (ironic question showing doubt)

2. I'll bet she wants to work all **WEEK**end.	words mean what they say
I'll **BET** she wants to work all weekend.	words mean the opposite (ironic or sarcastic)
I'll bet **SHE** wants to work all weekend.	She wants to work, but no one else does.
3. That was a great way to spend an after**NOON**.	words mean what they say
That was a **GREAT** way to spend an afternoon.	words mean the opposite (ironic)
THAT was a **GREAT** way to spend an afternoon.	exclamation, emphatic speech

---

pronunciation tip **Fall low enough in pitch at the ends of sentences to show that you are finished. Otherwise your sentences may sound unfinished or uncertain.**

Tag Questions

A tag question has two parts, a statement and a yes–no question called a *tag*. She isn't ready, is she? Each part has a focus word. You like **TEA, DON'T** you? When the tag falls in pitch, the speaker sounds more sure of the answer. When the tag rises in pitch, the speaker sounds less sure of the answer.

Tag Question	Meaning
1. We can catch the **BUS** here, **CAN'T** we? (↘)	sure (I believe this is a bus stop.)
We can catch the **BUS** here, **CAN'T** we? (↗)	not sure (I'm not sure that this is a bus stop.)
2. You won't for**GET, WILL** you? (↘)	sure (I feel certain that you won't forget.)
You won't for**GET, WILL** you? (↗)	not sure (I'm afraid that you may forget.)

g. Partner Practice: Variations in wh-questions

Most wh-questions end with a falling pitch line. Sometimes wh-questions end with a pitch rise to show surprise or the need for clarification. Notice the change in focus. Practice the dialogues with a partner.

Dialogue One

A. Where are you **GO**ing?

B. I'm going to **EUR**ope.

A. **WHERE** are you going?

B. To **EUR**ope.

Dialogue Two

A. What did the airline **TELL** you?

B. The planes are all **CAN**celed due to bad **WEA**ther.

A. **WHAT** did they tell you?

B. The **PLANES** are all CANceled.

h. Partner Practice: Dialogue

Statements with rising intonation can be questions seeking clarification or showing surprise. Large pitch changes show more emotion. Listen and discuss the meaning of the pitch lines in this dialogue. Replay the tape and practice the dialogue with a partner. Switch roles.

Not My Bag

A. That's not my bag. Those aren't my groceries.

B. That's not your bag? Those aren't your groceries?

A. No. I bought cheese, chips, salsa, and Coke.

B. You bought cheese, chips, salsa, and Coke? I didn't know you liked salsa.

A. I don't. I'm having a party, and I'm serving salsa.

B. You're having a party? And you didn't invite me?

practice tip Replay the tape and listen to the first part of this chapter with your book closed. Through careful listening you will learn the music of English.

i. Abbreviations

Abbreviations have a specific focus and intonation pattern. Listen and repeat the following abbreviations.

	List Abbreviations That You Use
1. CE**O** (Chief Executive Officer)	
2. CP**A** (Certified Public Accountant)	______________________
3. NP**R** (National Public Radio)	______________________
4. AT**M** (Automatic Teller Machine)	______________________
5. VC**R** (Video Cassette Recorder)	______________________

Two-letter abbreviations sometimes link two vowels.

1. P.**E.** ⟶ pee‿[y]**ee** (Physical Education)
2. E.**R.** ⟶ ee‿[y]**ar** (Emergency Room)
3. A.**M.** ⟶ a‿[y]**em** (midnight to noon)
4. R.**N.** ⟶ ar‿**ren** (Registered nurse)

Listen to your instructor say these abbreviations and figure out the pattern. Check (✓) the correct answer. Then practice the above abbreviations.

1. USA Melody: ____ The pitch stays on one line.
   ____ The pitch steps down.
2. USA Focus: ____ The first letter gets the focus.
   ____ The last letter gets the focus.

j. Partner Practice: Sentences

1. One partner says the abbreviation. The other partner says the sentence. Take turns.

Example First partner: CN**N** (Cable News Network)
Second partner: My friend is a reporter for CN**N**.

1. CE**O** The company has a new CE**O**.
2. CP**A** I am studying to be a CP**A**.
3. NP**R** I heard him interviewed on NP**R**.
4. VC**R** My brother bought a new VC**R**.
5. AT**M** I got cash from the AT**M**.

2. Write sentences with abbreviations that you use and dictate them to your partner.

____

____

k. Partner Practice: Short conversations

Take turns asking and answering questions using abbreviations. One partner asks the question. The other partner answers using the abbreviations. Ask and answer your own questions about other abbreviations.

Example A: How long have you been in the US**A**?

B: I've been in the US**A** for five years.

1. What do you think of UFO's? (unidentified flying object)
2. Who do you know who has an MBA? (Masters in Business Administration)
3. What is your favorite P.E. class?
4. Where is the ATM located?
5. How much TV do you watch?
6. Is 4 A.M. morning or afternoon?

l. Join the Chorus

Listen first. Then divide into groups A and B. Practice with your group until you sound like a chorus speaking in unison. Tap the desk as you say the focus word to keep up with the rhythm. Switch groups.

Get To The Airport Early

A: I'm going on va**CA**tion.

B: Gotta make a reser**VA**tion.

A: I wish you could come a**LONG**.

B: I wish I could come a**LONG**.

A: **A**.M., **P**.M.,* day or **NIGHT**.
Gotta get to the airport **EAR**ly.
Don't want to miss my **FLIGHT**.

B: DeTROIT, NEWark
WASHington, BOSton
ChiCAgo, ToRONto
J-F-**K**.

*****A**.M. and **P**.M. in this context show contrast. Usually the focus is on the last letter: 4 A.**M**., 2 P.**M**.

A: Find the **TICK**et. Stand in **LINE**.

B: Check the **LUG**gage. Get a **SEAT**.

A: Buckle **UP**. Settle **DOWN**.

B: Taking **OFF**. Up and a**WAY**.

A: **A**.M., **P**.M., day or **NIGHT**.

Gotta get to the airport **EAR**ly.

Don't want to miss my **FLIGHT**.

B: SeATTle, MiAMi

PORTland, DALlas

VanCOUver, PHOEnix

L-A-**X**.

A: C-E-**O**, V-I-**P**

B: CP**A** or Ph.**D**.

A: LA**X** or JF**K**

B: PD**Q** ASA**P**

A: I wish you could come a**LONG**.

B: I wish I could come a**LONG**.

A: **A**.M., **P**.M., day or **NIGHT**.

B: Gotta get to the airport **EARL**y . . .

A: Oh, **NO**! I missed my **FLIGHT**!

B: That's 'cause you didn't take **ME** along!

Abbreviations

PDQ = pretty darn quick

ASAP = as soon as possible

LAX = Los Angeles International Airport

JFK = John F. Kennedy Airport

CEO = Chief Executive Officer

VIP = very important person

CPA = Certified Public Accountant

Ph.D. = Doctor of Philosophy

Reductions

gotta = I've got to

'cause = because

Phrasal Verbs*

COME a**LONG** = accompany or go with someone

BUCkle **UP** = buckle your seat belt

SETtle **DOWN** = relax, get calm and comfortable

TAKing **OFF** = plane leaving the ground

* Phrasal verbs are "two-word verbs." The focus is on the second word. Practice phrasal verbs listed in Chapter 9.

Longer Sentences

Sentences with more than four or five words are organized into thought groups. The melody is more complex, and people make individual choices about the melody patterns for thought groups in longer sentences. The best way to learn these more complex melodies is to listen and repeat what you hear until it becomes automatic.

1. Listen to the words from the song, "Home on the Range." Each thought group has its own focus word and intonation pattern. Replay the tape and say the words with the speaker. Tap your desk for the focus words.

Where seldom is **HEARD** / a discouraging **WORD** /

and the **SKIES** / are not cloudy all **DAY**./

How often at **NIGHT** / when the heavens are **BRIGHT** /

from the **LIGHT** /of the glittering **STARS** /

have I stood there a**MAZED** / and I asked as I **GAZED** /

"Does their **GLO**ry /exceed that of **OURS**?"/

2. The following charts show one possible choice for the intonation of three longer sentences. Find the word on the chart that jumps up to the highest pitch in each sentence. It is often an early content word. Other stressed words jump up in pitch, but not as high.

1. I WATCHED the **BUS** / TURN the **COR**ner. /

4 Extra High		
3 High	WATCHED **BUS**	**COR-**
2 Middle-Low	I the	TURN the
1 Extra Low		ner.

2. I've been LIVing in Cali**FOR**nia / since LAST **MAY**.

4 Extra High		
3 High	LIV **FOR**	**M** LAST
2 Middle-Low	Cal I've been ing in i nia	**A** since
1 Extra Low		**Y.**

3. She SPENT all her **MON**ey / before she KNEW what **HAP**pened. /

4 Extra High		
3 High	MON SPENT	HAP- KNEW
2 Middle-Low	She all her ey	what before she
1 Extra Low		penned.

More to Say

A slight rising pitch line and pause after the focus word in each thought group indicates that the speaker has more to say. The falling pitch at the end of the sentence shows that the speaker is finished.

In a series

1. I'm taking history, math, and beginning English.
2. We're going to plant two rows of daisies, some rose bushes, and some daffodils.
3. I'd like the soup of the day, a Caesar salad, and the tomato pasta.

Two phrases

1. I believe you, but I'd like more proof.
2. He can fix the printer, but not today.
3. When you leave, please turn off the lights.

Giving a choice (The following are not "yes–no" questions.)

When answering questions with this kind of intonation, select one of the choices.

1. Do you want coffee or tea?
2. Are you planning to fly or take the train?
3. Is Lauren an M.D. or an R.N.?
4. Is his name Andrew or Andy?

m. An Ad

Listen to the ad. Draw a slash (/) every time you hear a pause. Listen to the pitch lines.

1. We don't make the mattress, we make it softer.
2. We don't make the boots, we make them drier.
3. We don't make the house, we make it livelier.
4. We don't make the snowboard, we make it stronger.
5. At BASF we don't make a lot of the products you buy, we make a lot of the products you buy better.*

Replay the tape several times. Pay attention to the focus words and the pitch lines.

* By permission. BASF Corporation.

n. Partner Practice: Add a thought group

Pretend that you are trying to get airplane reservations to go to a family reunion. You waited too long and the tickets are expensive. Furthermore, it is hard to get a reservation when you want to travel. Tell your friend what happened and what you plan to do.

1. Finish each sentence by writing another thought group.

Example In my experience, *it pays to make plane reservations ahead.*

1. As you probably **HEARD**, ______
2. As a **RULE**, ______
3. When I heard the **NEWS**, ______
4. Generally **SPEAKing**, ______
5. You may not be**LIEVE** this, but ______
6. As you can i**MAG**ine, ______
7. As a matter of **FACT**, ______
8. Under the **CIR**cumstances, ______

2. Say your sentences to your partner. Monitor the thought groups. Emphasize the focus words and pause. Use a pitch line at the end of the first thought group indicating that you are not finished and have more to say. Use a falling pitch line to indicate that you are finished with the sentence.

o. Partner Practice: Compare the pictures

Partner A looks at the drawing below. Partner B looks at the drawing on page 156. Exchange information about your pictures. Let your partner know when you are finished with each sentence by falling in pitch. If you use a longer sentence, signal the end of the first part with a slight change in pitch and a pause.

Partner A's drawing

Partner B's drawing

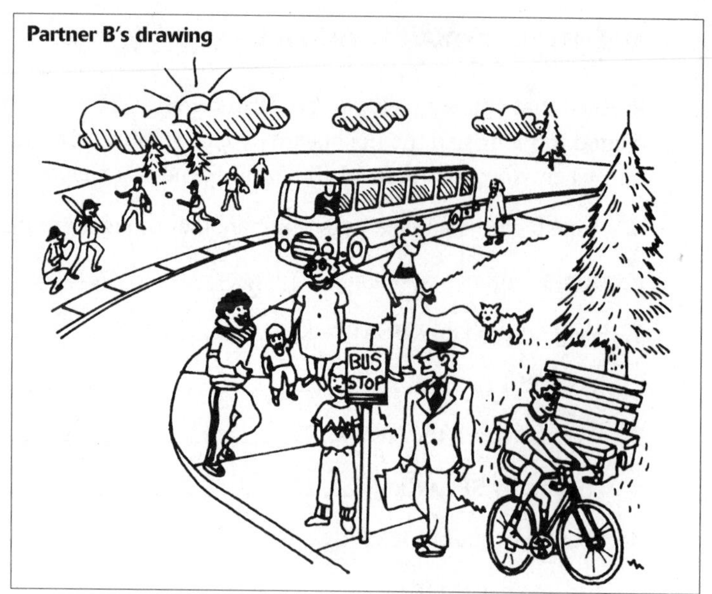

Sample Conversation

A: My picture shows people waiting at a **BUS** STOP. There's a **WO**man waiting with a large **BAG**.

B: My picture shows a **BUS** STOP, **TOO**, but there's a **MAN** waiting, and he's carrying a **BRIEF**case.

A: There's a woman pushing a BAby in a **STROL**ler. Are there babies in **YOUR** picture?

B: **NO**. But there's a picture of a young **CHILD.** He is walking with an older **WO**man. Maybe it's his **GRAND**MOther, or a **BA**by SITter.

p. Dictation

Listen to each sentence read two times. Write what you hear.

1. ______________________________
2. ______________________________
3. ______________________________
4. ______________________________
5. ______________________________

q. Talk: In my opinion . . .

Prepare a short two-minute talk explaining why you agree or disagree with one of the following statements.

- To stay healthy, people need vitamins and other supplements along with eating a balanced diet.
- Men should be the primary wage earners in a family while women take most of the responsibility for home and children.
- Divorce could be avoided if more couples lived together before marriage in order to test their relationship.
- Although cellular phones are popular and useful, they should be outlawed in cars because they are a safety hazard.
- The money spent on space programs would be better spent on community programs for homelessness, hunger, and education.

1. To prepare for your talk, practice some different ways to begin a sentence. Pause and change pitch to signal the end of each of the following thought groups. Repeat each phrase several times aloud.

To Express Your Opinion	To Disagree
In my opinion . . .	I can't agree with that because . . .
Not everyone will agree, but I think . . .	I'm not convinced that . . .
I'm convinced that . . .	I don't see it quite like that. I think that . . .
From my point of view . . .	From a different point of view . . .
I personally believe that . . .	I personally do not believe that . . .
I honestly believe that . . .	I can't go along with that . . .

2. Plan your ideas and take notes. Practice with a tape recorder. Use falling intonation to show confidence. Convince your listener that your reasons are good.

3. When giving your talk, use notes and look away from your paper. Start out by saying the topic or sentence you are discussing. Look at your audience as much as possible.

pronunciation tip Remember that commas and periods give clues about where to end thought groups. However, speakers may use additional thought groups that are not shown by punctuation.

Finishing Up

REVIEW

1. Write a question with rising intonation and draw the pitch line.

   ____

2. Write two questions with falling intonation and draw the pitch lines.

   ____

   ____

3. Write a sentence with an abbreviation. Draw a pitch line that will show that you are finished talking. Draw a dot over the stressed initial in the abbreviation.

   ____

Practice what you wrote with your partner. Discuss the pitch lines and what they mean.

TALK TIMES

In-class Preparation: Discussion

During Talk Times you will be contacting a music store to inquire about a possible purchase. Prepare for this by interviewing your partner about his or her taste in music. Then make a list of questions to ask when you contact the store.

1. Find out about your partner's taste in music. Practice the following interview questions that you will ask your partner. Monitor end-of-the-sentence intonation. The wh-questions fall in pitch. For more natural speech, use these reductions:

- (WHATcher) What is your favorite kind of music? Do you like folk, jazz, Latin, reggae, pop, rock 'n' roll, country/western, classical, alternative, Hawaiian, Irish, or another kind?
- (WHO'S your [ər]) Who is your favorite musical performer or recording artist?
- (WHAT'S the) What is the title of your favorite CD?
- (WHAT'S ONE øf [ə] your [ər]) What is one of your favorite songs?

2. With your partner, make a list of questions to ask the music store. Discuss the kinds of things you want to find out. What is important to you? What kind of music will you ask about?

Possible topics for questions:

- the kind of music the store sells
- discounted tapes or CDs
- the location and hours
- the possibility of listening to recordings in the store
- recordings in stock by your favorite artist or musician
- the store's return policy

Talk Times in Your Daily Life: Buying music

Call or go to three music stores to inquire about a purchase. Write down the questions you will ask. Ask two or three questions per inquiry. Self-monitor and assess what happened before you make your next call. Target focus words, pitch changes, and pauses. Pay attention to the intonation at the ends of sentences and questions.

ON YOUR OWN

1. Figure out the ways to practice with the audio tapes that work the best for you. Experiment with different methods. (1) Once you are familiar with an exercise, try closing your book. Listen and repeat what you hear on the tape without the book. (2) Replay the tape and listen to a phrase or sentence until you can say it easily along with the speaker. This is a good way to learn the pattern for longer sentences.

2. Record the sentences in Exercise k, page 151, using abbreviations. Monitor for focus. Then record the sentences you completed in Exercise n, page 155. Monitor the thought group signals.

3. Record the paragraph about the Beatles on the Targeting Pronunciation Web page.

4. Continue to add words to your personal glossary. Find out how to pronounce them and then use them in conversations. Continue to look for opportunities to converse in English here at school, at work, and in the community.

---

a helpful hint Listen to recordings of songs, especially folk songs or songs from Broadway shows. Listen many times. Eventually you will be able to sing or say the words along with the singer. Then try saying the words without the music. Keep the same rhythm.

9

More Intonation Patterns

To make your speech easier to understand and more native-like, learn about stress and intonation in two-word combinations such as compound nouns. Many common words are made up of two smaller words. For example, air + plane = airplane. Some of these compounds are spelled as one word, such as "notebook." Some are spelled separately, such as "gas station."

It's not always clear from looking at two words if they should sound like a compound noun or another kind of phrase. For example, "apple tree" and "apple pie" have different intonation and stress patterns. This chapter helps you hear the differences between compound nouns and other two-word combinations.

Compound Nouns

a. Listening: Compound noun intonation

1. Listen to the humming and the words.

Melody: grandfather software — Circle the answer. The (first–second) word is higher in pitch.

Stress: ice cream cash register — Circle the answer. The (first–second) word gets strong stress.

2. Trace the pattern.

dishwasher ▬ ▬ •   phone call ▬ ▬

---

guideline The first word of most compound nouns is strongly stressed. Raise the pitch. The second word falls in pitch and is lightly stressed.*

---

* The pronunciation of some compounds can vary occasionally in different regions.

3. Computer words are often compound. Can you add to the list?

DISK DRIVE	KEYBOARD	SPELL CHECK	______
FAX MAchine	comPUter SCREEN	TOOLBAR	______
CYberSPACE	EMAIL	SCREEN SAver	______
DESKTOP	WORD PROcessor		______

b. Partner Practice: Match the words

1. Match a noun from column 1 with a noun from column 2 to create a compound noun. Write the word in column 3.

2. Take turns saying the compound words. The first word is strongly stressed. Make the stressed syllable longer and higher in pitch. Practice saying the compound nouns in sentences.

	1	**2**	**3**	**1**	**2**	**3**
Example:	cheese	burger	cheeseburger			
	1. seat	paper	______	7. high	thing	______
	2. news	recorder	______	8. back	school	______
	3. super	dish	______	9. free	account	______
	4. baby	market	______	10. every	way	______
	5. soap	belt	______	11. bank	pool	______
	6. tape	sitter	______	12. swimming	ache	______

c. Make a List

Add compound nouns that start with the words below. Practice saying them. Change pitch.

Car	**Book**	**Coffee**	**School**	**Parking**	**Sun**
carphone	bookshelf	coffeepot	schooldays	parking lot	sunflower
______	______	______	______	______	______
______	______	______	______	______	______
______	______	______	______	______	______
______	______	______	______	______	______

d. Partner Practice: Short conversations

Look away from your book and listen. Replay the tape and underline the stressed word in the compound noun. Say the dialogues with your partner.

1. A: Where is the SALES SLIP?
   B: Next to the CREdit CARD.
2. A: I need to make a PHONE CALL.
   B. There's a PAY PHONE at the corner.
3. A: I like to watch GAME SHOWS.
   B: I prefer SOAP Operas. ("Soap operas" are daytime serial TV or radio dramas.)
4. A: Please send the information about your INcome TAX.
   B: Do you have a FAX maCHINE?
5. A: I can't balance my CHECKBOOK.
   B: You can wait for your next BANK STATEment.
6. A: It must be LUNCHTIME by now.
   B: I'm dying for a CHEESEBURger.

e. Partner Practice: Role play

One partner is a visitor from another country who arrived with a shopping list. The other partner is the host who suggests places to shop. Switch roles and use a different shopping list.

1. To prepare for the role play, practice the pronunciation of the items on the shopping lists and the places to shop. All these are compound nouns. Use the correct stress.

One Shopping List	The Other Shopping List	Places to Shop
address book	tennis shoes	drugstore
postcards	popcorn	coffee shop
raincoat	watchband	bookstore
applesauce	pancakes	supermarket
hiking boots	birthday card	department store
watermelon	peanut butter	shopping mall
sunscreen	blue jeans	
hair dryer	candy bar	
paperback	milkshake	
hamburger	sport coat	
newspaper	travel books	

2. In the role play, the visitor and the host take turns asking and answering questions about where to buy things on the shopping lists. Monitor for compound nouns. Remember to say the unstressed structure words when needed, such as, "an," "a," "the," "some," "can."

Examples an **AD**dress BOOK at a **BOOK**STORE some **TRA**vel BOOKS

Sample Conversation

Visitor: Do you know where I can buy some shoelaces?

Host: They sell shoelaces at the supermarket around the corner.

Visitor: Thank you. Do you know where I can get a toothbrush?

Host: You can buy a toothbrush in the drugstore at a near-by shopping mall.

More Compound Words

The intonation of these compound words is different from the intonation of compound nouns that sound like CHECKBOOK. How is it different?

1. OverSLEEP UNderNEATH NORTHEAST AFterNOON
2. New JERsey New BRUNSwick New YORK St. GEORGE San AnTONio

f. Join the Chorus

Divide into groups A and B. Practice with your group until you sound like a chorus with one voice. Tap the desk as you say the focus word to keep up the rhythm. Switch groups and say the chant again. Add more verses. What else is missing?

It's Missing, It's Gone

A: I CAN'T **FIND** it. Have you **SEEN** it?

B: I'm SO **SOR**ry. I HAVEn't **SEEN** it.

A: (pause) It's **MISS**ing.

B: (pause) It's **GONE**.

A: I CAN'T FIND my **RAIN**COAT.

I CAN'T FIND the **PHONE** BOOK.

WHAT HAPpened to my **BRIEF**CASE?

B: It's **MISS**ing. It's **GONE**.

A: WHERE'd you PUT the **NEWS**PAper?

I CAN'T FIND the **PEA**nut BUTter.

Have you SEEN my **BIRTH**day CARD?

B: You've **LOST** it? It's **GONE**?

Chorus

A: PLEASE, WON'T you **HELP** me?

B: I'm SORry, but I'm **BUSy** now.

A: WON'T you HELP me **FIND** it?

B: MAYbe LAter **ON**.

B: I CAN'T FIND my **CREdit** CARD.

I CAN'T FIND my **HIKing** BOOTS.

What HAPpened to my **CHECK**BOOK?

A: It's **MISSing**! IT's **GONE**!

B: I CAN'T FIND my **SHOPping** LIST.

Have you SEEN my **CAR** KEYS?

What HAPpened to my **TENnis** SHOE?

A: It's **MISSing**. It's **GONE**.

Chorus

B: PLEASE, WON'T you **HELP** me?

A: I'm SORry, but I'm **BUSy** now.

B: WON'T you HELP me **FIND** it?

A: MAYbe LAter **ON**.

Descriptive Phrases

The following two-word descriptive phrases have the same focus and intonation pattern. The last content word gets the focus and the intonation falls at the end. walking **slowly** a rainy **day**

1. Look away from your book and listen to these phrases. Replay the tape until you are familiar with the pattern.

Noun Phrases	**Verb Phrases**
an OLD **FRIEND**	the ANtelope **PLAY**
a TALL **TREE**	PAINTing **PICtures**
GLITTering **STARS**	WALKS **QUICKly**
a disCOURaging **WORD**	SLEEPing **SOUNDly**

2. Listen to your instructor and repeat some sentences ending with descriptive phrases. The intonation steps or glides down in pitch. Tap the desk when you hear the focus word.

Sentences Ending with Noun Phrases	Sentences Ending with Verb Phrases
The garden is full of BLOOMing **FLO**wers.	We FINished PULLing **WEEDS.**
I picked up the COlor **PHO**tographs.	James spent the day deVELoping **PIC**tures.
We hiked along the NARrow **TRAIL.**	We WALKED **SLOW**ly.
I invited my HUSband's **SIS**ter.	Patty reFUSED **GRA**ciously.
Yesterday I got a call from an OLD **FRIEND**.	She CALLS in**FRE**quently.

g. Check Your Listening

You can't tell from looking whether two words that go together should sound like a compound noun or a descriptive phrase. You can find out by listening. You might think that the following phrases are compound nouns. The intonation and the stress sound like descriptive phrases or names.

fast food   science fiction   iced tea   instant coffee   clock radio

1. Listen to the two-word combinations. For each combination, decide if you hear the pattern for a descriptive phrase or a compound noun. Which word gets more stress?

			Compound Noun	Descriptive Phrase
Examples	applesauce	I ate some applesauce.	✓	___
	apple pie	I ate some apple pie.	___	✓
1.	fresh bread	Here is the fresh bread.	___	___
	French bread	Here is the French bread.	___	___
2.	sleeping bear	I saw a sleeping bear.	___	___
	sleeping bag	I saw a sleeping bag.	___	___
3.	orange juice	I'd like some orange juice.	___	___
	orange sherbet	I'd like some orange sherbet.	___	___
4.	fresh cream	I want some fresh cream.	___	___
	ice cream	I want some ice cream.	___	___
5.	space shuttle	What's the schedule for the space shuttle?	___	___
	last shuttle	What's the schedule for the last shuttle?	___	___

2. Work with a partner. One partner says a sentence with one of the two-word combinations above. The other partner says the sentence with the other word.

Example Partner A: Here is the French bread.

Partner B: Here is the fresh bread.

h. Partner Practice: Descriptive phrases and compound nouns

One of the following sentences ends with a compound noun. The other ends with a descriptive phrase. The focus and the intonation should sound different. The focus words are shown in bold type.

1. Add an adjective of your choice to complete the descriptive phrase.

Example I bought a **SWEAT**SHIRT.

I bought a __________ **SHIRT**. (green, blue, new, striped)

Compound Nouns	**Descriptive Phrases**
1. I bought some **SUN**GLASses.	1. I bought some __________ **GLAS**ses.
2. They went on a **BUS** RIDE.	2. They went on a __________ **RIDE**.
3. Here's some to**MA**to JUICE.	3. Here's some __________ **JUICE**.
4. I made a **PHONE** CALL.	4. I made a __________ **CALL**.
5. I like your **TEN**nis SHOES.	5. I like your __________ **SHOES**.
6. John gave me a **COOK**BOOK.	6. John gave me a __________ **BOOK**.

2. Practice the sentences. One partner says the sentence with the compound noun. The other partner says the sentence with the descriptive phrase. Take turns.

i. Partner Practice

One partner asks either (a) or (b). The other partner answers. The focus words are shown in bold type.

Examples	A: What's he doing in the DARK **ROOM**?	He's **SLEEP**ing.
	B: What's he doing in the **DARK**ROOM?	He's developing **PIC**tures.
1.	a. What are you doing with the **BLACK**BOARD?	Writing on it with **CHALK**.
	b. What are you doing with the BLACK **BOARD**?	Building a **BOOK**CASE.
2.	a. What's a **FREE**WAY?	A fast **HIGH**WAY.
	b. What's a FREE **WAY**?	There is no **CHARGE.**

3.	a.	What are you doing with that HOT **DOG**?	Giving him a **DRINK**.
	b.	What are you doing with that **HOT** DOG?	Eating it for **LUNCH**.
4.	a.	Where does the **PRES**ident live?	In the **WHITE** HOUSE.
	b.	Where do you **LIVE**?	In the WHITE **HOUSE**.
5.	a.	Where does your rich **UN**cle live?	He lives on a REAL e**STATE**.
	b.	What kind of **WORK** does he do?	He sells **REAL** eSTATE.
6.	a.	Why are you **LATE**?	I made a SHORT **STOP** on the way **HOME**.
	b.	Did JAson play in the **BASE**BALL GAME?	Yes, he played **SHORT**STOP.

j. Join the Chorus

Divide into groups A and B. Practice with your group until you sound like a chorus with one voice. Tap the desk to keep up the rhythm. Stress the focus word at the end of each phrase. Wh- questions fall in pitch. Yes-no questions rise in pitch.

Wishes

A: What do you do with a hungry tiger?

B: Keep it away from the sleeping baby.

A: What do you do with a shiny car?

B: Cover it up on a rainy day.

A: What should I do with an apple pie?

B: Put it down on a kitchen table.

A: What do you think of the gorgeous sunset?

B: I like it better than the cloudy sky.

A: What did you order with the mushroom omelet?

B: Buttered toast and some fried potatoes.

A: Did you make a wish on a falling star?

B: I made a wish on a falling star.

A-B: I wished for—a gorgeous sunset, a mushroom omelet, a sleeping baby, a shiny car, and an apple pie.

k. Song: "This Land Is Your Land"

During the Great Depression of the 1930s Woody Guthrie roamed across many states on his way to California to look for work. He wrote this and other songs as he traveled on foot with his guitar. The lyrics of this song translate easily into conversational speech.

1. Listen to the song. Fill in the missing focus words. They are listed here in alphabetical order:

above around below forest deserts island lifting me rolling

shining valley walking waters your my

2. Compare answers with a partner. Replay the song.

1. As I was __________ that ribbon of **HIGH**way,

   I saw __________ me that endless **SKY**way,

   I saw __________ me that golden __________

   This land was **MADE** for you and __________.

   Chorus

   This land is __________ land,* This land is __________ land,

   From Cali**FOR**nia to the New York __________

   From the redwood __________

   To the Gulf Stream __________,

   This land was **MADE** for you and **ME.**

2. I've roamed and **RAM**bled, and I followed my **FOOT**steps,

   To the sparkling **SANDS** of her diamond __________;

   And all __________ me, a voice was **SOUND**ing,

   "This land was **MADE** for you and __________."

   Chorus

3. When the sun came __________, and I was **STROLL**ing,

   And the wheat fields **WAV**ing, and the dust clouds __________,

   As the fog was __________, a voice was **CHANT**ing,

   "This land was **MADE** for you and __________."

   Chorus

3. Discuss the vocabulary. roam ramble fog chant stroll dust clouds

In the song you hear this intonation: This land is **MY** land. This land is **YOUR** land. The pronouns are stressed to show contrast and to emphasize that the country belongs to everyone.

Compare what you hear in the song with the basic focus pattern for new information: This is my **LAND.**

Song Exercises

1. Word Stress. There are many two-syllable words in this song. Some are compound nouns. Write the two-syllable words from the song on the chart. Say the words as you trace the pattern with your finger.

PAper

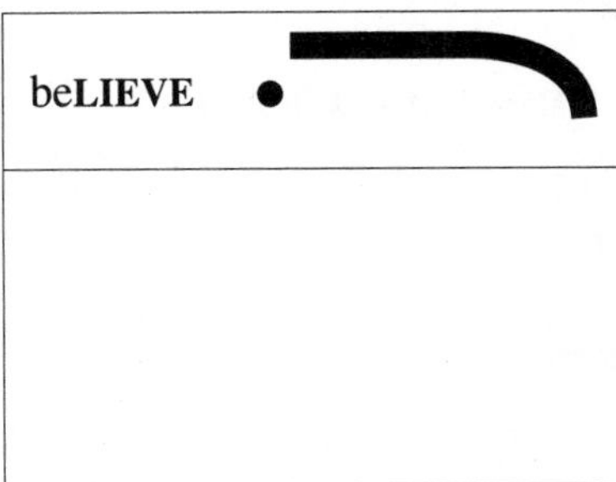

Compound Nouns

2. Descriptive Phrases. Add the focus word to these phrases. Practice saying the phrases. Focus on the last word. Sometimes a compound noun is part of a descriptive phrase. The compound nouns in the phrases to follow are written inside brackets.

a golden ______________ her diamond ______________

an endless ______________ the [dust clouds] ______________

the sparkling ______________ the [wheat fields] ______________

3. Important Endings: "ed" and final "s." Fill in the missing endings. Practice saying these phrases from the song. Slow down and lengthen the focus words, but link them to the next word in the sentence.

1. I've roam____ and ramble____ / and I follow____ my footstep ____ /
2. to the sparkling sand____ / of her diamond desert____ /
3. and the wheat field____ waving / and the dust cloud____ rolling /

4. Practice saying each verse as if you are telling a story. Lengthen the focus words and signal the end of the sentence by falling in pitch. Join in with a small group to say one of the verses for the class.

1. As I was **WALK**ing / that ribbon of **HIGH**way, / I saw a**BOVE** me / that endless **SKY**way. / I saw be**LOW** me / that golden **VAL**ley. / This land was **MADE** / for you and **ME.** /
2. I've roamed and **RAM**bled / and I followed my **FOOT**steps / to the sparkling **SANDS** / of her diamond **DE**serts / and all a**ROUND** me / a voice was **SOUND**ing / "This land was **MADE** / for you and **ME.**"/
3. When the sun came **SHIN**ing / and I was **STROLL**ing / and the wheat fields **WAV**ing / and the dust clouds **ROLL**ing / as the fog was **LIFT**ing / a voice was **CHANT**ing / "This land was **MADE** / for you and **ME.**"/

Phrasal Verbs

Phrasal verbs have two words that are pronounced as a unit. "Turn on." "Pull over." The second word is called the particle. (A particle is a very small piece, a fragment.) In a phrasal verb the particle is usually a preposition that comes after the verb.

Contrast Phrasal Verbs and Compound Nouns

1. Listen and compare the stress and intonation of the phrasal verbs and the compound nouns.

Phrasal Verbs	Compound Nouns
work out	workout
drop out	dropout
print out	printout
cover up	cover-up
run off	runoff
tear off	tearoff

2. Circle the answer.

Rule: In phrasal verbs, the (first–second) word gets the strong stress.

3. Sometimes the particle can be separated from the verb.

Examples Take it **away**. Put them **down**. Print it **out**.

I. Partner Practice

One partner says either (a), the compound noun, or (b), the phrasal verb. The other partner says the matching sentence.

1. a. WORKOUT — That was quite a workout.
   b. WORK **OUT** — How did the plan work out?
2. a. DROPOUT — He's a college dropout.
   b. DROP **OUT** — Did he drop out of the race?
3. a. PRINTOUT — The ink on the printout is faded.
   b. PRINT **OUT** — I need to print out some extra copies.

4.	a.	COver-UP	The criminals were involved in a cover-up.
	b.	COver **UP**	Please cover up the baby.
5.	a.	RUNOFF	The runoff is from the melting snow.
	b.	RUN **OFF**	The thief tried to run off with my wallet.
6.	a.	TEAR-OFF	There is a tear-off at the bottom of the page.
	b.	TEAR **OFF**	Don't tear off the label.

m. Cartoon: *Drabble*

Read the cartoon emphasizing the focus words.

Find and write the compound noun: ____________________

the descriptive phrase: ____________________

the phrasal verbs: ____________________ ____________________

DRABBLE by Kevin Fagan

Names

The last name gets stronger stress than the first name. The pitch steps or glides down. Names and descriptive phrases have the same pattern.

SHIRley TEMple	The ROCKy **MOUNT**ains	FROzen **PIZ**za
MICHael **JOR**dan	AMERican **AIR**LINES	DIet **CO**la
JOHN **MA**jor	NiAGra **FALLS**	BOILing **WA**ter
THOmas **JEF**ferson	MEXico **CI**ty	WINter **JACK**et

n. Partner Practice: Conversation with names

Make a list of the names of your favorite TV program, movie, or stars. Draw a large dot over the stressed syllables. Underline the focus word. Talk about your choices with your partner.

Example Sixty Minutes

______________________ ______________________

______________________ ______________________

______________________ ______________________

______________________ ______________________

o. Partner Practice: Talk about where you live

1. Say these names. The second word gets strong stress.

SeATtle, **WASH**ington CALgary, Al**BER**ta FIFTH **AVE**nue LINcoln **BOUL**evard

Names ending in "street" sound like compound nouns.

FOURTH STREET **GIN**ger STREET

2. Write the names of some streets and places in your community. Check to find out the correct pronunciation. Draw large dots over the stressed syllables and underline the words with strong stress.

Examples Princeton Avenue MacDougall's Drugstore

______________________ ______________________

______________________ ______________________

______________________ ______________________

______________________ ______________________

3. What cross streets are near where you live? Write them below.

Examples AriZONa **AVE**nue and **FOURTH** Street

SUNset **BOUL**evard and CoLUMbus **AVE**nue

______________________ ______________________

______________________ ______________________

4. Discuss where you live with your partner. Tell the name of the city, the state, and your street. Talk about near-by cross streets and the names of places in your community. Monitor your own and your partner's pronunciation. Find out if your partner can understand you. Exchange suggestions.

p. Dialogue

1. Listen and practice the following dialogue with a partner. Pay attention to the phrasal verbs, the compound nouns, the descriptive phrases, and the names.

A Great Weekend

1. A: I'm going away for the weekend. Would you and your roommate like to come along?
2. B: My roommate usually can't get away. She's an X-ray technician at Memorial Hospital and only gets off one weekend a month.
3. A: Sounds like a hard work schedule!
4. B: It is, but she likes her job. Where are you planning to go?
5. A: Sightseeing in the countryside near Angel's Ranch. I need some sunshine and a rest from the traffic jams and the car exhaust.
6. B: Sounds good to me. There's a phone booth across the street from Charlie's Market. I'll try to get hold of my roommate.
7. A: (B returns.) So what did she say? Can she take off for the weekend?
8. B: Yes! She can! The good news is that her backache is almost gone. And her headaches aren't a problem anymore. She still gets carsick but not if we pull off the highway every ten or fifteen minutes and let her walk around.
9. A: Terrific! It sounds like a great weekend.

2. Replay the tape and listen to A's comment (9) again. The intonation gives you extra information. Do the words mean what they say or do they mean the opposite?

3. List the phrasal verbs, compound nouns, and names in the dialogue. Say these in sentences. Practice the correct focus and intonation.

Phrasal Verbs **Names**

______________	______________	______________
______________	______________	______________
______________	______________	______________

Compound Nouns

______________	______________	______________
______________	______________	______________
______________	______________	______________
______________	______________	______________
______________	______________	______________

q. Role Play: Luxury home

One partner sells real estate and works for Star Realty. The other partner is a prospective buyer looking for a home with two bedrooms and two bathrooms. The real estate agent tries to interest the buyer in the large luxury home described in an ad. The buyer tells the agent that the home in the ad is too large and expensive, but agrees to take a look at the house anyway.

1. To prepare for the role play, listen to the ad for a luxury home. It is a series of phrases rather than complete sentences. The structure words are missing. Clarify any new vocabulary.

> **For Sale:**
> **LUXURY HOME**
> Elegant Spanish style home, prime Beverly Hills location, near movie star mansions. Five bedrooms, six bathrooms, maid's room, exercise room, separate guest house. Large courtyard. Glamorous entry hall with spiral staircase. Newly remodeled gourmet kitchen, own fireplace. Living room view, fruit trees, flower gardens, swimming pool. Pool house, hot tub, tennis court. Priced to sell, bargain. See today. Call Star Realty: 310-829-9511. Ask for John Handel or Betty Hoffman.

2. Replay the tape. Listen carefully for the compound nouns because you cannot always predict the intonation from looking at two words. Sometimes a compound noun can be part of a descriptive phrase. For example, glamorous [entry hall]. The compound noun is inside brackets.

3. Make a list of compound nouns that you hear in the ad. Underline the stressed word. Compare lists with a partner.

______________	______________	______________
______________	______________	______________
______________	______________	______________

4. Listen to your instructor and repeat the four names in the ad. Use the correct focus.

Beverly Hills   Star Realty   John Handel   Betty Hoffman

5. Listen to the sample conversation. Then make up your own conversation between the real estate agent and the prospective buyer. Switch roles. Monitor your own and your partner's speech for compound nouns, descriptive phrases, and phrasal verbs.

C = customer A = real estate agent

A: My name is John Handel. I'd like to tell you about a new listing of an elegant house in Beverly Hills. It has a swimming pool, a guest house, and a lovely view of fruit trees.

C: That sounds wonderful, but how large is it?

A: It has five bedrooms and six bathrooms, but that's not all . . .

C: That sounds much too big for my family. We only need two bedrooms and two bathrooms. Does it have a swimming pool?

A: A gorgeous one. And a tennis court, too.

C: I've always wanted a swimming pool, and I'd like to learn how to play tennis. But it's probably much too expensive.

A: Oh, no! It's a real bargain. You really should see it today. It's going to sell very quickly. It has a glamorous entry hall with a spiral staircase, and it's near the homes of famous movie stars.

C: I really don't want to live near any movie stars. Anyway, it must be very expensive.

A: Why don't you just take a look? There's a newly remodeled gourmet kitchen.

C: A new gourmet kitchen? I love to cook. Well, maybe I could just take a quick look.

Finishing Up

REVIEW

Write at least two examples for each pattern and practice saying them in sentences.

- **compound nouns** Stress the first word. Come down in pitch on the last word.

  ____

- **descriptive phrases** Focus on the last word. Change pitch.

  ____

- **names** Emphasize the last name. Change pitch.

  ____

- **phrasal verbs** Focus on the particle. Change pitch.

  ____

TALK TIMES

In-class Preparation: Role play

One partner works for the "Y" (YMCA, a community organization with a health club) and tries to interest people in the program. You answer questions about the schedule with enthusiasm. You know what you're talking about, so you fall in pitch noticeably at the end of each sentence. The other partner is considering joining the "Y" and wants to find out about the program and what classes fit into his or her schedule.

1. Practice saying the list of available classes. Listen to your instructor say the following with compound noun and descriptive phrase intonation. Repeat what you hear.

Compound Nouns		**Descriptive Phrases**
EXercise CLASS	VOLley BALL	CP**R**
aeRObics CLASS	BOdy SCULPTing	CARdioVAScular **JAZZ**
STRETCH CLASS	POwer WALKing	FITness after FIFty-**FIVE**
SWIMming CLASS	WAter WORKout	
YOga CLASS	RACquetBALL	

2. Role play with your partner. Switch roles.

Partner A: Look at the "Y" schedule. Your partner will be asking for information about it. Describe some of the classes, and try to convince your partner to join.

TIME	**MON.**	**TUES.**	**WED.**	**THURS.**	**FRI.**	**SAT.**	**SUN.**
7 AM	aerobics	swimming	yoga	water workout	CPR	water workout	stretch class
10 AM	power walking	water workout	body sculpting	fitness after 55	swimming	volley ball	exercise class
NOON	cardio/jazz	swimming	stretch class	aerobics	volley ball	CPR	racquetball
5 PM	aerobics	power walking	cardio/jazz	water workout	body sculpting	fitness after 55	water workout
7 PM	swimming	cardio/jazz	racquetball	yoga	aerobics	cardio/jazz	yoga

Partner B: Look at your personal calendar below. Ask about classes available during your free time, marked by asterisks. Fill in your calendar. Look at the list of classes. Ask questions about the times of classes you are interested in.

TIME	MON.	TUES.	WED.	THURS.	FRI.	SAT.	SUN.
7 AM	*	*	*	*	*	*	*
10 AM						*	*
NOON	*	*		*		*	*
5 PM			*		*	*	*
7 PM	*	*		*		*	*

Talk Times in Your Daily Life: Choosing a health club

Call or visit three health clubs in your community, including a YMCA. Make a list of questions to ask.

Sample topics

- the activity schedule
- the cost (dues, the payment plan)
- child care
- parking
- how to see the facilities or arrange a tour
- other

Self-monitor and assess what happened in order to improve the next call. Decide what targets you are going to monitor. List them below and give examples.

____

____

____

ON YOUR OWN

1. **Practice regularly with the audio tapes for short periods of time.** Monitor carefully. Try saying short segments of speech from memory. Whenever possible, look away from your book as you listen and speak.

2. **Record the chant, "Wishes," page 167, and the dialogue, "A Great Weekend," page 173.** Get together with another student or record both parts yourself. Monitor for compound nouns and descriptive phrases.

3. **Record the paragraph about science fiction on the Targeting Pronunciation Web page.** Pay attention to the compound nouns and the descriptive phrases.

4. **Keep noticing words that you want to pronounce more clearly.** Add them to your personal glossary. Use your dictionary or ask a native speaker how to say them. Most nonnative speakers have to exaggerate the stressed syllable by lengthening it and changing pitch.

5. **Continue conversing in English as much as possible each day, especially with native speakers.** Notice how much easier this is. Call someone in the class to talk about this chapter.

---

a helpful hint

Use a tape recorder to hear things about your speech that you did not hear at first. Silently read a page or two from any book about a topic that you are interested in. Close the book and tape record yourself talking about what you just read. Monitor for one or two targets. Listen to your tape, decide what you want to improve, and make another tape.

10

Important Endings

Some nonnative speakers do not clearly hear all the syllables and sounds in English words. It's hard to remember to say all the important final syllables if you don't always hear them.

Listen to These Words. Pay Attention to the Endings.

Past tenses:	PAINTed I PAINTed it.	WANTed They WANTed it.	comPLETed He comPLETed it.
Plural nouns:	PRIces HIGH PRIces	BOXes BIG BOXes	SENtences LONG SENtences
Verbs:	WATCHes She WATCHes it.	FACes She FACes it.	MISses He MISses it.

Part 1.
"ed" Endings

a. Check Your Listening

1. Past or Present?

You will hear a sentence in either the present or the past tense. Check (✓) the tense you hear. Replay the tape until you are sure of your answers.

Example a. **It tastes good.** _✓_ Present   b. It tasted good. ____ Past

1. ____ Present ____ Past
2. ____ Present ____ Past
3. ____ Present ____ Past
4. ____ Present ____ Past
5. ____ Present ____ Past
6. ____ Present ____ Past

2. "ed" or "ed"?

In some past tenses, the "ed" is an extra syllable with a schwa vowel. *ADDed*
In other past tenses, the "e" is silent. *hoped.*

Listen to the past tense. Do you hear an extra syllable with a schwa vowel or is the "e" silent? Check (✓) the correct column.

Examples painted _✓_ Extra syllable ____ Silent "e"

picked ____ Extra syllable _✓_ Silent "e"

Past Tense	**"ed"** (ə)	**"ed"** (silent)
1. rented	____	____
2. rained	____	____
3. applied	____	____
4. appreciated	____	____
5. used	____	____
6. ended	____	____

b. Figure Out the Rule

The "ed" in these verbs is an extra syllable. Look at the final sound of the regular verb and write it on the line next to the verb. The final letter may not indicate the final sound.

Example ended end _d_ skated skate _t_

seated	seat	____	wanted	want	____
needed	need	____	handed	hand	____
voted	vote	____	wasted	waste	____

The past tense of these verbs has a silent "e." Look at the final sound of the regular verb. Write it on the line.

Example baked bake _k_

stayed	stay	____	robbed	rob	____
locked	lock	____	moved	move	____
loaned	loan	____	closed	close	____
washed	wash	____	stopped	stop	____

---

rule **"ed" sounds like a separate syllable when the regular verb ends with a ____ or ____ sound. All other verbs have a silent "e."**

---

c. Partner Practice: Past and present

One partner says either sentence (a) or (b). The other partner says the other sentence. Monitor your own and your partner's pronunciation.

Example First partner: I dreamed about a trip.

Second partner: I dream about a trip.

1. a. I dream about a trip.
   b. I dreamed about a trip.
2. a. They live in a small house.
   b. They lived in a small house.
3. a. They love a cat.
   b. They loved a cat.
4. a. I want a pound of apples.
   b. I wanted a pound of apples.
5. a. We volunteer at the shelter.
   b. We volunteered at the shelter.
6. a. I print all the documents.
   b. I printed all the documents.
7. a. We exercise at the "Y."
   b. We exercised at the "Y."
8. a. I believe it all.
   b. I believed it all.

d. Linking "ed"

You can identify the past tense when you hear "ed" linked to the next word. Listen to the different kinds of linking. Then turn off your tape recorder and practice.

1. The Flap

Use a flap when linking "ed" to a vowel. Review the flap, p. 104.

tired out laughed at it used it up

locked her car walked alone liked his personality

2. Linking "ed" to a t or d

To link the past tense to a t or d, say the final sound once, but hold it longer. Keep your tongue on your gum ridge and briefly stop the air. Then say the next word. The **:** means to hold the sound.

moved: twice listened: to her mother

3. Linking "ed" to Other Consonants

When "ed" links to a word starting with a consonant, start to say the final d. Stop the air briefly before linking to the next word. Listen and compare the following phrases.

push the door—pushed the door skip lunch—skipped lunch

stop quickly—stopped quickly

pronunciation tip When you talk, listen carefully to your own speech to make sure you are saying the "ed." Self-monitoring is an important part of speaking clearly in English.

e. Join the Chorus

1. Listen first. Then divide into groups A and B. Practice until you sound like a chorus speaking in unison. Tap the desk as you say the focus words to keep up the rhythm. Link the "ed" ending to the next word.

The Visitor

1. A: I walked up the stairs.
   B: I stopped at the door.
   A: I pushed on the bell.
   B: I stamped on the floor.

2. A: She peeked through the crack.
   B: And switched on the light.
   A: She stared at my bag,
   B: Surprised at the sight.

3. A: I glanced at her face.
   B: I hoped she could see
   A: That although I had changed
   B: It really was me.

4. A: She pulled at the knob.
   B: The door opened wide.
   A: She paused and she smiled,
   B: And she asked me inside.

5. A: I had dreamed of this moment.
   B: All regrets vanished fast.
   A: We imagined the future
   B: Reunited at last.

2. Work with a small group. Prepare one verse to say with your group for the class.

f. Improve Your Monitoring

1. Listen to each sentence. Decide if the speaker says the underlined past tense or substitutes the present tense without the "ed." Check (✓) the word you hear.

Example She looked at the book. looked ✓ look ____

1.	Yolanda answered all the questions.	____ answered	____ answer
2.	My friend reported the accident to the police.	____ reported	____ report
3.	The baby bumped his head when he fell.	____ bumped	____ bump
4.	Alice finished all her work on time.	____ finished	____ finish
5.	Sam improved his grades.	____ improved	____ improve
6.	Roberta owned her own house.	____ owned	____ own
7.	She managed her mother's affairs.	____ managed	____ manage
8.	Yesterday we talked about our plans.	____ talked	____ talk

2. Practice saying the sentences correctly. Self-monitor. Listen for the "ed" and the linking.

g. Partner Practice: Idioms

1. Match the definitions with the idioms. Write the letter of the definition on the line next to the sentence with the idiom. Discuss your answers with the instructor.

Idioms

1. She brushed up on her Spanish before she went to Peru. ____
2. Jane jumped at the chance for an interview. ____
3. Harry dropped a bombshell when he announced that he was moving to Australia. ____
4. I wasted my breath when I tried to tell my brother what to do. ____
5. I washed my hands of the matter when he refused to consult a lawyer. ____
6. They lived it up after they won the lottery. ____

Definitions

a. acted quickly on an opportunity
b. reviewed, refreshed her memory
c. withdrew from the situation
d. lived extravagantly
e. made an unexpected shocking announcement
f. spoke without accomplishing anything

2. Take turns saying the sentences. Monitor linking "ed" to the next word.

h. Partner Practice: Dialogue

1. Listen to the dialogue. Monitor for "ed" endings.

Basket on the Bus

1. A: You'll NEver **GUESS** what happened on the **BUS** last week.
2. B: What **HAP**pened?
3. A: The bus driver pulled **O**ver and a little girl carrying a large **BAS**ket hopped on.
4. B: What **KIND** of basket?
5. A: It looked like a **PIC**nic BASket. A loaf of **BREAD** was wrapped up in a **NAPK**in, and I thought I smelled **COOK**ies.
6. B: She was **PRO**bably headed for* a **PIC**nic.
7. A: **MAY**be, but she seemed a little **NER**vous. The bus was **CROWD**ed. She climbed **O**ver the other **PAS**sengers and sat next to **ME**.
8. B: Did she **TALK** to you?
9. A: She **START**ed to talk to me, but changed her **MIND.**† Suddenly, she jumped **UP**, set the basket on my **LAP**, and hopped off the **BUS**.
13. B: It sounds as if you in**HER**ited a basket of **FOOD**.
14. A: Not e**XAC**tly. I seem to have inherited a **PUP**py! He was asleep under the **NAP**kin. The "cookies" were **DOG** BIScuits, and now I'm enrolled in DOG TRAINing **SCHOOL**.

2. Replay the tape several times, looking away from your book. Listen for the focus words and the intonation. Listen for compound nouns and phrasal verbs.

List the compound nouns: Stress the first word.

____________ ____________ ____________

List the phrasal verbs: Stress the particle.

____________ ____________ ____________

____________ ____________

3. Practice these phrases from the dialogue. Use a flap to link "ed" to the next vowel.

1. what happened‿on the **BUS**
2. pulled‿**O**ver
3. carried‿a large **BAS**ket
4. seemed‿a little **NER**vous
5. started‿to **TALK** to me
6. changed‿her **MIND**
7. inherited‿a **PUP**py
8. wrapped‿in a **NAP**kin
9. inherited‿a basket‿of **FOOD**
10. enrolled‿in DOG TRAINing **SCHOOL**

4. Practice the dialogue. Remember to link the words and say all the important endings. Switch roles.

* **headed for** Going to, going in the direction of.
† **changed her mind** Altered her ideas or plans.

i. Role Play: Technology in the twentieth century

You and your partner are writing an article about the history of technology in the twentieth century. You both have some of the research. What information are you missing? See Partner A's information below and Partner B's information on page 187.

1. To prepare for the role play, review the pronunciation of the information on your timeline with the instructor. Draw dots over stressed syllables in longer words. Underline the focus words.

Example Philips <u>Electronics</u> as a means of preserving food <u>commercially</u>

Partner A's Information

1902 Willis Carrier invented and produced the first air conditioner.

1903 *

1908 Henry Ford introduced the Model-T Ford, the first affordable automobile.

1909 *

1917 Clarence Birdseye developed a way of freezing food and packaging it commercially.

1937 *

1940 RCA produced the first commercial color TV.

1948 *

1952 Pan Am offered the first daily transatlantic roundtrip jetliner flight from New York to Paris. BOAC started the first daily jetliner service from New York to London.

1963 Philips Electronics demonstrated the first compact audio cassettes commonly used in tape recorders.

1969 *

1975 IBM introduced a new type of printer for computers, the laser printer.

1981 *

1982 RCA introduced the first compact disc players, and CDs were destined to replace long-playing records.

1989 The World Wide Web, which began in Switzerland, started connecting people around the globe to cyberspace.

1993 *

1997 British and Scottish scientists cloned a sheep called "Dolly."

Partner B's Information

1902 *

1903 The Wright brothers piloted the first airplane to make a successful flight.

1908 *

1909 A Belgian-born chemist patented and produced *Bakelite,* the first successful plastic.

1917 *

1937 Xerography introduced the first method of photo copying.

1940 *

1948 Columbia Records produced the first 33-⅓ RPM long playing (LP) phonograph record.

1952 *

1963 *

1969 Apollo 11, the first manned space ship, landed on the moon.

1975 *

1981 IBM introduced the first personal computer, commonly called a "PC."

1982 *

1989 *

1993 A research group at the University of Illinois developed the first World Wide Web browser for navigating the Internet.

1997 *

2. In the role play, talk about technology and fill in your timeline. Monitor for past tenses and linking.

Example A: Do you know if anything interesting happened in 1903?

B: Yes. The Wright brothers perfected the first airplane to make a successful flight.

A: I see that in 1952 the airlines started transatlantic jet service. What happened before 1952?

B: Well, in 1907 someone figured out how to make plastic. The first plastic was called *Bakelite*.

Review "ed" Endings

1. Look away from your book and listen to a true story about a gorilla.

Binti, The Heroine

In 1996, a mother gorilla at the Chicago Zoo __________ a three-and-a-half year old boy who __________ into the gorilla pit. As his parents __________ in horror, their toddler suddenly __________ into the pit and fell eighteen feet to the cement below. A mother gorilla named Binti __________ him from danger. With her own baby on her back, Binti gently __________ the child and __________ of the pit to safety. She __________ the child from the other gorillas and __________ him to a rescue worker. Unconscious, the boy was __________ immediately to a hospital. He soon __________ from a concussion and some bad bruises, and the gorilla made animal history. Binti was __________ with saving the life of a human child.

2. Replay the tape. Listen and fill in the missing words with "ed" endings.

3. Check your monitoring. Listen to some sentences about Binti. Decide if the speaker says the underlined past tense correctly or if the speaker substitutes the present tense without the "ed." Check (✓) the word you hear.

Example

A mother gorilla <u>rescued</u> a three-and-a-half year old boy.	_✓_ rescued	____ rescue
1. A three-and-a-half year old boy <u>tumbled</u> into the gorilla pit.	____ tumbled	____ tumble
2. His parents <u>watched</u> in horror.	____ watched	____ watch
3. A mother gorilla <u>saved</u> him from danger.	____ saved	____ save
4. She gently <u>picked</u> up the child in her arms.	____ picked	____ pick
5. Binti <u>climbed out</u> of the pit to safety.	____ climbed	____ climb
6. She <u>protected</u> the child from the other gorillas.	____ protected	____ protect
7. She <u>delivered</u> him to a rescue worker.	____ delivered	____ deliver
8. He soon <u>recovered</u> from a concussion.	____ recovered	____ recover

4. Practice saying the previous sentences in the monitoring exercise correctly. Then, replay the paragraph about Binti until you can say it along with the speaker. Look away from the page as much as possible.

5. Retell the story in your own words. Monitor for past tenses, linking, and focus words.

Part 2.
"s" Endings

"S" endings are important to English pronunciation and grammar. The following examples show different kinds of "s" endings.

1. My <u>books</u> are due at the library. (plural noun)
2. The library <u>opens</u> at noon today. (third-person verb)
3. My <u>sister's</u> house is near the library. (possessive)
4. <u>It's</u> a good day to visit her. (contraction)

There are different ways of pronouncing and spelling "s" endings. The following plural nouns and third-person verbs all end in the letters "es." Tap the desk for each syllable as you listen to these words.

tapes	charges
bites	wishes
hopes	beaches

a. "ə es" or "es"?

In some of the following plural nouns and third-person verbs, the "es" has a silent "e." In others, "es" is a separate syllable with a schwa vowel. Listen to your instructor say the words. Decide if you hear one or two syllables. Check (✓) the appropriate answer.

		"ə es"	"es" (silent e)
Example	makes (one syllable, silent "e")	____	✓
	teaches (two syllables, schwa vowel)	✓	____

	"ə es"	"es" (silent e)
1. shades—<u>shades</u> of gray	____	____
2. taxes—Pay your <u>taxes</u>.	____	____
3. judges—ten <u>judges</u>	____	____
4. dates—Check the <u>dates</u>.	____	____
5. writes—<u>writes</u> a story	____	____
6. drives—<u>drives</u> a truck	____	____
7. washes—<u>washes</u> his clothes	____	____
8. changes—<u>changes</u> the name	____	____

b. s or z?

These "s" endings sound like s.

picks up ⟶ pick sup   fits in ⟶ fit sin   Kip's address ⟶ Kip saddress

These "s" endings sound like z.

days are long ⟶ day zaar long   cleans up ⟶ clean zup

summer's over ⟶ summer zover

Listen to the underlined words with the "s" ending. Decide if you hear s or z linking to the next word. Check (✓) the answer.

Example The boy's arm is broken. ___ s _✓_ z

She eats everything. _✓_ s ___ z

1. The dogs are hungry. ___ s ___ z
2. The phone's ringing. ___ s ___ z
3. The cars are honking. ___ s ___ z
4. He drives away. ___ s ___ z
5. She skates very well. ___ s ___ z
6. It's to the right. ___ s ___ z

Introducing Sibilants

When is final "es" pronounced as a separate syllable? The rule has to do with sibilants. Sibilants are sounds that hiss or buzz. The air flows out through a narrow place in the mouth to make a hissing or a buzzing noise. The following words and sentences end with sibilant sounds. Link the final sibilant to the next word.

Sibilants That Hiss (voiceless)

s	bus	The bus is late.	The buses are late.
sh	rush	Rush around.	She rushes around.
ch	match	Match all the colors.	The matches are gone.
x (ks)	box	The box is empty.	The boxes arrived.

Sibilants That Buzz (voiced)

z	does **buzz**	Does it buzz?	It buzzes loudly.
j	age	the age of reason	I waited for ages and they never arrived.
	ba**dge**	His badge is crooked.	Their badges are silver.

At the ends of words j is often spelled "ge" or "dge."

c. Join the Chorus

1. Listen first. Divide into groups A and B. Practice the chant until you sound like a chorus speaking in unison. Tap the desk to keep up the rhythm. Switch groups.

S's, Messes

A: Catch the buses,

B: Buy some dresses,

A: No excuses,

B: Clean your messes.

A: Fix the boxes,

B: Switch the faxes,

A: The buzzer buzzes,

B: Pay your taxes.

A: Sandy beaches,

B: Forty wishes,

A: Juicy peaches,

B: Wish for riches.

A: Noses, nurses,

B: Vases, matches,

A: Roses, purses,

B: Spaces, patches.

A: Age in stages,

B: Do those stretches,

A: Turn the pages,

B: Time whizzes by.

d. Figure Out the Rule

Write the final sound of the following words on the line next to the word. Remember, the final letter may not indicate the final sound. Say the word in the parentheses. It has an "s" ending.

Example dress __s__ (dresses) ride __d__ (rides)

"es" (ə)			"es"		
excuse	____	(excuses)	give	____	(gives)
buzz	____	(buzzes)	hide	____	(hides)
wish	____	(wishes)	state	____	(states)
box	____	(boxes)	make	____	(makes)
beach	____	(beaches)	name	____	(names)
stage	____	(stages)	mile	____	(miles)

rule The "s" ending that comes after a __________ sound is a separate syllable with a schwa vowel. The "s" ending that comes after all other consonant sounds is not a separate syllable.

pronunciation tip When you see a new word that ends with "es" that does not follow a sibilant, do not pronounce the "e." It is silent.

Examples: forgives explodes interferes

e. Improve Your Monitoring: Final "s"

2. Listen to the sentences. Decide if the speaker says the underlined word with the "s" ending or if the speaker omits the final "s." Check (✓) the word you hear.

Plural Nouns

Example I bought two <u>bags</u> of popcorn ____ bags __✓__ bag

1. The <u>charges</u> on my bill are wrong. ____ charges ____ charge
2. Steve is twenty <u>years</u> old. ____ years ____ year
3. Two of your <u>tires</u> look worn. ____ tires ____ tire

Third-person Verbs

Example	He <u>pays</u> his bills on time.	___ pays	_✓_ pay
1.	She <u>likes</u> to ride horses.	___ likes	___ like
2.	Jane always <u>balances</u> her checkbook.	___ balances	___ balance
3.	Mark <u>leaves</u> for work at eight o'clock.	___ leaves	___ leave

Contractions

Example	<u>It's</u> very hot today.	_✓_ It's	___ It
1.	<u>That's</u> to our advantage.	___ That's	___ That
2.	<u>Where's</u> the entrance?	___ Where's	___ Where
3.	<u>What's</u> your name?	___ What's	___ What

Possessives

Example	The <u>teacher's</u> name is Mr. Rowland.	_✓_ teacher's	___ teacher
1.	Someone found <u>George's</u> wallet.	___ George's	___ George
2.	I like the <u>clown's</u> costume.	___ clown's	___ clown
3.	The <u>plumber's</u> tools are in his truck.	___ plumber's	___ plumber

2. Practice with a partner. Take turns saying the previous sentences with examples of "s" endings. Make sure you say the final "s." Monitor your own and your partner's speech.

f. Partner Practice: Idiomatic expressions and final "s"

1. Say the following sentences with everyday expressions. Pay attention to the "s" ending.

Idioms	**Definitions**
1. Paul <u>laid his cards on the table</u> and stated what he could afford to pay. ___	a. a successful result after much struggle
2. After many delays my sister finally got a visa. <u>All's well that ends well!</u> ___	b. an expression of approval or disapproval
3. The committee voted <u>thumbs up</u> (or thumbs down) on the new project. ___	c. discouraged, depressed, and sad
4. I heard it straight <u>from the horse's mouth</u>. ___	d. a very short distance
5. She lives <u>a stone's throw</u> from the school. ___	e. from a reliable source
6. He's been <u>down in the dumps</u> lately. ___	f. was honest and open

2. Match the definitions and the idioms. Write the letter of the definition on the line next to the appropriate sentence. Check your answers with the class.

3. Take turns saying the sentences. Make sure to say the final "s" and link it to the next word.

Use the Idiom in a Sentence

Work with a partner. Finish the following statements using the above idioms. Then say the completed sentences. Look away from your book as you speak. Monitor linking and "s" endings.

Example I feel sorry for Jane. She's been *down in the dumps* ________ lately.

1. I'm sure it's true because I heard it ________________.
2. They liked the movie and gave it an enthusiastic ________________.
3. I'm glad I live ________________ from the bus stop.
4. It's better to ________________ and let them know right away.
5. After much struggle, the city finally agreed to give us a permit. ________________.

g. Practice sh zh ch and j

sh

1. To say sh, start by saying s. Continue saying s and slide your tongue further back on the top of your mouth until you hear sh. It helps if you round your lips a little. **Sh**! Hu**sh**! The baby's sleeping.

2. Listen and repeat words with sh.

share ma**ch**ine tra**sh** ocean fi**sh**ing fa**sh**ion **sh**ow spe**ci**al permi**ss**ion

Contrast s and sh. Sue–**sh**oe so–**sh**ow see–**sh**e mass–ma**sh**

3. Look away from your book and listen to the sentences. Replay the tape.

Shoe Shopping

She saw my **sh**oes at a **sh**op in Sidney.

They're **sh**owing my **sh**oes in a bro**ch**ure from **Sh**anghai.

I saw my **sh**oes in a fa**sh**ion **sh**ow in **Ch**icago.*

They **sh**ipped my **sh**oes to a **ch**ic **sh**op in San Francisco.

* The "ch" in "brochure," "Chicago," and "chic" sound like "sh."

4. Practice "backward build-up." Say the last word of each sentence. Then say the last two words. Continue adding words until you have built the whole sentence from back to front. Keep up the rhythm.

Example **SI**Dney. in **SI**Dney. SHOP in **SI**Dney. a SHOP in **SI**Dney.

at a SHOP in **SI**Dney, and so on.

Replay the tape and say sentences along with the speaker

zh

1. Say sh with voicing. zh only appears in the middle and at the ends of words.

2. Listen and repeat words with zh.

It's a pleasure to meet you. He's on time as usual. She's wearing beige.

Words ending with "sion" sound like zh. decision occasion television.

ch

1. To say ch, start to say "tip." Stop the air and hold the t. Then slide your tongue back and say sh. ch has two steps: (1) t, (2) sh.

2. Listen and repeat words with ch.

chip **ch**amp ri**ch** mat**ch** fu**tu**re tea**ch**er

Contrast sh and ch. **ship–chip** **sh**oe–**ch**ew **dish–ditch**

mush–much ma**sh**ing–mat**ch**ing

j

1. To say j, feel your gum ridge. Then, start to say "**d**-ay." Stop the air and hold the d. Slide your tongue back and say "d-jay." j has two steps: (1) d (2) zh.

2. Listen and repeat words with j.

jump for **j**oy **j**am and **j**elly at a **g**ym a colle**ge** degree

a char**ge** account a ma**j**or disaster a ma**g**ic show

h. Partner Practice: Contrast sh and ch

One partner says (a) or (b). The other partner responds. Take turns.

1.	a.	Where are the di**sh**es?	In the dishwasher.
	b.	Where are the di**tch**es?	By the side of the road.
2.	a.	She's busy **sh**opping.	What is she buying?
	b.	She's busy **ch**opping.	Is she making salad?

3. a. I gave him my **sh**are. How much did he get?
   b. I gave him my **ch**air. Did he sit down?

4. a. Please wa**sh** my car. Is it very dirty?
   b. Please wa**tch** my car. When are you coming back?

5. a. The table was **sh**ipped When will it arrive?
   b. The table was **ch**ipped. Can you repair it?

i. Partner Practice: Contrast sh and j

One partner says (a) or (b). The other partner responds.

1. a. How do you spell "**sh**eep"? S-H-E-E-P
   b. How do you spell "**j**eep"? J-E-E-P

2. a. I found the **sh**ale.* Was there a lot of it?
   b. I found the **j**ail. Were there bars on the windows?

3. a. The crowd began to **ch**eer. They were happy.
   b. The crowd began to **j**eer. They were not happy.

4. a. I was **sh**ipped on a boat. Were you going overseas?
   b. I was **g**ypped on a boat. Did someone take your money?

5. a. How do you spell "**sh**erry"? S-H-E-R-R-Y
   b. How do you spell "**J**erry"? J-E-R-R-Y

j. Have Fun with Tongue Twisters

1. Look away from your book and listen. Replay the tape several times.

JERry PUT a **CHER**ry in his **SHER**ry.

There's a CHEAP **JEEP** in BACK of the **SHEEP**.

The JUDGE on the **SHIP** WORE a BADGE on his **JACK**et.

The MARCHing **MAR**tians had a MILKSHAKe for **LUNCH**.

* **shale:** Claylike layers of rock.

2. Practice "backward build-up." Say the last word of each tongue twister. Then say the last two words, and so on, until you have completed the tongue twister. Keep up the rhythm.

Example **SHER**ry his **SHER**ry in his **SHER**ry **CHER**ry in his **SHER**ry

a **CHER**ry in his **SHER**ry PUT a **CHER**ry in his **SHER**ry

JERry PUT a **CHER**ry in his **SHER**ry.

3. Replay the tape until you can say the tongue twisters along with the speaker.

k. Group Practice: Strip story

1. Some sibilants have unusual spellings. In "Portugal" the "tu" sounds like ch. Listen to the words from the following story and circle the sibilant sound you hear. Notice the spelling and the pronunciation.

Example assumed (s) - sh

ssi- permission	sh ch	x- exotic	ks gz	ti- premonition	sh ch
ci- specialized	sh ch	c- ocean	sh ch	ti- negotiated	sh ch
su- sure	sh ch	su- unusual	zh sh		

2. Look away from your book and listen to the story. Pay attention to the pauses and phrasing signals.

Part 1

Chuck* was sightseeing near the seashore in Portugal.

He stopped at a shop near the ocean that specialized in exotic shells.

The shop sold him an unusual shell in a fancy glass box.

Chuck negotiated a good price.

He left the store satisfied, but with a premonition that something was about to happen.

Sure enough, as he shifted into reverse and backed out of his parking space, Chuck heard a large crunch.

* Chuck is a common nickname for Charles.

Part 2

Chuck soon realized that he had crashed into a signpost.

He assumed that he hadn't done much damage because he was going slowly.

Chuck was surprised to find that the jeep's fender was smashed.

The package with the exotic shell had jumped out of the jeep and landed on the sidewalk.

The shell and the fancy box both got chipped before Chuck could ship them home.

Under the circumstances, the shopkeeper gave Chuck permission to replace them at no charge.

3. Work in groups of six. Photocopy Parts 1 and 2 of the story and cut it into strips. Each person in the group receives one line to memorize. Discuss the order of the story. When the story is assembled, each group will say one part of the story for the class.

y is not a sibilant.

y is different from ch and j. The air does not stop, or hiss or buzz. To say y, squeeze the back of the tongue between the molars as you push the whole tongue forward. Don't touch anything with the front of your tongue.

yes yam yellow you yesterday

Add words that start with y ______________________________

I. Partner Practice: y

Listen to your instructor first. Then take turns saying the words and sentences. Contrast j and y.

jail–Yale Did his father go to jail?

No! His father went to Yale. The convict is in jail.

jam–yam What's the difference between "jam" and "yam?"

Jam is made out of fruit. A yam is a sweet potato.

joke–yolk Is the yolk funny?

No! The joke is funny. A yolk is part of an egg and it's yellow.

jell–yell What is "yell"? Is it the same as "jell"?

No! To "yell" is to talk very loudly. Jell-o has to jell in the refrigerator.

I like yellow jello!

m. Join the Chorus

Divide into groups. Listen first, and then practice with your group until you can say the poem in unison. Link the words in each thought group and monitor for sibilants.

From *Through The Looking Glass*

"The time has **COME,**" the Walrus **SAID,**

"To talk of many **THINGS**:

Of **SHOES**—and **SHIPS**—and **SEAL**ing WAX—

Of **CAB**bages—and **KINGS**—

And why the **SEA** is boiling **HOT**—

And whether **PIGS** have **WINGS.**"

—Lewis Carroll

Finishing Up

REVIEW: "ED" AND "S" ENDINGS

1. Look away from your book and listen to the paragraph about a famous American athlete.

2. Replay the tape and fill in the missing words with "ed" or "s" endings.

From the time Jesse Owens was a boy he had __________ of becoming an athlete and participating in the Olympic __________. This dream came true when he __________ the United __________ Track Team and __________ in the 1936 Berlin __________. Adolf Hitler had __________ to use the __________ to validate his __________ about the superiority of the Aryan, or white, race. Owens, a 23-year-old black American runner, stole the show by winning four gold __________. It is said that Hitler __________ out of the stadium in anger. Owens not only __________ a victory against Nazism, but made __________ history by breaking all previous track __________.

3. Listen to the paragraph until you can say it along with the speaker.

4. Retell the story in your own words. Self-monitor for "ed" and "s" endings and linking.

TALK TIMES: MAKE YOUR NEW PRONUNCIATION A HABIT

In-class Preparation: Renting a video

1. Write the following information and discuss it with your partner.

- two of your favorite actors ______________________________
- two of your favorite films ______________________________
- the type of film you want to rent (action, drama, comedy, mystery, etc.) ________
- the name of a video store in your area ______________________________

2. Make a list of questions you can ask the person who works in the video store. Possible topics: availability of a certain film, names of films with a certain actor or director, rental rates, what time the film has to be returned. Underline the focus words.

Example Do you have a copy of Titanic? /I missed seeing it /when it was in the theaters. /

3. Draw a dot over the stressed syllables in these words:
drama comedy mystery foreign

Practice the compound nouns.

ACtion FILM VIdeoTAPE MOvie STAR LOVE STOry aWARD WINner

Practice the descriptive phrases and names.

SPEcial ef**FECTS** POpular **MO**vie FAvorite di**REC**tor

TOM **HANKS** JULIA **ROB**erts

Talk Times in Your Daily Life: Renting a video

Call or visit a video store in your community to inquire about renting a video. Prepare sample questions. You do not actually have to rent the film, even if they have the one you are asking about. Thank them, and either leave or say you have changed your mind. Target "ed" and "s" endings.

ON YOUR OWN

1. **Practicing regularly with the audio tapes is important to your progress.** Practice in a quiet place so that you can concentrate and self-monitor. Repeat the exercises that are the most challenging.

2. **Record the chant "The Visitor," page 183.** Link the past tenses. Then record the dialogue "Basket on the Bus," page 183, either with a partner or by yourself.

3. **Record the chant "S's, Messes," page 191.**

4. **Keep adding new words to your glossary.** Discover what part of the word was troublesome, the vowel sounds, the consonant sounds, or the word stress.

5. **Continue conversing in English whenever possible.**

---

a helpful hint

Plan ahead. If you know you will be making a presentation in a class or at a meeting, plan what you will say. Talk from notes made up of key focus words. Make sure the pronunciation of these key words is correct. Use a tape recorder to prepare your talk. Monitor carefully, decide what you want to improve, and make another recording.

11

Putting Words Together

English speech is easier to understand when you recognize how native speakers put words together. What you see in print is not what you hear in conversational English.

- **Linking.** Words are linked together into a chunk that can sound like one long word. "The cat is hungry" sounds like "theCATizHUNgry." You might never know this if you learned English from the printed page where each word is written separately and you can't hear the melody of the whole chunk. You practiced familiar chunks of speech in Chapter 3.
- **Reductions.** When words are linked into chunks, structure words such as "you" and "or" are not usually pronounced the way they are spelled. Vowels are reduced to schwa. Sometimes consonants are dropped. These shortened words are called *reductions*. The more informal the speech, the more reductions you will hear.

black and blue ⟶ blacken blue	care at home ⟶ carrot home
day to day ⟶ data day	box is full ⟶ boxes full
short or tall ⟶ shorter tall	will he ⟶ Willy
off and on ⟶ often on	would he ⟶ Woody

Reductions and Chunks of Speech

a. Listening

Listen to these common chunks of speech without looking at your book. First you will hear the full form. Then you will hear more native-like speech with reductions and a schwa vowel. Replay the tape. Concentrate on what you hear.

Full Form	Reduced Words
1. salt and pepper	ə and
2. a year and a half	ə and ə a
3. It's out of order.	ə of
4. Do you think so?	ə do ə you
5. Thanks for everything.	ə for
6. He's an old friend.	ə an

b. Common Reductions: Parts of speech

Native speakers reduce unstressed structure words in everyday speech by omitting sounds or substituting schwa vowels.

1. Listen to the sentences with examples of reduced words.

Pronouns. Linked reduced pronouns often sound like new words.

1. her — What's her name? → WHATser **NAME**?
   Ask her later. → ASKer **LA**ter.
2. his — What's his name? → WHATsiz **NAME**?
   When's his appointment? → WHENziz apPOINTment?
3. he — Is he ready? → izzy REAdy?
   What does he want? → WHATsy **WANT**?
4. them — Ask them what they want. → ASKum WHAT they **WANT.**
5. him — I gave him a ride. → I GAVim a **RIDE.**
6. you — Do you like it? → d'ya LIKE it?
7. your — Do you have your passport? → d'ya HAVE yer **PASS**PORT?

Prepositions. The vowels in these reduced prepositions sound like schwa.

1. to — It's next ə to the table.
2. of — That's one ə of the best.
3. for — Thanks ə for the invitation.
4. at — They left ə at dawn.

Conjunctions. The vowels in these reduced conjunctions sound like schwa.

1. or — Now or later?
2. and — doctors and nurses
3. that — I hope that it stops raining.

Articles. The vowels in these articles sound like schwa.

1. the — Please hand me the pencil.
2. a — I would like a copy.
3. an — Do you have an extra one?

Helping Verbs. The vowels in these helping verbs sound like schwa.

1. have — I should have waited.
2. was — I was listening.
3. can — He can speak Spanish.
4. do — What do you think?

2. Look away from your book and replay the tape. Repeat what you hear.

c. Partner Practice: Sentence completion

1. Listen and fill in the structure words you hear.

1. I'd like __________ borrow __________ book.
2. Janet __________ appointed __________ __________ steering committee.
3. What __________ __________ think __________ __________ outcome?
4. __________ __________ package ready?
5. When __________ __________ call?
6. __________ forgot __________ bring __________ tape.
7. Half __________ __________ pictures __________ missing.
8. __________ dropped __________ off __________ __________ corner.

2. Compare answers with your partner. Take turns saying the sentences. Reduce the unstressed words.

---

practice tip Try whispering the unstressed reduced words in the above sentences and saying the stressed words in a full voice. Whispering helps emphasize the difference between the stressed and the reduced words.

---

questions and answers

1. **What is the difference between a reduction and a contraction?**
   A contraction is a reduction that is formally part of written English.
2. **Are reductions ever written?**
   Not usually. Reductions are part of standard spoken English, not standard written English.

   Sometimes common reductions are spelled out in dialogues in plays, novels, or comic strips.

   Occasionally you see reductions in advertising or titles of films or products. For example, "Good 'n Plenty" is a candy bar. "Pic 'n Save" is a discount store.

d. Partner Practice

1. Listen to the dialogue and pay attention to the reduced speech.

Kids 'n Cars

Child: When are we going to get there?

Parent: Sooner than you think. Why don't you look at one of your books?

Child: I'm tired of my books. There's nothing to do, is there?

Parent: Look out of the window and count the trucks.

Child: What kind of trucks?

Parent: Any kind of trucks.

Child: I'm sort of tired of counting trucks.

Parent: Then maybe you'd like to take a nap.

2. Replay the tape. Practice the dialogue, repeating one line at a time.

3. Say the whole dialogue with your partner. Switch roles.

e. Join the Chorus

1. Listen to this rhythmic poem. The stressed words stand out. You will hear common reductions of structure words such as "him," "his," "and," "at," and "to."

Sneezles*

1. Christopher Robin
Had wheezles and sneezles.
They bundled him into his bed.
They gave him what goes
With a cold in the nose,
And some more for a cold in his head.

2. They wondered if wheezles
Could turn into measles,
If sneezles would turn into mumps.
They examined his chest
For a rash and the rest
Of his body for swellings and lumps.

3. They sent for some doctors
In sneezles and wheezles
To tell them what ought to be done.
All sorts of conditions
Of famous physicians
Came hurrying round at a run.

4. They all made a note
Of the state of his throat.
They asked if he suffered from thirst.
They asked if the sneezles
Came after the wheezles,
Or if the first sneezle came first.

* Some of the verses are not included here.

5. Christopher Robin

   Got up in the morning,

   The sneezles had vanished away.

   And the look in his eye

   Seemed to say to the sky,

   "Now, how to amuse them today?"

   —A.A. Milne

2. Divide into small groups. Work with your group to prepare one verse of the poem to present to the whole class. Practice until you can say your verse in unison. Pay attention to final sounds, reductions, and linking.

Review the Flap

The flap is part of many common reduced chunks of speech. Pronounce a flap somewhere between a "d" and a "t." Tap your tongue lightly on your gum ridge.

f. Partner Practice: The flap

1. Listen to these examples of reductions with a flap.

1.	aLOTta	There's <u>a lot of</u> smog today.
2.	THOUGHTa	I already <u>thought of</u> that.
3.	OUTta	Let's get <u>out of</u> this lane.
4.	STAYta RIGHTta	<u>Stay to</u> the <u>right of</u> the road.
5.	GOta	Should we <u>go to</u> the market?
6.	MOSta	<u>Most of</u> the time.
7.	HAFta	I <u>have to</u> finish by noon.
8.	WANna	I <u>want to</u> change jobs.

("Wanna" is a common reduction for "want to." It is similar to a flap because the tongue taps the gum ridge for the n sound.)

2. Practice with your partner. One partner says the reduction by itself. The other partner says the sentence. Take turns. Make up your own sentences with these reductions.

Example Partner A: alotta

Partner B: There's <u>a lot of</u> smog today.

g. Partner Practice: Two short conversations

1. Look away from your book and listen to the conversations using reduced speech.

Conversation 1

A. I'm ready to take a break.

B. Good. I'm ready for a Big Mac and a Coke.

A. I'd rather take a walk than eat.

B. O.K. Let's walk over to McDonald's. Then we can walk and eat.

Conversation 2

A: Are you ready to order?

B: In a minute. I have to decide what I want to eat.

A: Do you think we ought to get it for here or to go? (Food "to go" is food you take with you to eat later.)

B: We've got to be back in thirty minutes. Maybe we'd better get it to go.

2. Replay the tape. Underline the focus words.

3. Practice saying the dialogues. Pay attention to the linking and the reductions. Switch roles.

---

more questions and answers

1. **Is it O.K. to reduce sounds when speaking English?**
   Yes. Educated native speakers all reduce unstressed words. This is part of English speech rhythm. It's <u>not</u> O.K. to reduce consonants in most clusters or grammatical endings.

2. **Do I have to reduce sounds when speaking English in order to have clear speech?**
   No. You need to be able to understand reductions because native speakers use them.

3. **If I want to sound more like a native speaker do I have to use reductions?**
   Yes.

4. **Are the same words always reduced?**
   Not always. Reductions can vary with the speaker and the situation. In general, the more informal the conversation, the more reductions you hear.

More Practice with Reduced Speech

h. Partner Practice: Common expressions

Listen to the conversations. Speaker B uses some common expressions. Can you figure out the meaning? Practice the conversations reducing the underlined structure words. Switch roles.

1. A: How do you know she's afraid?

   B: Look at her! She's as white as a sheet.

2. A: How did you figure out the answer?

   B: It is obvious. It's as plain as the nose on your face.

3. A: Is the box too heavy?

   B: Not at all It's as light as a feather.

4. A: Is Bill strong enough to carry it?

   B: Bill? He's as strong as an ox.

5. A: Are you busy these days?

   B: Not really. Lately I've been as free as a bird.

6. A: Did you fix the chair?

   B: Yes. It's as good as new.

7. A: What color is his sweater?

   B: It's as green as grass.

8. A: Why are you shivering?

   B: I'm as cold as ice.

9. A: Are you comfortable?

   B: I'm as snug as a bug in a rug.

10. A: Is the new air conditioner noisy?

    B: Not a bit! It's as quiet as a mouse.

i. Song: "Leaving on a Jet Plane"

The melody and rhythm of this song follow closely the intonation and stress patterns of spoken English. Listen and fill in the structure words that are missing. Replay the tape several times. Compare answers with a partner.

1. All _______ bags _______ packed, _______ ready _______ go.
   _______ standing here outside _______ door.

   _______ hate _______ wake you up _______ say good-bye.
   _______ _______ dawn _______ breaking, _______ early morn.
   _______ taxi's waiting, _______ blowing _______ horn.
   Already _______ _______ lonesome _______ _______ cry.

   Chorus

   _______ kiss _______ _______ smile _______ _______
   Tell _______ that _______ wait _______ _______.
   Hold _______ like _______ never let _______ go.
   _______ _______ leaving _______ _______ jet plane.
   Don't know when _______ _______ back again.
   Oh, Babe. _______ hate _______ go.

2. There's _______ many times _______ played around.
   _______ many times _______ let you down.
   _______ tell you now, they don't mean _______ thing.

   Every place _______ go, _______ think _______ you.
   Every song _______ sing, _______ sing _______ you.
   When _______ come back _______ wear _______ wedding ring.

   Chorus

3. Now _______ time _______ come _______ leave you.
   One more time, let _______ kiss _______.
   _______ close _______ eyes _______ I'll _______ on _______ way.

   _______ dream _______ _______ days _______ come
   When _______ won't _______ _______ leave alone
   _______ _______ times _______ won't _______ _______ say . . .

   Chorus

—words and music by John Denver

j. Song Exercises

1. Important Endings: Contractions and final "s" and "ed"
Fill in the missing endings. Practice these phrases from the song. Pay attention to the linking.

1. All my bag _______ are pack _______, I _______ ready to go.
2. It _______ early morn.
3. The taxi _______ waiting.
4. He_______ blowing his horn.
5. so many time _______ I _______ play _______ around
6. Dream about the day _______ to come

2. Sounds: r and vowel + r
Say these phrases from the song and monitor for r and ər. Look in the song for additional r words to practice. Remember to curl your tongue tightly to say r. Listen for a good r sound.

Vowel + r	**r and r Clusters**
outside y**our** d**oor**	I'm **r**eady to go
I'm standing h**ere**	**br**ing your WEDding **R**ING
early m**orn**	dawn is **br**eaking
tell h**er**	**dr**eam about
one m**ore** time	a**r**ound
blowing his h**orn**	al**r**eady

3. Divide into three groups. With your group, practice saying one verse as if you are telling a story. Lengthen the stressed words and shorten the unstressed structure words. Tap the desk for the focus words. Say your verse for the class.

1. All my BAGS are **PACKED**. / I'm READy to **GO**./ I'm **STAND**ing here / outSIDE your **DOOR**. / I HATE to WAKE you **UP/** to say good-**BYE**. / But the DAWN is **BREAK**ing, / it's EARly **MORN**. / The taxi's **WAIT**ing, / he's BLOWing his **HORN**. / AlREADy I'm so **LONE**some / I could **CRY**. /

2. There're so many **TIMES** / I PLAYED a**ROUND**. / So many **TIMES** / I let you **DOWN.** / I TELL you **NOW** / they DON'T MEAN a **THING.**/ Every PLACE I **GO,**/ I **THINK** of you. / EVERY SONG I **SING**, / I'll **SING** for you. / When I COME **BACK** /I'll WEAR your **WED**ding RING. /

3. Now the TIME has COME to **LEAVE** you. / One more **TIME,**/ let me **KISS** you./ Then CLOSE your **EYES**, / and I'll BE on my **WAY**. / I'll DREAM about the DAYS to **COME** / when I WON'T have to **LEAVE** / a**LONE,**/ about the TIMES I WON'T have to **SAY** . . . /

   All groups: 'Cause I'm **LEAV**ing on a **JET** PLANE. / DON'T **KNOW** / WHEN I'll be **BACK** aGAIN. / Oh, **BABE**, / I HATE to **GO**.

pronunciation tip Remember to say all the structure words. Although reduced, these small words, like "the" and "to," build and connect a sentence grammatically. Speaking English with missing structure words can be distracting to listeners who know the language.

k. Partner Practice: Dialogue

1. Look away from your book and listen to the dialogue.

Willpower

1. A: This is incredible! I can't believe it's not ice cream. It tastes just like real chocolate ice cream.
2. B: Believe it or not, it's not ice cream. It's frozen yogurt—soft frozen yogurt.
3. A: Do you know how many calories it has? I'm on a special diet.
4. B: That depends. Do you want the chocolate or the vanilla? Do you want the nonfat or the regular? What kind do you want?
5. A: I want the good kind. I want it with fat, lots of rich, dark chocolate fat.
6. B: I thought you were worried about calories.
7. A: I am worried about calories. You didn't ask me what kind I should have. You asked me what kind I wanted to have.
8. B: Well, what kind do you want to order?
9. A: I'll have a small dish of vanilla nonfat yogurt, please.
10. B: Now that's what you call "willpower!"

2. Replay the tape. Pay attention to the reductions. Then practice the dialogue with a partner. Switch roles.

l. Role Play: Two invitations

You and your partner are friends. You both receive invitations to events taking place on the same date. You would like to go together to both events, but are not sure it is possible. One friend receives an invitation to a cousin's wedding. The other friend receives an invitation to a retirement dinner for someone important at work. What are you going to do?

1. To prepare for the role play, review the pronunciation of the information on the invitations on page 213. Decide which invitation is yours and which is your partner's.

2. In the role play, talk by phone with your friend to discuss your invitations. Consider the times and the locations of both events in order to decide what to do.

Wedding Bells Are Ringing

Linda Pasternak and Bob Holbrook
request your presence at their wedding
5 o'clock Saturday, June 12

Metropolitan Historical Society Gardens
10292 Riverton Drive, East Lakeville, Ohio
R.S.V.P. by June 1
Reception and dancing following the ceremony

30 YEARS' DEVOTED SERVICE

Our Division Manager, Lewis Anthony, is retiring.

LET'S HONOR LEW

Saturday, June 12, 7 o'clock
Cocktails and Dinner

The Mesquite Grill
258 W. 20th Street • West Lakeville, Ohio
R.S.V.P. by June 5 • Dress: informal

Finishing Up

REVIEW

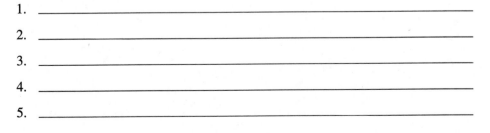

Write the sentences that you hear. Check the answer key to see if you are hearing the reductions clearly.

1. ______________________________
2. ______________________________
3. ______________________________
4. ______________________________
5. ______________________________

TALK TIMES

In-class Preparation: Role play

One partner's car will be in the repair shop for a week. That partner needs a car to get to work and contacts a car rental agency to ask about renting a car. The other partner works for the car rental agency. Both partners need information, and both have information that the other partner needs.

1. To prepare for the role play, write two lists of questions that you might ask. What does the car agency need to know and what does the customer need to know?

Possible topics for questions:

Information the Car Agency Needs

- the kind of car you want to rent
- the date(s) that you need it
- how long you plan to keep the car
- how you will be paying (major credit card, etc.)
- driver's age (over 25, under 25)
- other

Information the Customer Needs

- the cost (daily, weekly)
- any extra charges, such as taxes
- the kinds of cars available
- the insurance needed
- location of the nearest agency
- other

2. Practice your questions with your partner. Monitor stress and unstress. Make the stressed syllables sound much longer and higher in pitch than the unstressed ones even if you do not always reduce the vowels to schwa. Use the appropriate intonation for "wh" and "yes–no" questions.

3. In the role play, exchange information about renting a car from a car agency. Monitor your own and your partner's speech. Switch roles.

Talk Times in Your Daily Life: Renting a car

Make three to five calls to car agencies for information. You can look for the phone numbers in the yellow pages of a local phone book or call 1-800-555-1212 to get the toll free numbers for various car agencies. Pick three things to ask about during each call. Monitor your speech for stressed and unstressed words. Lengthen the focus words.

ON YOUR OWN

1. **Practice with the audio tapes.** Your independent work with the audio tapes reinforces the new pronunciation that you learned in class. Regular well-monitored practice for 10–20 minutes a day makes permanent change more likely.

2. **Record the sentences to review "The Flap," page 207.** Record the dialogue, "Willpower," page 212, either with a partner from class or by yourself. Pay attention to the intonation and the r words.

3. **Record the dialogue about calling directory assistance on the targeting pronunciation Web page.**

4. **Are you using any words that people do not understand?** Are there words you want to pronounce more clearly? Write them on your glossary and find out how to pronounce them.

5. **Continue to converse in English with as many people as possible.** Feel your comfort level increase.

---

a helpful hint

Listen to an interesting book recorded on audio tape. These "books on tape" are often available at a public library. Make sure you are comfortable with the English dialect on the tape you choose. Replay small sections so that you can concentrate on the pronunciation.

12

Thought Groups

Make your speech easier to understand by organizing what you say into smaller pieces called *thought groups*. These thought groups are like short songs, each with a melody and a focus word. Signal the end of a thought group in three ways: lengthen the focus word; change pitch; pause. These signals sound stronger in English than you might expect compared to your native language. Pay attention to the signals in these sentences.

Let's stop the **CAR** / and go get some **COF**fee. /

I drove all after**NOON** / before I got a flat **TIRE**. /

a. Guidelines for Thought Groups

Individual speakers make different choices about dividing sentences into thought groups.

guideline 1 **Slow speakers use more thought groups than fast speakers. They pause more often and lengthen the focus words more noticeably.**

1. Listen to two speakers say this sentence from Ernest Hemingway's short story "A Clean,Well-Lighted Place."

First speaker: "It was **LATE** / and everyone had left the **CAFE** / except an old **MAN** / who sat in the **SHA**dow / that the leaves of the **TREE** / made against the electric **LIGHT**."

Second speaker: "It was **LATE** / and everyone had left the cafe except an old **MAN** / who sat in the shadow that the leaves of the **TREE** / made against the electric **LIGHT**."

2. Listen to two speakers say this sentence from Amy Tan's *The Kitchen God's Wife.*

First speaker: "It was an American **SONG** / about **LOVE**, / and I heard right a**WAY** / that she had a very sweet **VOICE**, / the kind of **VOICE** / that sounded as if her heart had been **BRO**ken / many **TIMES**./"

Second speaker: "It was an American song about **LOVE**, / and I heard right a**WAY** that she had a very sweet **VOICE**, / the kind of voice that sounded as if her heart had been broken many **TIMES**./"

---

guideline 2 **Speakers with more melody and more pauses are easier to understand.**

---

1. Look away from your book and listen to two speakers respond to the question, "Where can I find a telephone?" Which speaker uses more thought groups?

First speaker: There's a phone in the next block in front of the **MAR**ket /across the street from that tall stone **BUILD**ing./

Second speaker: There's a **PHONE** / in the next **BLOCK** / in front of the **MAR**ket / across the **STREET** / from that tall stone **BUILD**ing./

b. An Ad for Delta Air Lines

1. Listen to the ad without looking at your book.

2. Replay the tape. Mark the thought groups with a slash (/) when you hear a pause. Underline the focus words. Notice the pitch changes at the ends of thought groups and the pitch fall at the ends of sentences. Clarify any new vocabulary.

[1]We don't need a radar screen, or a weather balloon, or even the *Farmer's Almanac.* [2]But we can forecast with confidence that the next time you need to fly overseas, the weather inside your big Delta Jet will be absolutely clear. [3]That's because Delta is the only U.S. airline to fly smoke free worldwide. [4]Delta quit smoking long before most airlines started to, shall we say, cut back. [5]So if you prefer to keep puffy clouds outside the airplane where they belong, insist on flying Delta. [6]Even our cozy Crown Room Clubs in major airports around the world are smoke free. [7]At Delta, we make one thing perfectly clear—your next flight.

3. See Chapter 9 to review the intonation for compound nouns and descriptive phrases. Listen to the following phrases and check (✓) the correct column.

Phrases	Compound Noun	Descriptive Phrase
Example radar screen	✓	___
1. weather balloon	___	___
2. *Farmer's Almanac*	___	___
3. fly overseas	___	___
4. absolutely clear	___	___
5. quit smoking	___	___
6. puffy clouds	___	___
7. major airports	___	___

4. Listen and repeat the ad one sentence at a time. Put your tape recorder on pause and look away from the book whenever possible.

Oral Presentations: New information

Whether you are giving an oral presentation or presenting unfamiliar information in casual conversation, strong thought-group signals will make your speech easier to understand. Emphasize the focus words so that people will know what you think is important. Rephrase some of the new information in different words.

---

guideline 3 **The thought-group signals in an oral presentation should be very easy to hear, especially when the information is unfamiliar.**

c. Thought-group Signals: A paragraph

1. Look away from your book and listen to the paragraph about biodegradable plastic.

2. Replay the tape several times. Draw a slash (/) where the speaker pauses or slows down. Underline the focus words.

Plastic Plants

[1]Americans buy over sixty billion pounds of plastic goods a year. [2]Even with recycling, more than one-third gets dumped into landfills and stays intact forever.* [3]The concern about pollution from plastic waste has motivated researchers to develop biodegradable plastics from natural sources. [4]For example, there are plastic bags and golf tees being made from corn and other leaves and seeds. [5]In Korea, scientists have genetically engineered aspen trees to produce a plastic that biodegrades in about ten months. [6]Soy protein has been used to make plastic foam. [7]There are more than 600 kinds of bacteria that produce polymer in their cells that can be used to make biodegradable plastic products. [8]In March 1997, the *London Times* reported that farmers could be growing plants for plastic within a decade. [9]If plastic plants become a new cash crop for farmers, we could throw away plastic bags and bottles without worrying about pollution.

3. Practice saying the paragraph with a partner and discuss the information. Monitor for thought groups.

---

pronunciation tip When you are reading out loud, periods and commas give clues about where to signal some of the thought groups.

Thought-group Signals: Conversation

d. Song: "When I First Came to This Land"

Singing songs and telling jokes can help make moving to a new land and beginning a new life easier. This humorous song is about a farmer who came to the United States several hundred years ago. The words and music are by Oscar Brand, a twentieth-century folk singer.

1. Listen to the song. The focus words in the first verse are underlined. Underline the focus words in the remaining verses. Compare answers with a partner.

When I First Came to This Land

1. When I first came to this <u>land</u>, I was not a wealthy <u>man</u>.
   Then I built myself a <u>shack</u>, and I did what I <u>could</u>.
   I called my <u>shack</u> "Break my <u>back</u>."

Chorus:

For the <u>land</u> was sweet and <u>good</u>. I did what I <u>could</u>.

* *Mt. Holyoke College Journal*, January 24, 1997.

2. When I first came to this land, I was not a wealthy man.
Then I bought myself a cow. And I did what I could.
I called my cow "No milk now."
I called my shack "Break my back."

Chorus:

For the land was sweet and good. I did what I could.

3. When I first came to this land, I was not a wealthy man.
So I bought myself a duck. And I did what I could.
I called my duck "Out of luck."
I called my cow "No milk now."
I called my shack "Break my back."

Chorus:

For the land was sweet and good. I did what I could.

4. When I first came to this land, I was not a wealthy man.
So I got myself a wife, and I did what I could.
I called my wife "Joy of my life."
I called my duck "Out of luck."
I called my cow "No milk now."
I called my shack "Break my back."

Chorus:

For the land was sweet and good. I did what I could.

5. When I first came to this land, I was not a wealthy man.
Then I got myself a son. I did what I could.
I told my son "My work's done."
I called my wife "Joy of my life."
I called my duck "Out of luck."
I called my cow "No milk now."
I called my shack "Break my back."

Chorus:

For the land was sweet and good. I did what I could.

2. List new vocabulary words and discuss the meaning.

Examples **shack** A small crudely built cabin.

break your back Work very hard.

3. Say the lyrics of the song with your partner as if you are telling a story. Use clear thought group signals. Emphasize the focus words, fall in pitch, and pause at the end of each sentence.

4. Add new verses to the song.

Example When I first came to this land, I was not a wealthy man.

Then I got myself a store. I did what I could.

I called my store, "what a bore," or "I want more," etc.

e. A Conversation about Moving

In conversation, speakers often hesitate, gather their thoughts, rephrase, and start again. Sometimes they use incomplete sentences. This can make some conversations difficult for nonnative speakers to follow. When you talk, the same signals used in oral presentations can make your spontaneous conversation easier to understand.

- Use focus words to draw your listener's attention to what is important. Slow down and lengthen the focus word in each thought group.
- Change pitch. The biggest change of pitch is at the end of a sentence.
- Pause. Although pauses in spontaneous conversation are less predictable than the pauses in more formal speech, people often wait for a pause or falling pitch at the end of a sentence to know when to take a turn speaking.

1. First, think about an experience in your life when you moved. Take notes on your thoughts, writing down key ideas.

2. Work in groups of three or four. Take turns telling your group about your experience. Talk for one minute. Emphasize the focus words, and use speech melody and pauses to make your speech easy to understand. Self-monitor. Exchange suggestions about pronunciation with the members of your group.

f. Partner Practice: Longer sentences

Longer sentences can have several thought groups. Assemble a sentence about celebrations and holidays in English-speaking countries. Start by saying a thought group in column 1. Add a thought group from columns 2 and 3 to complete the sentence. Take turns, and monitor your own and your partner's speech.

Example Flower shops / sell more flowers in late May / because of Mother's Day.

1	**2**	**3**
1. Flower shops	• a day for remembering someone you love	• to celebrate Halloween.
2. In late October	• people celebrate birthdays	• is on February 14th.
3. Valentine's Day,	• a national British holiday	• by giving gifts and eating birthday cake.
4. In most English-speaking countries,	• children dress up in costumes and collect candy	• originated when wealthy people gave Christmas boxes to the less fortunate.
5. Boxing Day,	• sell more flowers in late May	• because of Mother's Day

1	2	3
1. Thanksgiving is celebrated	• look forward to presents from Santa Claus	• with a family gathering and a turkey dinner.
2. Children who celebrate Christmas	• people celebrate their country's independence	• on Canada Day (July 1st) and the Fourth of July.
3. In the United States and Canada	• the whole of Australia unites in celebration	• on December 25th.
4. On the first Tuesday in November	• by many people in the United States and Canada	• surrounding a horse race called the Foster's Melbourne Cup.

g. More about Pauses

Listen to phrases (a) and (b). Compare the thought groups. The focus words and the pauses change the meaning of the words. Check (✓) the appropriate meaning for each sentence.

a.

one 22" fish

b.

twenty 2" fish

Example	a.	the twenty-two-inch goldfish	_✓_ 22" fish	____ 2" fish
	b.	the twenty two-inch goldfish	____ 22" fish	_✓_ 2" fish
1.	a.	fifty-one-dollar raffle tickets	____ $1 a ticket	____ $51 a ticket
	b.	fifty one-dollar raffle tickets	____ $1 a ticket	____ $51 a ticket
2.	a.	fried chicken, potato salad, and a coke	____ three things	____ four things
	b.	fried chicken, potato, salad, and a coke	____ three things	____ four things
3.	a.	the computer software and keyboard	____ two things	____ three things
	b.	the computer, software, and keyboard	____ two things	____ three things
4.	a.	a car, phone, and tape deck	____ two things	____ three things
	b.	a carphone and tape deck	____ two things	____ three things

h. Partner Practice

1. First listen to your instructor say both sentences (a) and (b). Discuss how the pauses change the meaning.

2. One partner says either sentence (a) or (b). The other partner gives the appropriate response. Switch roles.

Examples a. What do you **THINK** / of the TWENty-two-INCH **GOLD**FISH ? /
____ It needs a much bigger bowl!

b. What do you **THINK** / of the **TWEN**ty / TWO-inch **GOLD**FISH? /
_✓_ They are very small. My fish are at least three inches long.

1. a. Robert is selling FIFTy-ONE-DOLlar **RAF**fle TICKets / for a trip to Ha**WA**ii. /
____ $51 a piece? That's pretty expensive for a raffle ticket.

   b. Robert is selling **FIF**ty / ONE-dollar **RAF**fle TICKets / for a trip to Ha**WA**ii./
____At $1 a piece, maybe I'll buy five of them.

2. a. I'd like fried **CHICK**en / with po**TA**to / **SA**lad/ and a **COKE**./
____Do you want butter and sour cream on your potato?

   b. I'd like fried **CHICK**en / with po**TA**to SAlad/ and a **COKE**./
____Would you like extra potato salad?

3. a. Jim's new com**PU**ter / **SOFT**WARE / and **KEY**BOARD / finally ar**RIVED**./
____What kind of computer did he buy?

   b. Jim's new com**PU**ter SOFTware / and KEYBOARD finally ar**RIVED**./
____It's too bad he couldn't afford to buy a new computer.

4. a. I'm planning to buy a new **CAR** / **PHONE** / and **TAPE** DECK. /
____What kind of car are you going to buy?

   b. I'm planning to buy a new **CAR**PHONE / and **TAPE** DECK. /
____It's too bad you aren't going to buy a new car.

pronunciation tip Speakers who emphasize the focus words, use more speech melody, and pause in the right place are easier to understand.

i. An Answering-machine Message

1. Look at the ad and listen to the message for a shop called *The Book Bakery*. Pay attention to the pauses and the thought groups. Replay the tape several times because you are going to be taping a similar answering machine message.

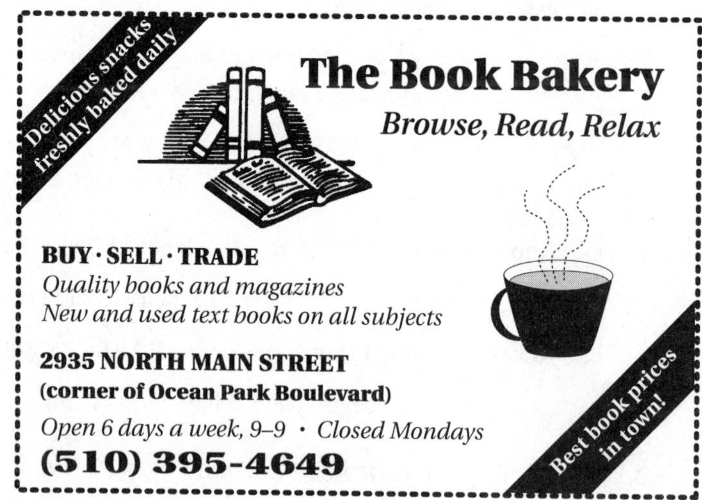

2. Silently read the following ad for the flower shop and the ad for the motorcycle shop on page 225. Write a one-minute answering-machine message for one of these shops. Do not try to tell everything in the ad.

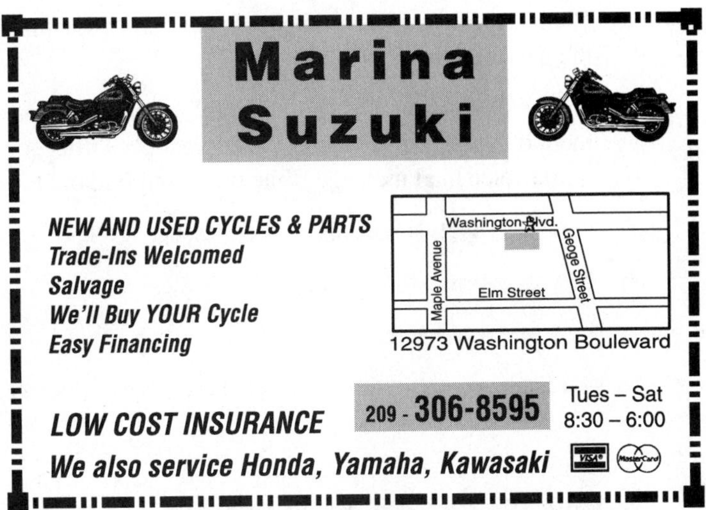

3. Say your phone ad for your partner. Use melody to sound friendly so that people will be interested in visiting your business. Target focus words and pauses to make your message easy to understand.

4. Use a tape recorder to improve your pronunciation. Tape a final version of your answering machine ad to play for the class. Listen to your tape along with the class and take notes on your pronunciation targets. Discuss and compare what you heard about your pronunciation with the class comments.

j. Paragraph: Voice mail

1. Look away from your book and listen to the following paragraph.

2. Replay the tape several times. Mark the thought groups with slashes (/) when you hear the speaker pause or slow down.

Voice Mail

[1]Voice mail has taken over the phone waves! [2]People find more and more often that when they call a business, they are greeted not by a human voice but by a "voice-mail center." [3]This is a recorded greeting that asks you to perform a series of tasks. [4]For example, it may tell you to "press one on your touch-tone phone" if you're calling about a sale, to "press two if you have questions about a faulty product," or to "press three to be put on a mailing list." [5]These recorded messages can be hard to follow and time-consuming for the caller. [6]If you're lucky, you can bypass the string of recorded messages by pressing zero, and eventually speak to a human customer-service representative. [7]Although electronic answering systems may be cost effective for businesses, they are unpopular with many customers.

3. Compare your decisions about thought groups with your partner. Practice saying the paragraph.

4. Home assignment. Call a local bank or government office, such as the Department of Motor Vehicles, the Social Security Office, or the Passport Office. Listen to the voice mail message. Take notes and find out the following:

- what the first two choices on the message are
- how to return to the main menu
- how to repeat the message

Make a list of your questions about the message to discuss in class.

k. Role Play: Nobel Prize winners

You and your partner are doing research on Nobel Prize winners. Although you both have some of the same information, check to see if your partner has information that you are missing. One partner asks questions to complete the chart, page 227. The other partner asks about the chart, page 228.

1. To prepare for the role play, review the pronunciation of the names, countries, dates, subjects, and comments in your information chart. Draw a dot over the stressed syllables in the longer words.

Example literature artificial hormones chemistry

Underline the focus word in the names and dates.

Example George Bernard <u>Shaw</u> 192<u>5</u>

2. In the role play, use sentences with thought groups to discuss the Nobel Prize winners. Monitor your own and your partner's pronunciation for word stress and focus words. Pretend you are a slow speaker who uses more thought groups.

Sample Conversation

A: I see that Enrico **FER**mi / won the prize for **PHY**sics / in 193**8**. / Do you **KNOW** / what it was **FOR**? /

B: It was for his early re**SEARCH** /on nuclear **CHAIN** reACtions. /Do you **KNOW** / where he was **FROM**?/

A: He was born in **IT**aly / and worked in the United **STATES**. /

B: Someone from **IRE**land /was honored in 1925 / for his **WORK** /as a humanitarian **PLAY**WRIGHT. / Do you know his **NAME**? /

Partner A's information

Name	**Country**	**Year**	**Subject**	**Comments**
1. George Bernard Shaw	*	*	Literature	*
2. Enrico Fermi	Italy/USA	1938	Physics	*
3. Sir Robert Robinson	England	*	*	for research of biological and medical importance including steroids, artificial sex hormones, and penicillin
4. *	USA	1964	Peace	*
5. *	Chile	1971	Literature	for his powerful poetry that brings alive a continent's destiny and dreams
6. Leo Esaki	Japan	*	Physics	*
7. Andrei Sakharov	*	1975	*	a noted physicist who was also recognized for his inspirational contributions to peace
8. *	USA	*	Medicine	for her research in genetics related to genes, chromosomes, and DNA
9. Rigoberto Menchu Tum	Guatemala	1992	*	*
10.*	Poland	1996	*	*

Partner B's information

Name	Country	Year	Subject	Comments
1. *	Ireland	1925	*	honored for his work as a humanitarian playwright
2. *	*	*	*	for early research on nuclear chain reactions that provided the foundation for many branches of physics
3. *	*	1947	Chemistry	*
4. Martin Luther King	*	*	*	a Christian minister who led Black Americans in an historic civil rights movement based on nonviolence
5. Pablo Neruda	Chile	*	*	*
6. Leo Esaki	*	1973	*	for pioneering many advances in computers and other electronic equipment
7. *	USSR/ Russia	*	Peace	*
8. Barbara McClintock	*	1983	Medicine	*
9. Rigoberto Menchu Tum	*	*	Peace	for her work on behalf of the world's indigenous peoples; the youngest person to receive the Peace Prize
10. Wislawa Szymborska	*	*	Literature	for her remarkable poetry about the nature of everyday life and personal relations

I. Join the Chorus

Listen and then sing along. Move your hand or your foot to keep up with the rhythm. Work with a group to learn one verse to chant for the class. Practice with your group until you sound like one voice.

Pronunciation Rap

1. If you want to speak English in a way that's cool
   Put it in your body as you learn each rule,
   Tap the rhythm and feel the beat
   Put that language in your feet

Chorus

(And) Practice—It's the only way.
Make small talk—every day.
(I said) Practice—It's the only way.
Make small talk—every day.

2. Whether you whisper, whether you shout
   Stress that syllable, stretch it out
   Ice cream in the <u>de</u>sert makes a great des<u>sert.</u>
   Pre<u>sent</u> me with a <u>pre</u>sent of a brand new shirt.
3. Reduce those "of's" and reduce those "and's"
   Have a cup o' coffee, Wash your face 'n' hands
   Drop that "h" when you *"give 'er a kiss,"*
   With all this rhyming, you just can't miss!

Chorus

4. Remember to link those final "S's."
   Add those endings, no more guesses.
   She likes apples while she sits on beaches .
   When <u>he's</u> hungry he goes for peaches."
5. "E-d" endings must be clear.
   Shout them out for all to hear!
   And, when is it *post<u>ed</u>,* when is it *<u>picked</u>*?
   When is it *toast<u>ed</u>* , when is it *<u>ticked</u>*?

Chorus

6. Articulate!—And you'll do great
   You won't say *A* when you mean to say *eight.*
   You won't get *Kay,* when you want to get *cake*
   (See the difference a sound can make!)
7. Put in pauses, where they need to go
   Change those pitches—make 'em high, make 'em low
   Start rapping and tapping, and you'll feel grand
   'cause when you talk, they'll understand!

Chorus

8. Well, that's the way to get things done—
   Ten parts rhythm, and ten parts fun.
   In the shower, and in your bed,
   Practice intonation till it fills your head!

SISTERS AND BROTHERS, GET INTO THE FLOW—
INTONATION IS THE WAY TO GO!!

—Ellen Stein

m. Talk: The new millennium

Imagine yourself near the end of the twenty-first century. Think about some of the possible changes in the world, such as living conditions, technological advances, or new ways of travel. The purpose of the talk is to express yourself clearly and to monitor your pronunciation.

1. Write a short talk (about three minutes), describing the future as you imagine it or want it to be. Your talk should only be as long as you can keep up the monitoring. Include an introduction, a few main ideas about the new millennium, and a conclusion.

Sample topics to choose from:

- living conditions
- clothing
- education
- health/medicine
- religion
- government
- technology
- travel
- other

2. Underline the focus words and use these to make notes. Talk from your notes.

3. Use a tape recorder to practice. Listen for your targets. Check the length of your talk. Decide how you want to improve your talk and re-tape it.

Targets

- Word stress. Lengthen and raise the pitch of the stressed syllables.
- Sentence stress. Emphasize the focus words. Stress the content words, and unstress the structure words.
- Thought groups. Use focus words, pitch changes, and pauses to make your talk easy to follow.

Finishing Up

REVIEW

1. Listen to the following dialogue and draw slashes where you hear the end of thought groups. Underline the focus words. See the first sentence in the dialogue as an example.

Ordering A New VCR

A: I'd like to order the VCR / on page 198 of your catalog. / How much does it cost?

B: We're having a special this month on VCRs. That one is one hundred forty-five dollars and ninety-nine cents ($145.99). The shipping is about fifteen dollars ($15), depending upon where you are. How would you like to pay for this? By check or credit card?

A: Credit card.

B: I'm going to need your credit card number and a shipping address. May I have the type of card and the card number first, please.

A: Wells Fargo Master Card number 555**2** 949**1** 216**8** 917**8**.

B: Let me repeat the number. Is it 553**2** . . .

A: No. The first four digits are 55**5**2.

B: O.K. 55**5**2 949**1** 216**8** 917**8**. What's the expiration date?

A: Uh oh! I think this card has expired. I'm sorry, but I'll have to call you back later.

2. Practice saying the dialogue with a partner. Monitor for thought groups and focus words. Switch roles.

TALK TIMES

In-class Preparation

You've decided to shop by phone from a mail-order catalog store and have a catalog with good selections. Decide what you want to buy.

1. To prepare for your conversation with the service representative at the catalog store, make a list of questions about your purchase or how to order by mail. For example, ask about the availability of the item, colors in stock, accuracy of sizes, the shipping time, how to place an order.

____

____

____

____

____

2. The catalog representative will want information from you as well. With a partner, make a list of information that you may need before you call the catalog store. For ideas about this, look at the sample-order page from a catalog and review the previous dialogue "Ordering a New VCR."

Talk Times in Your Daily Life: Shopping by phone

Collect a few mail-order merchandise catalogs of your choice and make three to five phone calls to the toll-free numbers at the backs of the catalogs. Write out questions to get information about items you're interested in, such as articles of clothing, things for the house and garden, books, electronic equipment, and so on. When you make the call, it is not necessary to actually place an order. Say that you are getting information, thank the person, and say that you will call back later. The clerks will be glad to answer questions for a possible customer.

- Use a tape recorder in the room to record your part of each conversation. You will not be recording the clerk's voice. Listen to the tape and assess your targets to improve the next call.
- Target thought groups and focus words. Use pauses and pitch changes.

ORDER 24 HOURS A DAY

CALL: 1.800.282.7790 **FAX:** 1.800.245.8968

The Catalog Store
600 Catalog Avenue, Fort Wayne, IN 46804

ORDERED BY (attach label from back of catalog):

Daytime phone: ____________

Evening phone: ____________

SHIP TO (if different):

Name ____________

Address ____________

City ____________ State ____ Zip ____

(If your address is a P.O. box, please give street for UPS)

#	PAGE #	STYLE #	DESCRIPTION	SIZE	QTY.	PRICE	TOTAL PRICE
1							
2							
3							
4							
5							
6							
7							
8							

☐ Check or Money Order ($15 charge for returned checks)

☐ MasterCard ☐ VISA

Card # ☐☐☐☐☐☐☐☐☐☐☐☐☐☐☐☐

Signature ____________ Exp. Date ☐☐/☐☐

SUBTOTAL	
Add sales tax	
Delivery charges	
Express delivery	
GRAND TOTAL	

DELIVERY CHARGES PER ADDRESS

Up to $25................................$4.99
$25.01–$50.00.........................$6.99
$50.01–$75.00.........................$8.99
$75.01–$100.00.....................$10.99
$100.01–$150.00...................$12.99
$150.01–$200.00...................$13.99
over $200.00..........................$14.99

EXPRESS DELIVERY:
All shipments UPS or USPS Priority Mail unless noted here:

☐ Parcel Post
☐ Express Delivery

ON YOUR OWN

1. **Continue practicing regularly with the audio tapes.** Remember, it takes time to change old pronunciation habits.

2. **Record Exercise h., Longer Sentences.** Record the sentences about celebrations and holidays in English-speaking countries. Choose any two sets of sentences in Exercise j.

3. **Record the poem "Today Someone Brought You Flowers," on the Targeting Pronunciation Web page.** Each line of the poem is a thought group. Underline the focus words.

4. **Keep noticing words that you want to pronounce more clearly and add them to your glossary.** Go over all the words on your glossary. Make a tape using your words in sentences.

5. **Review the ten pronunciation targets, page 11.** Decide which three targets on the list are the highest priority for your speech.

WHAT'S NEXT?

Congratulations! You now have a better understanding of how to pronounce English more clearly. Perhaps you have changed some of the ways you pronounce English and have increased your comfort level when speaking. Fill out the questionnaire to rate your progress and your effort.

Assess your progress

Circle 1, 2, or 3 1 = Not at all true 2 = Somewhat true 3 = Definitely true

1. I learned a lot about English pronunciation and what it sounds like. 1 - 2 - 3
2. I can understand conversations in English more easily. 1 - 2 - 3
3. People seem to understand my speech more easily. 1 - 2 - 3
4. I have more confidence speaking English and my comfort level has increased. 1 - 2 - 3
5. I know ways to make my speech easier to understand if I am asked to repeat something. 1 - 2 - 3
6. I know what my personal pronunciation targets are and which targets I need to improve. 1 - 2 - 3
7. I can discover many of my own pronunciation errors and know how to correct them. 1 - 2 - 3
8. I am better able to monitor my pronunciation when I practice and during conversations. 1 - 2 - 3

9. I can communicate more effectively in situations that were difficult for me. 1 - 2 - 3

10. I feel that I still have more work to do on my pronunciation, but I can see that I have made progress 1 - 2 - 3

Assess Your Effort

1. I practiced on my own with the tapes almost every day for 10–20 minutes. 1 - 2 - 3
2. I made small talk in English frequently. 1 - 2 - 3
3. I completed the Talk Time assignments. 1 - 2 - 3
4. I attended class regularly and participated in the activities. 1 - 2 - 3
5. I looked for native speakers to converse with. 1 - 2 - 3
6. I used a tape recorder or video recorder to help improve my pronunciation. 1 - 2 - 3
7. I became familiar with the sound of my own voice on tape. 1 - 2 - 3
8. I improved my monitoring skills by paying attention to my pronunciation for brief periods every day. 1 - 2 - 3
9. I took responsibility for discovering my own errors and correcting them. 1 - 2 - 3
10. I remembered to congratulate myself for taking on the challenge of learning new ways to pronounce English. 1 - 2 - 3

Keep Working toward Your Goals

Your pronunciation will continue to change and improve over time. Gradually the changes become automatic. Copy and insert this "To Do" list into your daily planner or calendar as a reminder.

---

to do

1. **Set aside short but regular practice times to review *Targeting Pronunciation* and the tapes. Review the practice tips for the audio tapes, page 20.**
2. **Check out the extra-practice material and the spelling tips on the Houghton Mifflin Website.**
3. **Use a dictionary to check the pronunciation of new words. Ask native speakers for help.**
4. **Continue conversing in English as much as possible.**
5. **Continue to refine my listening and monitoring skills.**
6. **Be patient and have fun. Remember, it takes time to reach my goals.**

APPENDIX A

Glossary

chunk of speech A familiar phrase or short sentence that is heard as a single unit.
Examples What do you think? See you later.

consonants Voiced and unvoiced sounds that are made by stopping or slowing down the air as it travels up the speech pathway.
Examples b d f v m n l s z

consonant cluster A series of two or more consonant sounds in a row. Many words start or end with consonant clusters. Some clusters cross word boundaries.
Examples street looks looks twice

content words The words in a sentence that contain most of the meaning. Content words are stressed.
Example I FOUND a DOLlar on the **SIDE**WALK.

continuant A sound made from air that travels from the lungs up the speech pathway continuously without stopping. All vowel sounds and most consonant sounds are continuants.
Examples r s v th z m w

descriptive phrase A short phrase with a specific stress pattern. The last word gets the strongest stress, or focus.
Examples HUNgry **TI**ger CRUNchy RED **AP**ple

flap A t sound that is made when the tongue lightly taps the gum ridge before unstressed vowels.
Examples BETty GET a RIDE

focus word The one content word in each thought group that gets the most emphasis and draws attention to new and important information.
Example I LOST my **WAL**let.

gum ridge The place behind the upper front teeth where you put your tongue to say t, d, and n.

intonation The melody of speech. A series of rising and falling speech tones that affect meaning and help us sort out what we are hearing.
Examples John is leaving? John is leaving.

linking Words within a phrase are linked, or connected, and sound like one long word.
Examples spear it → spirit missed her → mister

phrasal verb A two-word verb made up of a verb followed by a small word called a *particle.* The stress is on the particle.
Examples STAND **UP** PUT **OFF**

pitch A single musical tone or note. A high pitch is a high tone. A low pitch is a low tone.

reduction Native English speakers reduce the length of weak unstressed words by substituting a schwa vowel or omitting consonants.

Examples day to day ——→ DAta **DAY** let her go ——→ LETter**GO**

schwa The vowel sound heard in most unstressed words and syllables. There is also a stressed schwa. The symbol for schwa is ə .

Examples DOZen (unstressed) bus (stressed)

sentence stress The pattern of stressed and unstressed words in a sentence. The more important words are emphasized. The less important words are shorter and lower in pitch.

Example I forGOT to SET my a**LARM.**

sibilants A group of consonant sounds that hiss and buzz. The air flows out of the mouth in a narrow stream.

Examples s z sh zh ch j x

speech pathway The route that the air travels from the lungs up through the vocal cords and out the mouth or the nose to make speech sounds.

speech sound What you hear when someone talks. A sound is different from a written letter. Letters do not always sound the same way in English.

Examples s is the sound at the beginning of **s**oup, **c**ertain, and **sc**ene.

steps and glides Specific intonation patterns used at the ends of sentences. Most sentences end by either stepping or gliding down in pitch.

Examples I teach math. (glide) I'm a professor. (step)

stress (light) Dictionaries refer to light stress as *secondary stress* and show this with a light stress mark. A lightly stressed syllable sounds lower in pitch and weaker than the main stressed syllable.

Examples appreciate (ə **prē′** shē āt′) baseball (BASE′ BALL′)

stress (strong) In words, one syllable gets the main emphasis or stress. The vowel sounds longer and easier to hear than the vowels in other syllables.

Examples MESsage comMITtee

stops Sounds made by air that stops at the lips, the gum ridge, or the back of the throat as the breath travels out the speech pathway.

Examples b and p d and t k and g

structure words The small words in a sentence that are important grammatically, but are less essential to the meaning.

Examples you him to an a for if on

syllable A small word or part of a word that gets one beat. Each syllable has one vowel sound.

Examples fold (1 syllable) FOLDer (2 syllables) unFOLDed (3 syllables)

Talk Times Planned times for practicing and monitoring speech targets in real-life situations in order to make more lasting pronunciation changes.

thought group A spoken phrase heard as an intonational unit. Each thought group has a focus word. Longer sentences are divided into thought groups.

Examples We want to **TALK** to you/so leave us a **MES**sage./

voiced sounds Sounds made with vibrating vocal cords. All vowels are voiced. Only some consonants are voiced.

Examples b d g z v

voiceless sounds Consonant sounds in which the vocal cords do not vibrate as the air travels from the lungs up the speech pathway.

Examples p t k s sh ch f

vowel The main sound in a syllable. The air flows freely without slowing down or stopping along the speech pathway.

Examples payment

vowel, clear The fifteen English vowel sounds heard in stressed syllables are called "clear."

Examples iy see I it ey say E yes æ fat

vowel, unclear Unstressed reduced vowels (schwa) go by quickly, are hard to hear clearly, and are called "unclear."

Examples Adam Adam can **GO** now.

word stress The pattern of stressed and unstressed syllables in a word.

Examples reTURN imPORtant

Checklists, Charts, and Forms

The checklists, charts, and forms in this Appendix can be photocopied for classroom use. They are listed below along with the chapter and pages where they are first suggested.

Name ______________________________ **Week of** ____________________

1. Small Talk Report (photocopy for classroom use)

Small talk helps build your confidence. You can make small talk almost anywhere that there are people speaking English. Your comfort level will improve every week.

How many times did you make small talk this week? Rate your comfort level for each conversation.

Situation *(Write the day, Where and with whom?*	**What Happened?**	**Comfort Level** *rate 1–10 (10 = the most comfortable)*

Name ______________________________ **Assignment** __________ **Date** ________

2. Instructor Observations (photocopy for classroom use)

Your pronunciation will sound more effective if you work on the targets that are checked:

__ **1. Word stress**
Signal the correct syllable more strongly. Make it longer, louder, and higher in pitch than the unstressed syllables.
Be careful not to omit or add syllables.

__ **2. Finishing words and linking**
Say the sounds at the ends of words. Link the words in each thought group.
Say all the grammatical endings of words. **Examples** ed s es ll 've 'd ll 've 'd

__ **3. Thought groups and end-of-the-sentence intonation**
Use more pauses and melody to divide longer sentences and organize your speech.
Use more speech melody, more ups and downs.
Glide or step down in pitch at the ends of sentences to show you are finished.
Include all the small grammatical words such as *at, to, the, a.*

__ **4. Focus words**
Slow down and lengthen the most important content word in each thought group. Change pitch.
Choose the right focus word.

__ **5. Special patterns**
compound nouns phrasal verbs abbreviations names

__ **6. Sounds**
Consonant sounds: th sh ch j s z x f v w r l m n b p t d g k flap

Vowel sounds: iy I ey E æ ər ə a uw U ow ɔ ay aw ɔy

__ **7.** Look over these notes, replay the tape of your speech, and listen for the examples.
Be sure to listen to the instructor's comments at the end of your tape.

__ **8.** Resubmit your tape: ____ It was hard to hear ____ not complete ____ not set at the beginning.

Strengths:

Priorities:

Name ______________________________ Assignment __________ Date ________

3. My Speech Checklist (photocopy for classroom use)

Use the following checklist of pronunciation targets to improve your self-monitoring and to keep track of what you hear when you listen to your tape. The more frequently you listen, the easier it will be to hear the targets.

- The instructor will tell you which targets to listen for this time. Put a check (✓) by those targets.
- Listen to your speech tape several times and write examples.

Targets

__ **1. Word stress**
Am I stressing the right syllable? Does the stressed syllable sound longer, louder, and higher in pitch than the unstressed syllables?
Problem words:

__ **2. Finishing words and linking**
Am I finishing all the words? Am I saying the "ed" and final "s" endings? Am I linking words? Words with missing sounds:

__ **3. Thought groups and end-of-the-sentence intonation**
Am I pausing? Am I gliding or stepping down in pitch at the end of most sentences? Am I using enough melody? Am I saying all the small grammatical words such as *at*, *to*, *the*, and *a*?

__ **4. Focus words**
Am I focusing on one important word in each thought group? Did I focus on the right word?

__ **5. Special patterns** Write examples.
compound nouns phrasal verbs abbreviations names

__ **6. Sounds** Circle the problem sound. Write examples of words with problem consonants or vowels.
Consonant sounds: th sh ch j s z x f v w r l m n b p t d g k flap

Vowel sounds: iy I ey E æ ər ə a uw U ow ɔ ay aw ɔy

Describe one strength you observed when listening to your tape:

Name ______________________________ Date ______________

4. Talk Times Plan (photocopy for classroom use)

1. **Targets.** Write the targets each day you plan a Talk Times: for example, Monday-word stress, Friday-focus, etc.
2. **Situation.** Write where you were and whom you were talking to, for example, at work-John, at a market-clerk, at the movies-person in line, etc.
3. **Notes.** Write notes about what you plan to say and what happened when you said it.
4. **Comfort Level.** Rate 1–10: 1 = least comfortable, 10 = most comfortable.

Day Targets	**Situation** *(where and with whom?)*	**Notes** *(what you plan to say and what happened)*	**Comfort Level** *(rate 1–10)*

Name ______________________________ **Date** ____________

5. Sample Talk Times Plan

1. **Targets.** Write the targets each day you plan a Talk Times: for example, Monday-word stress, Friday-focus, etc.
2. **Situation.** Write where you were and whom you were talking to, for example, at work-John, at a market-clerk, at the movies-person in line, etc.
3. **Notes.** Write notes about what you plan to say and what happened when you said it.
4. **Comfort Level.** Rate 1–10: 1 = least comfortable, 10 = most comfortable.

Day Targets	**Situation** *(where and with whom?)*	**Notes** *(what you plan to say and what happened)*	**Comfort Level** *(rate 1–10)*
Monday: Word stress	Call an airline. Talk to the agent.	I need inforMAtion about TICKets to LONdon. Do the SUMmer fares end in SepTEMber or OcTOber? **Notes:** had trouble understanding the agent, forgot to monitor all the stressed syllables.	1
Tuesday Word stress	Call a different airline.	I would like some inforMAtion about two TICKets to BOSton. Are there any DIScount seats aVAILable? **Notes:** A lot better! getting easier, was able to monitor somewhat because I practiced the sentences.	3
Wednesday Word stress Pauses.	Lunchtime. Conversation with Jane.	What do you think of the new RESTaurant / on the mall? / We went there for desSERT / on SUNday. / The food was deLIcious. / I'd like to go back next WEEKEND. / **Notes:** monitored all the stressed syllables, paused or slowed down at the end of each sentence. It's getting easier to use English, especially with friends.	4
Friday Word stress	Ended up making small talk. Forgot to monitor for any targets, but did talk to someone at the market.	was standing in line at the market and asked a man what time it was, said "Thank you. I thought it was later." Also, I asked the manager where the crackers were. I couldn't find them and didn't ask again. **Notes:** Seemed OK. Still hard to talk to strangers.	2

6. Common Word Stress Patterns

The following chart shows examples of eight common word stress patterns of words from one-to-four syllables. The words in each line across the chart have the same stressed vowel sound. Practice vowel sounds by reading across the chart. Practice word stress by reading down the list of words under each pattern. Notice how the strongly stressed syllable and intonation are the same in each list.

There is a less common word stress pattern for four-syllable words. The stress is on the first syllable.
Examples TELevision KINdergarten ALternating EXercising EScalator

Common Word Stress Patterns

Vowel symbol	I	II	III	IV	V	VI	VII	VIII
1. iy	NEED	TEACHer	sucCEED	MEDium	rePEATed	disaGREE	imMEdiate	undeFEATed
2. I	PRINT	MIDdle	disMISS	PHYSical	staTIStics	uneQUIPPED	parTICular	poliTIcian
3. ey	FAME	LATEly	toDAY	MAINtenance	toMAto	underPAID	uRAnium	repuTAtion
4. E	MEND	BETter	aHEAD	ENergy	DeCEMber	personNEL	conVENtional	confiDENtial
5. æ	CAT	MAgic	atTACK	ANimal	fanTAStic	underSTAND	eVAPorate	manuFACture
6. ər	GIRL	JUry	preFER	GERmany	asSERtion	DOUGlas FIR†	inJURious	she is EARly†
7. ə	LUNCH	MOney	inSULT	NUMbering	asSUMPtion	interRUPT	inDUStrial	introDUCtion
8. a	JOB	FOLlow	forGOT	POSsible	disHONest	underSTOCKED	psyCHOlogy	horiZONtal
9. uw*	SOUP	MOvie	apPROVE	MOVable	apPROval	afterNOON	aLUminum	absoLUtely
10. U	BOOK	COOKie	unHOOK	BULletin	good-LOOKing	underSTOOD	it's BULLetproof†	overLOOKing
11. ow	SOAP	MOtor	aLONE	TOtally	enCLOsure	underSOLD	neGOtiate	macaROni
12. ɔ	TAUGHT	AUthor	apPLAUSE	ALternate	inSTALLment	after ALL	inAUgurate	aeroNAUtics
13. ay	FIGHT	ICing	JuLY	DYNamite	surPRISing	unasSIGNED	adVISable	undiVIded
14. aw	HOW	OUTer	aROUND	MOUNtainous	alLOWance	It's alLOWED.†	alLOWable	unacCOUNTed
15. ɔy	BOY	NOIsy	emPLOY	NOISily	aVOIDance	reapPOINT	emPLOYable	unemPLOYment

* This vowel has two pronunciations. Many common English words have a y sound before the uw vowel.
Examples: huge community confuse See page 37 for more examples.

† This phrase has the same stress and intonation as the words in this pattern.

Name ______________________________ Date ____________

7. Complete the word stress chart. (photocopy for classroom use)

Write three examples for each pattern on the chart. Look for words in newspapers, magazines, or advertisements. Write words that you hear on television and the radio. Listen for the stressed syllables, then use your dictionary to check the stress. Practice saying the words listed under each pattern. The intonation should sound the same.

LADder	reMOVE	APpetite	toMORrow	overWHELM	APpetizer	meMORial	occuPAtion

Longer words

You may find longer words that are almost like one of the above patterns, but with more syllables. Write these words below. These longer words may have suffixes or prefixes as shown on page 37, Longer Words: Prefixes and suffixes. Use a dictionary to check your prediction. Draw a dot over the strongly stressed syllable, and draw the pattern for each word.

Longer Words	Pattern	Longer Words	Pattern	Longer Words	Pattern
ordinarily					
environmental					
experimentation					

Name ______________________________ **Date** ____________

8. Personal Pronunciation Glossary (photocopy for classroom use)

Keep a list of words from your everyday life that you want to learn to pronounce. Use your dictionary to check the syllable stress and the spelling. Draw the pattern and trace it with your finger as you say the word. Signal the stressed syllable by saying it longer and higher in pitch. Use the word in a phrase or sentence.

Word Write the word and draw a dot over the stressed syllable. Write the number of syllables.	**Intonation Pattern** Draw the pattern and trace it.	**Notes** Write helpful information, such as phrases to practice.
oc.cu.PA.tion 4	●● ▬ ●	a good occuPAtion He changed occuPAtions.
__		
__		
__		
__		
__		
__		
__		
__		
__		
__		
__		
__		
__		
__		
__		
__		
__		
__		
__		

APPENDIX C

Consonants

The exercises in this Appendix provide extra practice with consonant sounds that many non-native speakers have difficulty pronouncing. The answers to the exercises are in the Answer Key on the Targeting Pronunciation Web page.

Consonant Chart

Voicing

There are different ways of describing consonant sounds. One way is to describe where they are made. Another way is to describe whether they are *voiced* or *voiceless*. The vocal cords vibrate when you say voiced sounds. The following chart shows voiced and voiceless consonant sounds. See Chapter 6 to review voicing and where sounds are made.

Sound symbols

The twenty-five sound symbols written inside the boxes on the chart stand for sounds. Each boxed symbol always sounds the same regardless of how the word is spelled. For example, k is the first sound of the words "**k**ey" and "**c**at," and the last sound in the words hi**k**e and a**ch**e. In English, one letter can have different sounds, and different letters can have the same sound.

Voiceless	Voiced	
p **p**ay–dro**p**	b **b**uy–ca**b**	m **m**y–co**m**e
t **t**ie–ma**t**	d **d**ime–sa**d**	n **n**o–ra**n**
k **k**ey, **c**at–pi**ck**	g **g**o–e**gg**	ng * ri**ng**
f **f**an–li**f**e	v **v**an–ha**v**e	l **l**ie–fa**ll**
s **S**ue–ni**c**e	z **z**oo–wa**s**	r **r**ain–ca**r**
sh **sh**ip–ma**sh**	zh * u**s**ual–televi**s**ion	h † **h**i–a**h**ead
th **th**ink–bo**th**	th **th**e–mo**th**er	w **w**ay–a**w**ay
ch **ch**ip–whi**ch**	j **j**am–pa**g**e	y **y**es–be**y**ond
x e**x**tra–bo**x**		

* This sound does not occur at the beginning of English words.
† This sound does not occur at the end of English words.

Consonants introduced in Chapters 6 and 10 are divided into the following five target groups for additional practice.

Target 1 f *and* v

a. Improve Your Monitoring: f and p

1. Listen to each sentence. Decide if the speaker says the underlined word that starts with an f sound or substitutes a similar word with a p sound. Check (✓) the word you hear.

Example	They tried to fool us.	___ fool	✓ pool
1.	The sun feels very hot today.	___ feels	___ peels
2.	He works too fast.	___ fast	___ past
3.	The fact of the matter is that he can't sing.	___ fact	___ pact
4.	She's fine now.	___ fine	___ pine
5.	It's a fashion magazine.	___ fashion	___ passion
6.	The bus fare went up.	___ fare	___ pear

2. Practice saying the sentences correctly. Self-monitor. Copy the intonation as well as the sounds.

b. Contrast f and p (voiceless)

p stops the air at the lips. f is a continuant. The air keeps flowing. Review stops and continuants in Chapter 6.

1. Listen to the sentences. Then practice saying them. Remember to keep your lips open for f and to close your lips for p.

1.	fool–**p**ool	Jim acted like a **f**ool. Jim swam in the **p**ool.
2.	fashion–**p**assion	The actor's clothes are in **f**ashion. The actor shows a lot of **p**assion.
3.	fast–**p**ast	My watch is a little **f**ast. The time is half **p**ast four.
4.	fine–**p**ine	I'm **f**ine, thank you. Look at the **p**ine tree.
5.	beef–bee**p**	The bee**f** is cooking. There's a bee**p** on the **ph**one.
6.	leaf–lea**p**	The lea**f** is green. Can you lea**p** across?
7.	laughed–la**pp**ed	The boy lau**gh**ed at the puppy. The puppy la**pp**ed up the water.

2. Write three words that start with f that you use in your everyday speech. Practice them in sentences. Monitor for f.

_______________ _______________ _______________

c. Contrast b and v (voiced)

1. Listen to the sentences.

1.	**b**erry–**v**ery	I like **b**erry pie. I am **v**ery sure.
2.	**b**an–**v**an	They ordered a **b**an on smoking. Our **v**an broke down.
3.	**b**et–**v**et	I **b**et the stores are closed. We took our cat to the **v**et.
4.	**b**ent–**v**ent	The coat hanger got **b**ent. Air conditioning comes through a **v**ent.
5.	**b**oat–**v**ote	The **b**oat left the harbor. I plan to **v**ote in the election.

2. Replay the tape. Repeat each word three times. Then say the sentence.

Example **b**ase-**b**ase-**b**ase The **b**ase is made of wood.
vase-**v**ase-**v**ase The **v**ase is made of glass.

d. Practice f and v (continuants)

Say the words and phrases. Monitor for f and v.

Verbs	Phrases	Nouns	Phrases
fill	**f**ill the gas tank	**f**ingers	**f**ive **f**ingers
fix	**f**ix the **f**lat tire	**f**ame	**f**ame and **f**ortune
forget	**f**orget it	**ph**one	a new **ph**one number
finish	**f**inish the job	**f**a**v**or	do a **f**a**v**or
a**ff**ord	I can't a**ff**ord it.	**v**isa	a tra**v**el **v**isa
dri**v**e	Dri**v**e care**f**ully.	di**v**orce	**f**iled for di**v**orce
violate	**v**iolate the law	**v**itamin	**V**itamin C
a**v**oid	a**v**oid a penalty	**v**inegar	oil and **v**inegar dressing
di**v**ide	di**v**ide the assets	**v**ideo	rent a **v**ideo
pre**v**ent	pre**v**ent crime	**v**acancy	Is there a **v**acancy?

---

pronunciation tip Unusual spellings for f: **Examples** **phone** **philosophy** **geography** **graph** **laugh**

---

e. Contrast w and v (voiced)

Look at the front teeth and lips in these pictures.

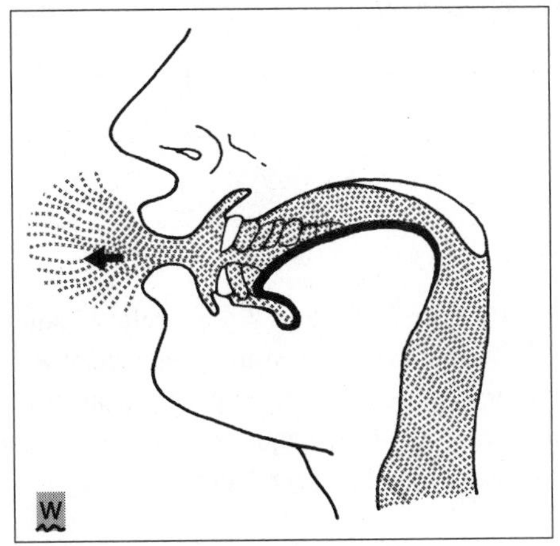

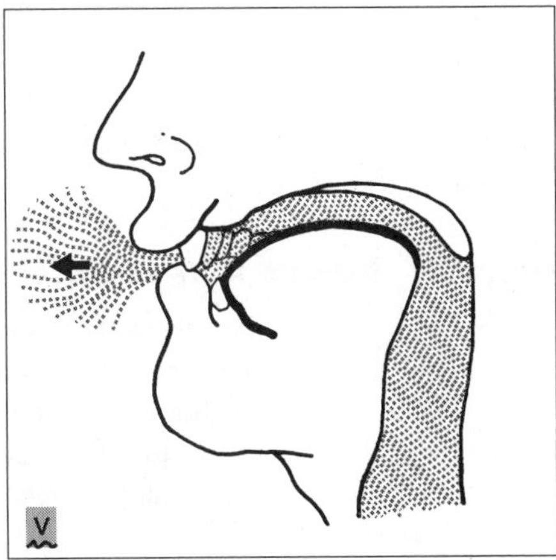

wine

vine

w word water windy wonderful Washington away always aware

1. Listen to the sentences contrasting w and v.

1.	whale–veil	There was a **wh**ale in the ocean.	The bride wore a long veil.
2.	wine–vine	People drink **wh**ite wine with fish.	The **wh**ite vine grew up the wall.
3.	wary–very	We were wary of walking at night.	We went for a very long walk.
4.	wet–vet	The streets were wet.	We took our dog to the vet.
5.	worse–verse	The weather got worse.	This is the first verse.

2. Replay the tape. Say each word three times. Then say the sentence.

Example west-west-west The sun sets in the west.
vest-vest-vest The vest is made of silk.

f. Improve Your Monitoring: w and v

1. Listen to each sentence. Decide if the speaker says the underlined word or substitutes a similar word with a different sound. Check (✓) the word you hear.

1.	My cold has gotten worse.	___ worse	___ verse
2.	Turn the wheel to the right.	___ wheel	___ veal
3.	The school is on the west side of the street.	___ west	___ vest
4.	We had veal for dinner.	___ wheel	___ veal
5.	I am very happy to see you.	___ wary	___ very

2. Practice saying the above sentences correctly. Monitor for v and w.

3. Write three words that start with v and w that you use in your everyday speech. Practice them in sentences. Self-monitor.

v ______ ______ ______

w ______ ______ ______

Target 2 Voiced and Voiceless th

To review these sounds, see Chapter 6. th and th are relaxed sounds. The air flows gently over the tongue. If there is too much tension in your tongue when you say "th," it will squeeze the air and sound like an s or a z. If your tongue pushes against your gum ridge and the air stops, the "th" becomes a t or a d. If you squeeze your tongue too hard, "the" can sound like "zuh" or "duh." "There" can sound like "zere" or "dare."

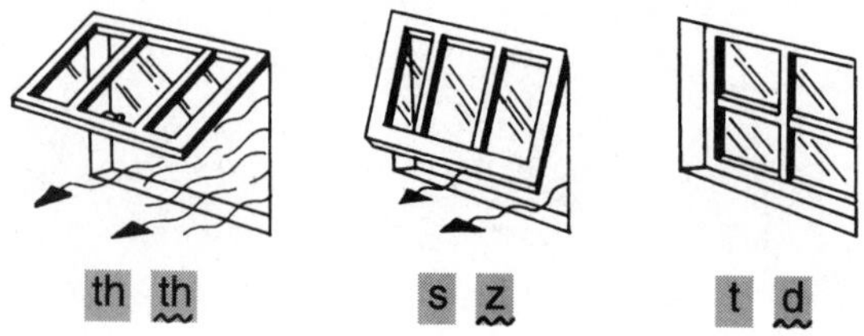

g. Stops and Continuants: d and th

Stop the air at the gum ridge for d. Allow the air to flow out for th.

1. Practice saying the word and sentences. Contrast d and th.

1. **d**ay–**th**ey — It was a sunny **d**ay. **Th**ey waited outside.
2. **d**en–**th**en — We can meet at The Lion's **D**en. **Th**en we'll have lunch.
3. **d**oze–**th**ose — Did you **d**oze during **th**e lecture? **Th**ose notes are not complete.
4. **d**are–**th**ere — He wouldn't **d**are to miss it. **Th**ere he is.
5. la**dd**er–la**th**er — It is hard to climb up a la**dd**er, if your hands are full of la**th**er.

2. Repeat each word three times. Then say the sentence. Remember to keep your mouth relaxed for th. Feel the difference between the stop and the continuant.

Example day-**d**ay-**d**ay — It was a sunny **d**ay.
they-**th**ey-**th**ey — **Th**ey waited outside.

3. Practice these "th" words. Then say them in sentences. Many common "th" words are unstressed.

this **th**e **th**at **th**ese **th**em **th**ose — Brea**th**e in. **Th**at was a smoo**th** ride.

h. Contrast th and s (voiceless)

These sounds are both continuants. The difference is that the air flows out gently for th. The air squeezes out and makes a hissing sound for s.

1. Listen to the word pairs and sentences several times. Contrast s and th.

sum–**th**umb	The sum of 4 + 3 is 7.	She hurt her **th**umb.
sink–**th**ink	I hope the boat won't sink.	I'm trying not to **th**ink about it.
worse–wor**th**	His flu is much worse.	It's not wor**th** it.
sank–**th**ank	My heart sank when I heard the news.	**Th**ank you for your help.
sick–**th**ick	She's been sick all week.	It's a **th**ick book.

2. Replay the tape. Repeat each word three times. Then say the sentence. Feel the difference between the air flowing out gently for th and the air hissing out for s.

Example sum-sum-sum The sum of 4 + 3 is 7.
thumb-**th**umb-**th**umb She hurt her **th**umb.

3. Practice saying the unvoiced "th" in ordinal numbers.

the nin**th** grade the four**th** floor the seven**th** day of the week
the ten**th** of the month

Target 3 Sibilants

s and z

The basic hissing and buzzing sounds are s and z. Other sibilants are related to these. Pronunciation problems with sibilants often come from the following:

1. Voicing. Some people switch s and z.
2. Omitting these sounds at the ends of words or when they are part of a consonant cluster.
3. Spelling. Predicting pronunciation from spelling is not easy because letters do not always sound the same in all words. (See the Targeting Pronunciation Web page for more tips about spelling.)

s

Practice words with s spelled in different ways.

1. Most common spelling at the beginning of words: **s**
Examples soup sip said sun
2. Less common spelling at the beginning of words: **c sc**
Examples cent century science
3. At the ends of words: **s ce se ss**
Examples makes courteous peace house mess

z

Practice the following examples of different ways to spell z at the ends of words. Lengthen the vowel before all the voiced final z sounds.

Examples plays praise prize

s ze: plays the piano My toes fro**ze.** the grand pri**ze**

se: Did you choo**se** it? Can you u**se** it? Did you lo**se** it? Pau**se** and rai**se** your hand.

i. Paragraph

1. Listen to the paragraph about James. You will hear many common words that are spelled with an "s" but pronounced with a z. Pay attention to the linking.

James was‿always‿a good student. He has‿a high‿GPA (grade point average). He's planning to go to graduate school soon. James shows‿every sign of success. He's friendly and polite, and he does good work. James‿is‿a busy guy! He has‿a daytime job, goes to school at night, raises orchids, and plays‿in a band.

2. Practice saying the paragraph one line at a time. After you have practiced, say the paragraph looking away from your book. Pretend you are telling someone about James.

j. sh ch (voiceless) and j (voiced)

Review how to say these sibilant sounds in Chapter 10, page 190.

sh

1. Say s and slide your tongue back to say sh. Sh! The baby's sleeping. Sh!

2. Listen and repeat the words and phrases.

Contrast s and sh. Sue–**sh**oe same–**sh**ame sip–**sh**ip

fini**sh** talking fooli**sh** question Spani**sh** food Dani**sh** pastry

3. Practice saying the following words with sh. Lengthen the stressed syllable with the dot over it. These letter combinations can all sound like sh **ti ci ch ss tion**

shortage	**sh**oulder	**sh**iny	**sh**ampoo
ma**ch**ine	permi**ss**ion	pa**ti**ent	so**ci**al
Engli**sh**	Spani**sh**	Swedi**sh**	fooli**sh**
na**tion**	fic**tion**	avia**tion**	ac**tion**

ch and j

1. Move your tongue from one sound to another to pronounce these combination sounds.

t + sh ⟶ ch

d + zh ⟶ j

2. Listen and repeat the words and phrases.

ch **ch**oke **ch**ain **ch**arity wat**ch** out cat**ch** it rea**ch** over Whi**ch** arrived? pea**ch** pie

j **j**oke **J**ane **G**ermany **j**oy pa**ge** eleven wa**ge** increase MANa**ge** MONey

ba**dge** of honor

k. Improve Your Monitoring: sh and ch

Listen to the words. Check (✓) the sound you hear. Then practice. Use the words in sentences. Monitor for sh and ch.

Example **cash**–catch ✓ sh ___ ch

1. **ship**–**ch**ip	___ sh ___ ch	4. **dish**–**ditch**	___ sh ___ ch
2. **sheer**–**ch**eer	___ sh ___ ch	5. **wash**–**watch**	___ sh ___ ch
3. **sheet**–**ch**eat	___ sh ___ ch	6. **mush**–**much**	___ sh ___ ch

l. Improve Your Monitoring

1. Listen to each of the sentences. Decide if the speaker says the underlined word or substitutes a similar word with a different sound. Check (✓) the word your hear.

1. Please have a **chair** while you wait.	___ **share**	___ **chair**
2. I'd like some **chips** with my lunch.	___ **ships**	___ **chips**
3. I'd like to **wish** you good luck.	___ **wish**	___ **witch**
4. I **watched** the basketball game.	___ **washed**	___ **watched**
5. Can you **cash** this check?	___ **cash**	___ **catch**
6. Did you **catch** a fish?	___ **cash**	___ **catch**
7. Jane dressed up as a **witch** for Halloween.	___ **wish**	___ **witch**
8. The **ditch** is full of dirt.	___ **dish**	___ **ditch**

2. Practice saying the sentences correctly. Self-monitor for intonation as well as four the sounds.

Another Sibilant: x

1. To say x link two sounds. k + s ⟶ x. English words do not start with an x sound.

2. Listen and then practice saying x in the following words and phrases. Monitor for the k + s combination.

fi**x** si**x** ta**x** tru**cks** pi**cks** coo**ks** sha**kes** e**x**plain e**x**tra e**x**ercise

mi**x** up bo**x** of candy ta**x** deduction fa**x** modem "**X**" rated movie ba**cks** up

3. "cc" is often pronounced k s. Practice the following examples.

accept I'm happy to **accept** your invitation.

accent I'm learning a new **accent**.

succeed You can't **succeed** without trying.

vaccine There is a **vaccine** for many diseases.

accident There was an **accident** at the corner.

Target 4 r and l

See page 113 to review how to make an r. See page 131 to review vowel + r sound.

m. Improve Your Monitoring: r and w

1. Listen to the following words contrasting r and w.

ride–wide right–white red–wed ray–way raid–weighed

2. Listen to sentence (a) or (b). Check (✓) the sentence you hear. Practice saying the sentences.

Example ___ It's a long ray. ✓ **It's a long way.**

1. ___ a. Be sure to take the right hat. ___ b. Be sure to take the white hat.
2. ___ a. I paid according to the rate. ___ b. I paid according to the weight.
3. ___ a. We saw the ray through the window ___ b. We saw the way through the window.
4. ___ a. I didn't like the rage. ___ b. I didn't like the wage.
5. ___ a. Let's travel to see the rest. ___ b. Let's travel to see the West.

n. Improve Your Monitoring: r and l

ride–lied right–light red–led ray–lay raid–laid

Listen to sentence (a) or (b). Check (✓) the sentence you hear. Practice saying the sentences.

1. ___ a. Did you find the rake? ___ b. Did you find the lake?
2. ___ a. Take the right backpack. ___ b. Take the light backpack.
3. ___ a. I finished the race first. ___ b. I finished the lace first.
4. ___ a. The road was full of bricks. ___ b. The load was full of bricks.
5. ___ a. I got ink on my wrist. ___ b. I got ink on my list.

o. Vowel + r

Some r sounds come after vowels. Notice the spelling variations on the following lists.

Listen to the first three words in each list. Use the sound of these words to figure out the pronunciation of the rest of the list. Practice the words on each list by saying them in sentences.

1. iy + r	**2.** ey + r	**3.** a + r	**4.** ow + r	**5.** ay + r	**6.** aw + r
here	air	far	four	fire	our
ear	fair	heart	pour	hire	sour
fear	there	park	door	dryer	flour
NEARly	VEry	sharp	more	wire	TOwer
EARPHONE	VARious	BARgain	ORder	reTIRE	POwer
YEARly	MERry	ARgue	STORy	adMIRE	fLOwer
apPEAR	CAREful	PARty	ORganize	reQUIRE	SHOwer

pronunciation tip Take your time. Glide from the vowel to the r and give yourself time to tighten and curl your tongue when you get to the r.

p. Paragraph

1. Listen to the paragraph and write the missing r and l words.

Learning to Drive

I first learned to __________ a __________ when I was about __________ or fourteen __________ old. I was too young to get a __________ license, but my older brother __________ used to __________ me __________ driving his __________. We would go over to the __________ in back of the __________ Market after the __________ closed. I would __________ around and __________ in circles. Sometimes we would __________ out to the __________ where the __________ were deserted, and Larry would __________ me loose.* My __________ never found out about it until __________ later. By then it was too __________. I already had by driver's license and __________ had graduated from college and was __________ in California.

***let loose:** to set free.

2. Replay the tape several times and put your tape recorder on pause to practice one line at a time. Then say the whole paragraph.

Target 5 Consonant Clusters

Practice pronouncing consonants when they are linked in clusters, either in individual words or across word boundaries. Review Chapter 7, page 127.

q. Improve Your Monitoring: r and l clusters

1. Listen to the words contrasting r and l.

crown–**cl**own **cr**ime–**cl**imb **fl**ows–**fr**oze **cr**owd–**cl**oud **gr**ass–**gl**ass

2. Listen to sentence (a) or (b). Check (✓) the sentence you hear. Practice saying the sentences.

Example ✓a. The children **pl**ayed at the church. __ b. The children **pr**ayed at the church.

1. ___ a. I saw a picture of a **cr**own. ___ b. I saw a picture of a **cl**own.
2. ___ a. It's a major **cr**ime. ___ b. It's a major **cl**imb.
3. ___ a. The river **fl**ows all winter. ___ b. The river **fr**oze all winter.
4. ___ a. There's a **cr**owd in the distance. ___ b. There's a **cl**oud in the distance.
5. ___ a. The **gr**ass is wet. ___ b. The **gl**ass is wet.

r. More r and l Clusters

1. Practice saying the words and sentences. Monitor the clusters and the linking.

fr: friend **fr**uit **fr**equently	My **fr**iend **fr**equently gives me fresh **fruit.**
tr: true **tr**avel **tr**uck	It's **tr**ue that we **tr**aveled by **tr**uck
br: brought **br**own **br**iefcase	My **br**other **br**ought his **br**own **br**iefcase.
cr: credit **cr**ib **cr**azy	We paid for the **cr**ib with a **cr**edit card.
dr: drop **dr**apes **dr**y-clearn	I **dr**opped off my **dr**apes at the **dr**y cleaners.
thr: three **thr**ew **thr**eaten	The pitcher **thr**ew **thr**ee good pitches in a **row.**
str: street **str**ipe **str**aight	They painted a **str**aight **str**ipe on the **str**eet.
bl: black **bl**ue **bl**ock	Her knee was **bl**ack and **bl**ue after tripping on the **block.**
pl: plan **pl**easant **pl**ay	We **pl**an to see a **pl**easant **pl**ay.
fl: floated **fl**ash **fl**ood	The car **fl**oated away during the **fl**ash **fl**ood.

2. Practice saying sentences with these words.

Nouns: **cr**eam **dr**ugs **fl**ag **fl**avor **fl**ower

Verbs: **tr**ust **dr**eam **dr**ive **bl**ame **bl**ow

s. Clusters across Word Boundaries

Practice saying the following compound nouns and descriptive phrases. Then say them in sentences. Make sure that you finish all the words and say all the underlined consonant clusters.

Compound Nouns	**Descriptive Phrases**
BACKPACK	cheap **SHIRT**
CHECKBOOK	COLlege **FRESHman**
COMic BOOKS	drunk **DRIVer**
DANCE GROUPS	ecoNOmic **PROgress**
HEALTH CLUB	FINal **REport**
HOUSE KEY	HELPing **HAND**
inSURance COMpany	HUman **BEing**
PAPer JAM	presiDENtial **POLitics**
PRESS CARD	PREvious **BILL**
rePORT CARDS	rich **FLAVors**
SPIder WEB	road **CLOSED**
SUN SCREEN	WELcome **HOME**

REVIEW

1. **List any of the English consonants that are difficult for you.** Repeat the exercises with these consonants.

   ____

2. **List any consonant sounds that you do not have in your native language.** Say them in words and sentences.

   ____

3. **For additional practice with paragraphs, poems, and dialogues, visit the Targeting Pronunciation Web page.** Monitor for difficult consonants.

APPENDIX D

Vowels

The exercises in this Appendix provide extra practice with vowel sounds that many nonnative speakers have difficulty pronouncing. The answers to the exercises are in the Answer Key on the Targeting Pronunciation Web page.

Introducing Fifteen Vowels: Vowel chart

The following chart shows the fifteen clear vowel sounds that you hear in stressed syllables. The most important thing about saying these vowels is to lengthen and raise the pitch of the stressed ones. The symbols for the vowel sounds are shown on the chart in gray boxes. You will need a blue, orange, and yellow highlighter pen to complete your vowel chart.

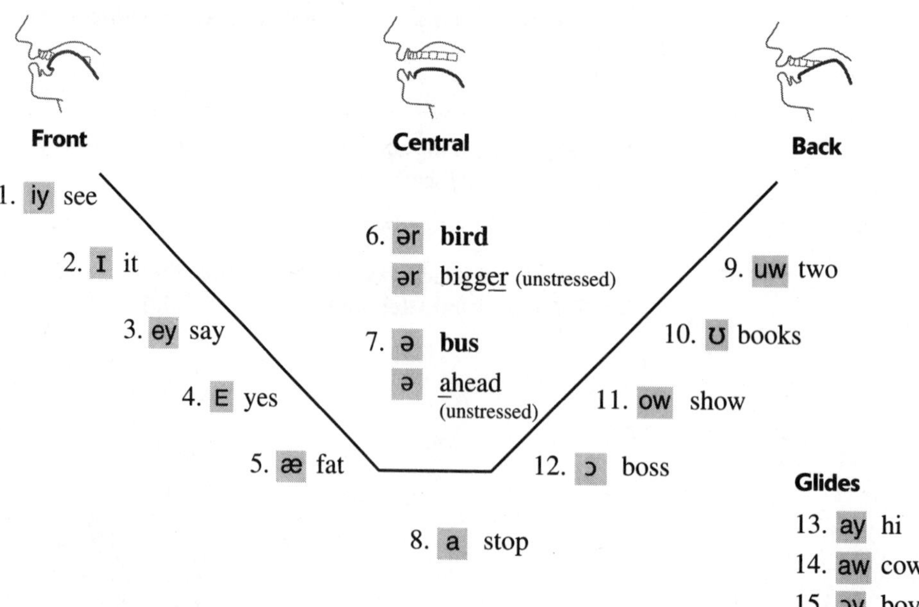

1. Listen to the fifteen clear vowels in key words and phrases.*

SEE IT SAY YES a FAT BIRD at a BUS STOP TWO BOOKS SHOW the BOSS HI, COWBOY

2. Replay the tape several times and repeat the phrases. You'll be using them again.

Vowels that are easily confused with each other are grouped into the following five target groups for additional practice.

Target 1 Long and Short Vowels

Five long vowels iy **see** ey **say** ay **hi** ow **show** uw **two**

Some of the fifteen vowels take longer to say than others because the middle of the tongue glides from one place to another. This takes extra time. Five of these long vowels are easy to recognize because they sound like the names of the alphabet letters: A, E, I, O, and U.

1. Listen and practice saying words and phrases with five long vowels.

- **E** w**e** m**e** t**ea** gr**ee**n t**ea** sw**ee**t dr**ea**ms He s**ee**med pl**ea**sed to s**ee** m**e**.

  To say iy, rest your tongue tip behind your lower front teeth and push the middle of your tongue forward toward your top teeth and then tense it. Whisper the key word: **SEE**

- **A** st**ay** d**ay** **eight** st**ay** all d**ay** a l**a**te d**a**te a p**ay** r**ai**se

  To say ey, start with "eh." Then slowly glide the middle of your tongue forward to start the word "**y**–es." Feel your tongue glide and tense. Whisper the key word: **SAY**

- **I** t**ie** m**y** **eye** f**i**ve t**ie**s l**igh**t in m**y** **eye**s The p**ie** was a surpr**i**se.

  To say ay, start with "ah." Then slowly glide the middle of your tongue forward to start to say the word "**y**–es." Feel it tense. Whisper the key word: **HI**

- **O** g**o** n**o**te **ow**n **Oh**, n**o**! My t**oe**s fr**o**ze! S**o** it g**oe**s!

  To say ow, pull your tongue toward the back of your mouth and tense it. Round your lips gently as you finish saying this vowel. Whisper the key word: **SHOW**

- **U** sh**oe** bl**ue** m**oo**n M**o**ve the n**ew** sh**oe**s. Exc**u**se me. May I have a s**ou**p sp**oo**n?

  To say uw, pull your tongue to the back of your mouth and up. Tense it. Round your lips slightly. Whisper the key word: **TWO**

2. For this exercise, let your tongue do the all the work. Whisper and alternate between two vowel sounds, "O" and "E." Concentrate on the feeling of your tongue movements, and keep your lips relaxed. Rest your tongue tip behind your lower teeth. Then pull the middle of your tongue back to whisper "O" and push it forward to whisper "E," moving your lips as little as possible. Whisper O—E O—E O—E. Try the same thing whispering U—E U—E U—E.

* The key words and phrases were adapted from *Improving Spoken English* by Joan Morley, University of Michigan Press, 1979, by permission of Joan Morley.

3. Color the long vowels on the vowel chart (numbers 1, 3, 9, 11, and 13) with a blue highlighter pen. Notice the two symbols inside gray boxes for these vowels. These symbols show where your tongue glides as you say the long vowels.

---

pronunciation tip **When saying long vowels, let your tongue do most of the work. Let your lips follow along in a relaxed way. It is your tongue that makes the vowels sound clear.**

Two More Long Vowels: aw **cow** ɔy **boy**

Vowels 14 and 15 glide more noticeably than most of the other long vowels. Notice the spelling variations.

1. Listen and practice saying words and phrases for two more long vowels.

- aw d**ow**n t**ow**n ar**ou**nd the f**ou**ntain a l**ou**d s**ou**nd

  To say aw start with "ah." Glide from "ah" to the "w" at the beginning of the word "**w**-ay." Round your lips slightly. Whisper the key word: **COW**

- ɔy The b**oy** found his t**oy**. Av**oi**d sp**oi**led milk. Destr**oy** the p**oi**son.

  To say ɔy, start with "oh." Glide from "oh" to the "y" at the beginning of the word "**y**-es." Tense your tongue. Spread your lips slightly. Whisper the key word: **BOY**

2. Color vowels 14 and 15 blue along with the other long vowels. Vowels 13, 14, and 15 glide a longer distance than the others. They are often called diphthongs.

Six short vowels ɪ **it** e **yes** æ **fat** a **stop** u **books** ɔ **boss**

The next six vowels take less time to say than the long vowels. They are called *short vowels.*

1. Listen and repeat the phrases. The words with short vowels are underlined.

SEE <u>IT</u> SAY <u>YES</u> a <u>FAT</u> BIRD at a <u>BUS</u> <u>STOP</u> TWO <u>BOOKS</u> SHOW the <u>BOSS</u>
HI COWBOY

2. On the vowel chart, color the six short vowels you just heard with an orange highlighter pen. You have now colored eleven of the fifteen vowels. The long vowels are blue. The short vowels, numbers 2, 4, 5, 8, 10, and 12 are orange.

a. Long and Short Vowel Contrasts

Listen first and replay the tape. Say the short and long vowel contrasts. Exaggerate the long vowel words. Even when you say long vowels quickly, you need to glide and tense your tongue.

1. ey main - E men The main road is closed for repairs. The men are fixing the road.
2. iy reach - I rich Can you reach the top? Is the man rich?
3. ay kite - a cot Sarah wants to fly a kite. Sarah wants to sleep on the cot.
4. ow phone - ɔ fawn The phone is ringing. The fawn is near its mother.
5. uw pool - U pull The hotel has a large swimming pool. Can your car pull a large trailer?

b. Improve Your Monitoring

1. Listen to each sentence. Decide if the speaker says the underlined word or substitutes a similar word with a different vowel sound. Check (✓) the word you hear.

1. The book's main idea was clever. ____ main ____ men
2. I bought some vitamin pills. ____ peels ____ pills
3. They put the pills in a paper bag. ____ paper ____ pepper
4. What time is it? ____ time ____ Tom
5. Andrew wants to leave the country. ____ leave ____ live
6. Please answer the phone. ____ phone ____ fawn

2. Practice saying the sentences correctly. Self-monitor for intonation as well as for vowel sounds.

Target 2 ər bird ə bus a stop BIRD at a BUS STOP

These are called *central vowels* because the tongue doesn't push way forward or pull way backward as it does for iy and uw. Rest your tongue tip behind your lower teeth for ə. Curl and tense your tongue tip for ər. Review a in Chapter 5, page 88.

Two schwa vowels: ə BUS ər BIRD

ə and the ər have a stressed and an unstressed version.

1. To say a schwa, keep your tongue very relaxed. Put your tongue tip gently behind your bottom teeth. Open your lips slightly. Say "uh" without moving or tensing any part of your mouth.

2. To say r, your tongue has to tighten. Open your mouth gently and say a schwa. Bring the rear sides of the tongue up to the inside of the upper back teeth. Curl and tense your tongue tip. Take your time. The tongue tip doesn't touch anything. Say "Brrr. Brrr. It's cold! Brrr."

3. Color vowels number 6 and 7 on the vowel chart yellow to call attention to the schwa.

4. Listen to these word pairs contrasting schwa and other vowel sounds. The schwa vowel comes first and sounds different from the other vowels.

but–bake but–beak but–bike but–boat but–boot

but–bit but–bet but–bat but–bought but–book but–bird

c. Compare Schwa and ər

1. Listen to the word pairs and the sentences. Replay the tape.

bu**n**–bu**rn** hu**t**–hu**rt** su**ch**–sear**ch** sh**ut**–sh**irt** to**n**–tu**rn** fu**n**–fe**rn** gu**ll**–gi**rl** bu**d**–bi**rd**

1. I'd like a hot dog on a **bun**. Don't let the hot dog **burn**.
2. He lives in a **hut**. He got **hurt**.
3. **Such** an interesting day! **Search** the Internet.
4. Button it sh**ut**. Button the sh**irt**.
5. I have a **ton** of homework. I have to **turn** it in tomorrow.
6. I have **fun** in my garden. I have a **fern** in my garden.
7. The **gull** flew over the sand. The **girl** sat on the sand.
8. Put the **bud** in a vase. Put the **bird** in its nest.

2. Say the word pairs and the sentences. Monitor your speech.

d. Learn about Shirley

1. Listen to the paragraph. The stressed ər words are underlined and the bold type shows focus.

The <u>girl's</u> name is <u>**SHIR**</u>ley, and she's in the <u>third</u> **GRADE**. Her personality is quiet and re-<u>**SERVED**</u>. <u>Shir</u>ley's mother <u>works</u> as a <u>**NURSE**</u>, and her father <u>works</u> as an <u>at**TOR**ney</u>. They're often in a <u>**HUR**</u>ry, and they <u>wor</u>ry about <u>**SHIR**</u>ley. <u>Shir</u>ley spends a lot of **TIME** with her pet <u>**GER**bil</u>.*

2. Practice saying the paragraph. Then answer the questions looking away from the book.

Example Who is <u>Shirley</u>? <u>Shirley</u> is a <u>girl</u> with a pet <u>gerbil</u>.

1. What is the girl's name and what grade is she in?
2. What kind of personality does Shirley have?
3. What kind of work do her parents do?
4. What else do you know about Shirley's parents?
5. How does Shirley spend a lot of her time?

***gerbil:** Pronounced JERbəl. A small rodent similar to a mouse that is often kept as a pet.

e. Improve Your Monitoring

1. Listen to each sentence. Decide if the speaker says the underlined word with the ər sound or substitutes a similar word with a schwa. Check (✓) the word you hear. Replay the tape to make sure.

Example	The business was hurt by a recession.	✓ **hurt**	___ **hut**
1.	The fern was tall and green.	___ **fern**	___ **fun**
2.	The search party found the missing hiker.	___ **search**	___ **such**
3.	Don't burn the soup.	___ **burn**	___ **bun**
4.	Let's give everyone a turn.	___ **turn**	___ **ton**
5.	The girl decided to study Russian.	___ **girl**	___ **gull**

2. Practice saying the sentences correctly. Self-monitor for intonation as well as for sounds.

f. Spelling Variations for a Stressed ər

The following words have the same vowel sound although they are spelled with different letters. Practice saying the words and monitor for ər .

"er"	"ir"	"ur"	"or"	"our"	"ear"
WERE	SIR	TURN	WORry	COURage	EARTH
PERfect	THIRsty	SURface	WORK	JOURnal	EARLY
NERvous	CIRcle	HURry	WORD	JOURnalism	EARN
eMERgency	THIRty	URgent	WORSE	adJOURN	HEARD
inTERpret	DIRty	ocCUR	WORKing	FLOURish	LEARNing

g. The Unstressed ər

The stressed and unstressed ər sounds vary with different English dialects. Some speakers curl their tongues very little and say an ər that sounds closer to a schwa. The majority of North American speakers curl and tighten their tongues for this sound. Practice some examples.

Comparatives:	BIGger	SMALler	HIGHer	LOWer
Jobs:	SINGer	LAWyer	ACtor	inVENtor
Directions:	EASTern	WESTern	NORTHern	SOUTHern
Nouns:	MUStard	PEPper	RAzor	YOgurt
Family members:	MOther	FAther	BROther	SISter

pronunciation tips 1. Your ear is your best helper for working on any "r" sound. 2. Take the time to curl and tighten your tongue tip. 3. Close your palm and curl your fingers as you say the r.

h. Paragraph

1. Listen to the paragraph. Replay the tape, and practice one line at a time. Monitor the r.

Farmers' Markets

Open-air farmers' markets that for centuries have been part of everyday life around the world have become an urban attraction in the United States. Farmers rise before dawn, load up their trucks, and drive many hours to set up their portable produce stands. Each day, markets spring up in various shopping malls and parking lots only to disappear five or six hours later when the farmers return home. These portable markets draw millions of customers every week. Eager shoppers gather in large numbers to support this growing industry. Many customers prefer stands featuring organic fruits and vegetables. People seem tired of supermarket fruit that was preserved to travel and ripen later. They like the friendly atmosphere, the fresh food, and the chance to interact with the farmers.

2. Finish the following sentences using your own words and tape your answers. Listen for r words that need improvement. Practice saying them and re-tape.

1. A new urban attraction in the United States . . .
2. For the farmers, these markets are hard work. They have to . . .
3. Each day portable markets spring up . . .
4. Eager shoppers . . .
5. Customers like a lot of things about shopping at these markets. For example, . . .

Target 3 iy see I it

1. To say both iy and I push the middle of your tongue toward the front of the mouth. For iy push your tongue further forward and then tense it. I is a short vowel and more relaxed.

2. Listen and practice saying the words and phrases.

iy **reach** the **ceiling** **easy teach**er **sea**son the **pi**zza the **re**cent **pea**ce

I **fi**x **di**nner the **ki**tchen **wi**ndow the **mi**ddle **si**ster **fi**nish the **my**stery quick**ly** **bu**sy **wo**men

3. Say the rhyming words* in each list and practice them in phrases. Write phrases of your own on the blank lines and practice them.

iy		I	
seek	seek help	sick	sick and tired
peek	peek out of the window	pick	pick the apples
leak	leak in the roof	wick	the burning candle wick
week	____________________	Dick	____________________
meek	____________________	stick	____________________
chic	____________________	kick	____________________

* The vowel sounds and the final consonant sounds are the same in rhyming words. Only the beginning sound is different.
Examples: cat-hat-mat big-pig-fig run-fun-ton date-wait-mate